Doing Business in the Middle East

Is business the solution to the problems of the Middle East? Some economists and policymakers argue that unleashing the Arab private sector is the key to sustainable growth and more liberal politics. Pete Moore's book is the first to examine, systematically and historically, relations between state authority and elite business representation in the region. By analyzing the cases of Kuwait and Jordan, he considers why organized businesses in Kuwait have been able to coordinate policy reform with state officials, while their Jordanian counterparts have generally failed. The author concludes that unleashing the private sector alone is insufficient to change current political and economic arrangements, and that successful economic adjustment requires successful political adjustment.

PETE W. MOORE is Assistant Professor in the Department of Political Science, University of Miami.

Cambridge Middle East Studies 20

Cambridge Middle East Studies has been established to publish books on the modern Middle East and North Africa. The aim of the series is to provide new and original interpretations of aspects of Middle Eastern societies and their histories. To achieve disciplinary diversity, books will be solicited from authors writing in a wide range of fields including history, sociology, anthropology, political science, and political economy. The emphasis will be on producing books offering an original approach along theoretical and empirical lines. The series is intended for students and academics, but the more accessible and wide-ranging studies will also appeal to the interested general reader.

A list of books in the series can be found after the index.

Doing Business in the Middle East

Politics and Economic Crisis in Jordan and Kuwait

Pete W. Moore
University of Miami

CAMBRIDGE
UNIVERSITY PRESS

PUBLISHED BY THE PRESS SYNDICATE OF THE UNIVERSITY OF CAMBRIDGE
The Pitt Building, Trumpington Street, Cambridge, United Kingdom

CAMBRIDGE UNIVERSITY PRESS
The Edinburgh Building, Cambridge, CB2 2RU, UK
40 West 20th Street, New York, NY 10011-4211, USA
477 Williamstown Road, Port Melbourne, VIC 3207, Australia
Ruiz de Alarcón 13, 28014 Madrid, Spain
Dock House, The Waterfront, Cape Town 8001, South Africa

http://www.cambridge.org

First published 2004

Printed in the United Kingdom at the University Press, Cambridge

Typeface Plantin 10/12 pt.   *System* LATEX 2ε [TB]

A catalogue record for this book is available from the British Library

Library of Congress Cataloguing in Publication data
Moore, Pete W.
Doing business in the Middle East: politics and economic crisis in Jordan and
Kuwait / Pete W. Moore.
   p.   cm. – (Cambridge Middle East studies ; 20)
Includes bibliographical references and index.
ISBN 0 521 83955 6
1. Kuwait – Economic conditions.   2. Jordan – Economic conditions.
3. Kuwait – Politics and government.   4. Jordan – Politics and government.
I. Title. II. Series.
HC415.39.M66   2004
330.95367 – dc22   2003069748

ISBN 0 521 83955 6 hardback

For Watson, Ike, and Joe

Contents

Acknowledgements   *page* x
Note on transliteration and translation   xii

1 Summers of discontent: business–state politics in the
   Middle East   1
   Comparing cases and subjects   5
   A single logic, two approaches   10
   Rents and sectors in the Middle East   13
   The micro approach: collective action by business   24
   Contributions and framework   27

2 Organizing first: business and political authority
   during state formation   30
   Among equals: merchant–ruler relations and state creation in
     Kuwait   30
   A less promising birth: the British, the Hashemites, and the
     creation of business–state relations in Jordan   57
   Conclusion   81

3 Politics and profits   85
   Good times in Kuwait   85
   Business and state under high rents in Jordan   101
   Conclusion   118

4 Crises at century's end   120
   Easy money and regrets in Kuwait   120
   Adjustment in Jordan   145
   Conclusion   174

5 Is business the solution?   176
   Addressing the alternatives   178
   Business, state, and economic liberalization in the Arab world   180
   Economic crisis, business representation, and the question of
     political reform   185

Appendix   Comparative associational data   191
Select bibliography   199
Index   210

Acknowledgements

The initial inspiration for this study was familial pressure. I come from a large Arab-American family which settled in a small Southern town in the early twentieth century. Throughout my graduate career, well-meaning aunts and uncles continually asked: "Haven't you finished school yet? When are you going to get a job? Why don't you go into business for yourself?" Had my Southern Arab-American mother, Jerri Moore, not supported me throughout my education, I would still be facing that grilling. As it turned out, those questions led me to think more broadly about how business actually took place in the Arab Middle East and what role politics played.

This study is based upon several years of field research in Jordan and Kuwait. A Fulbright grant allowed for study in Kuwait, while grants from the Social Science Research Council, the American Center of Oriental Research in Amman, and the Inter-University Consortium for Arab and Middle East Studies in Montreal provided funds to conduct research in Jordan.

To begin, I must thank my teachers and advisors. While I was a cadet at the Virginia Military Institute, Pat Mayerchak and Wayne Thompson taught me a love of teaching and international affairs. My graduate education in political science and Middle East studies was guided by two of the finest advisors around. It is well known that Edmund Ghareeb is a gentleman and scholar of the highest caliber. Edmund encouraged my interest in the Middle East and guided me through the dangers of Middle East politics in Washington, DC. My advisor at McGill University, Rex Brynen, displayed great patience with an American graduate student who constantly spoke in the first-person collective when referring to the USA and Canada. Through his intellect and work ethic, Rex has institutionalized a critical mass of Middle East specialists and resources in Montreal that make it the center of Middle East studies in Canada. His guidance and insight were crucial to the completion of this book.

I would like to thank several friends and scholars who took the time to read and comment on parts of this study. Jill Crystal, Richard Doner, and Gregory Gause read the entire manuscript and offered important critiques and guidance. Robert Barr, Benjamin Bishin, Jason Brownlee, Louise Davidson-Schmich, Steven Heydemann, David Kang, Bassel Salloukh, Jillian Schwedler, Kenneth Shadlen, Andrew Shrank, and Marie Joelle Zahar offered invaluable advice on sections of the book and the overall argument. I am very thankful for the research assistance of Maria Silvia Costa at the University of Miami. At Cambridge University Press, Karen Anderson Howes deserves great thanks for her editing of this typescript.

A number of friends in Jordan and Kuwait gave of their time to assist my research and make me feel at home. In Amman, Riad al-Khouri taught me about business from the ground up. Mustafa Hamarneh, Mamdouh Abu Hassan, Dr. Tayseer Abdel Jabber, Luay Jadoun, Hamdi Tabba, and Mohammed M. Tijani all assisted my research into business politics in Jordan. I want to thank the entire staff at the American Center of Oriental Research in Amman, in particular Kathy Nimri. I have great memories of my time in Amman due in large part to friends like Rafat Rayyan, Marc Lynch, Eric Thompson, and Jillian Schwedler. In Kuwait City, my effort to understand the politics of business was guided by Dr. Muhammed A. Al-'Awadi, Dr. Hassan Johar, Abdulwahab Al-Wazzan, and Jasem K. Al-Sadoun. Mona Farouki and Barton Marcois at the US Embassy in Kuwait could not have been more helpful in managing the Fulbright program. Many of the students at Kuwait University, in particular Zekirisa Alievski and Jasmin Kantaveoic, made my stay there immense fun.

For enduring my ill-tempered behavior during the writing of this book (and beyond) and for supporting me when I was down, my greatest debt is owed to my wife Jennie. This book is dedicated to our next generation.

1 Summers of discontent: business–state politics in the Middle East

August is not a pleasant month in Kuwait City. In the noonday heat, a cigarette lighter left in a car can burst into flames. Sandstorms arrive without warning, making immediate shelter vital. Understandably, August is a time many Kuwaitis choose not to remain in the country, giving the impression that politics is almost suspended during the summer months. How ironic, then, that two of Kuwait's most damaging political events, a massive fiscal collapse and invasion by Iraq's army, occurred in the month of August. These events were not unrelated. The crash of an extra-legal stock market, the Souq al-Manakh, in 1982 initiated a string of economic difficulties that would contribute to the Iraqi invasion nearly a decade later.[1] To cope with the fiscal and political fallout from each, the Kuwaiti state turned to its private sector. The public–private struggle to respond to these events would require enduring many more Augusts.

Kuwait, however, was not alone. Across the Middle East, declines in external sources of capital were testing state capacities to respond. Of all the Arab states, no other was tied to Kuwait's travails quite like the Hashemite Kingdom of Jordan. In addition to foreign aid from the West, Jordan was a major recipient of development aid from Kuwait. Hundreds of thousands of Jordanian professionals have worked in the public and private sectors in Kuwait since the 1950s. The same fiscal crisis that jolted Kuwait carried through to Jordan; and in the aftermath of Kuwait's liberation, those Jordanian workers were forced to return to Jordan. To deal with these crises, the Jordanian state also turned to its private sector. Decades of fiscal crisis and political struggle, therefore, have inexorably bound these two Arab countries. Moreover, the remedy each sought was oddly reminiscent of what the developmental economist Albert Hirschman argued long ago, "what lacks in late-late developers is not the capital to invest, but the will of entrepreneurs to invest."[2] Central

---

[1] Kuwait's insistence that loans to Iraq in the 1980s be repaid was one of the Iraqi regime's grievances against Kuwait.

[2] Albert O. Hirschman, *The Strategy of Economic Development* (New Haven: Yale University Press, 1958), pp. 34–36.

1

to this will is the status of relations between domestic business and the state. This book is about that relationship before, during, and after prolonged economic crisis. It seeks to explain variation in business–state relations and chart the political and economic effects that follow from such divergences.

Kuwait's and Jordan's political-economic crises have been quite similar to those of other developing countries throughout the 1980s and 1990s. In contrast to the common perception that developing countries are only now opening to globalization, Jordan and Kuwait, like many states in the Middle East, have long been supine in the face of the dangers and fortunes of regional and international shifts. Following the optimism of independence and the soft budget constraints of the 1960s and 1970s, many states witnessed economic near-reversal in the 1980s and 1990s. In Africa and the Middle East, declines in exogenous revenue and persistent low economic growth rates have strained fiscal systems and induced chronic debt. Few Latin American countries escaped similar fiscal shocks, and even the Asian Tigers experienced crisis by the late 1990s. In tandem with global market shifts, demographic pressures in every developing country have made acute the need for more productive growth; that is, not merely greater economic expansion (higher output) but longer-term investment and developmentally nutritious private-sector expansion. The policy responses to and political effects of these pressures have not been uniform. Some states have pursued successful reform, some have retrenched, some have undergone regime change, and others continue to struggle with reform implementation. However, in almost every case, state officials have attempted to balance the need for increased domestic revenue with the desire to entice more private-sector investment and employment.

In the Arab Middle East, similar economic dilemmas are set against varied political and social backgrounds. Compared with much of the developing world, the Arab states have weathered the economic crisis of the 1980s and 1990s with few of the expected political ramifications and virtually no meaningful democratization. Among the Arab states, however, variation in the extent of economic adjustment has been evident, albeit with no "Arab Tigers." Given that oil is a finite resource, the dawn of a new millennium may bring a rise in oil prices and perhaps some economic relief for debt-burdened Arab governments. However, if we are to understand and speculate on the region's economic future, we must first account for political-economic change during the crisis decades. By unpacking and examining change in business–state relations across two cases, this book's aim is to address a set of questions that explore a crucial element of state–society relations during economic crisis. How do business–state relations affect reform outcomes? Why do organized business representatives of some countries gain more voice in policy while others fail to gain influence? What effect does this specific state–society relationship have on broader political outcomes such as productive economic adjustment and political liberalization?

These questions are not in the abstract. In the post-colonial Arab world, business elites have at times played prominent roles in demanding greater political representation, creating domestic economies, and resisting the consolidation of authoritarian rule.[3] During those same years, however, private enterprises were sequestered in many countries, business elites were coopted through state patronage, and organized business representation was either bypassed or swallowed by an expanding public sector. Since the 1980s, the Arab private sector has made an institutional comeback as Arab states faced chronic fiscal crisis and persistent economic downturn. Why has this been the case? Because coping with these pressures requires states to craft economic reform policy, mediate domestic political influences, balance external pressures, and implement and monitor policy changes. The last two decades have clearly demonstrated that the Arab state cannot do all of this. The result, in nearly every Arab country, has been an increased role for private-sector actors at each of these stages. Almost everywhere associations of business representation have been resuscitated. In countries where business was either fully coopted or partially replaced (Syria, Egypt, Qatar, and Saudi Arabia), a combination of state-initiated openings and business reorganization has generated a louder voice for business and increased public–private coordination. In countries with a more historically resilient private sector (Kuwait, Yemen, Tunisia, and Morocco), business associations have come to play genuine roles in the formulation and implementation of economic policy. As some countries have gradually opened their political systems to wider participation, business has sought greater political representation and expression.

Collectively these trends have encouraged a reappraisal of the Arab private sector. International lending agencies and consultants now call for deeper domestic reforms to "unleash the private sector."[4] Popular

---

[3] Steve Heydemann, *Authoritarianism in Syria* (Ithaca: Cornell University Press, 1999); Jill Crystal, *Oil and Politics in the Gulf: Rulers and Merchants in Kuwait and Qatar* (Cambridge: Cambridge University Press, 1995); Robert L. Tignor, *Capitalism and Nationalism at the End of Empire: State and Business in Decolonizing Egypt, Nigeria, and Kenya, 1945–1963* (Princeton: Princeton University Press, 1998).

[4] See, for example, World Bank, *Claiming the Future: Choosing Prosperity in the Middle East and North Africa* (Washington, DC: World Bank, 1995); and Bernard Hoekman and Patrick Messerlin, *Harnessing Trade for Development and Growth in the Middle East* (New York: Council on Foreign Relations, 2002).

journalistic accounts regularly tout Arab business as a natural counter-weight to political Islam and a natural ally of Western ideals.[5] Government officials in Washington have also jumped on the bandwagon and overtly tie increased private-sector activity with peace in the region. The trend is to join a revived private sector, market reform, Arab–Israeli peace, and the defeat of terrorism into one causal chain.[6] Despite this advocacy and the growing comparative evidence that some form of public–private coordination is required for successful economic reform, the ability of Arab states and their private sectors to coordinate in their efforts toward reform has not been uniform.

Peter Gourevitch best summed up the vexing logic present in such business–state engagement during crisis: "State action is frequently corporatistic, in that state and groups borrow from each other the authority to do what they cannot do alone."[7] Political factors determine how the dilemma is addressed: in some cases business elites and state officials borrow enough to achieve sustained private–public coordination, while in other cases coordination remains elusive. The cases of Jordan and Kuwait exemplify these typical yet contrasting outcomes. Despite enduring decades of exogenously triggered fiscal crises, business–state coordination in reform attempts and business's ability to shape policy under fiscal crisis generally succeed in Kuwait, yet fail in Jordan. One can add to this divergence the counterintuitive theoretical aspect of such outcomes. Comparative political-economy literature privileging structural constraints and a country's revenue base posit that highly revenue-autonomous and sectorally dependent states, such as Kuwait, should experience either policy deadlock or policy drift as a result of resistant domestic business. Less dependent states, such as Jordan, should benefit from greater autonomy from business and an ability to implement unpopular reform.

This book's explanation of divergence in the Jordanian and Kuwaiti cases seeks to build upon structural and incentive-based models of business–state relations. The sectoral nature and revenue characteristics of the modern Arab state are important first factors to study in assessing how business and state interact and under what conditions coordinated relations evolve; however, they are not sufficient. Shifts in a

---

[5] Thomas Friedman, *The Lexus and the Olive Tree* (New York: Farrar, Straus, Giroux, 1999).

[6] See Pete W. Moore and Andrew Shrank, "Commerce and Conflict: How the US Effort to Counter Terrorism with Trade May Backfire," *Middle East Policy*, 10, 3 (September 2003), pp. 112–120.

[7] Peter Gourevitch, *Politics in Hard Times: Comparative Responses to International Economic Crises* (Ithaca: Cornell University Press, 1986), p. 230.

Table 1.1 *Per capita GNP: constant US dollars*

	1972–1976	1976–1980	1980–1984	1984–1988	1988–1993
Jordan	470	996	1,642	1,842	1,396
Kuwait	7,854	17,104	20,392	15,366	14,053

Source: World Bank, *World Tables 1987* (Baltimore: Johns Hopkins University Press, 1987); World Bank, *World Tables 1996* (Baltimore: Johns Hopkins University Press, 1996).

country's revenue or sectoral profile (declines or increases in oil and aid, for instance) herald domestic political change, but the direction and type are not givens. For example, David Waldner argues that "the [rentier] thesis fails to distinguish between constraining conditions and permissive conditions; the presence of externally derived wealth makes certain arrangements possible but it does not dictate their establishment."[8] The argument of this book proposes patterns of business–state relations as one set of constraining conditions on the ebb and flow of external revenue, an approach that requires attention above and below the level of the state. Divergence in the organizational nature of business representation (whether elite cohesion or breakdown) shaped the capacities of business elites to coordinate with public authorities during the exogenously driven crisis decades of the 1980s and 1990s. The pace and political terrain (i.e., the strength of the political opposition) during crisis determined state incentives toward coordination. Consequently, the task of my empirical analysis is to take account of how each country's business community evolved before and after European rule, how institutions of business representation changed over time, and how state actions vis-à-vis important social actors, such as business and political Islam, shaped the type and strength of political opposition during crisis. It is these factors that distinguish business–state relations in the region and ultimately shape future economic development and reform.

Comparing cases and subjects

At first glance, comparing Jordan, a lower-middle-income country, with Kuwait, one of the world's richest countries, seems a mismatch (see table 1.1). The differences are not trivial, but as candidates for comparing business–state relations Kuwait and Jordan exhibit key similarities: their

[8] David Waldner, *State Building and Late Development* (Ithaca: Cornell University Press, 1999), p. 107.

histories as post-colonial Arab states, the presence of large, functionally similar business organizations, and the timing of economic growth and crisis.

First, both are important Arab countries given their strategic locations, and each has been a regional leader in experimenting with political liberalization. Jordan and Kuwait both experienced British rule, which recognized and strengthened the local monarchies, and nurtured a new form of external dependence. The al-Sabahs in Kuwait and the Hashemites in Jordan have traditionally retained near-absolute political authority while hesitantly granting greater participation in formal politics over time. Jordan and Kuwait are small states, located in an insecure regional environment, and thus both monarchies relied on British and later American support (financial and military) to retain their power. Surrounded by large, aggressive neighbors, Jordan and Kuwait are equally sensitive to regional shifts and external threats. The two have exhibited similar ascriptive divisions and conflicting national identifications. In Kuwait, the distinctions run from the religious (Shi'a, Sunni), to citizenship status, to tribal affiliations and history. In Jordan, distinctions involve principally origin (West Bank or East Bank) but also include time of immigration to Jordan, tribal affiliation, and religious identification (Christian or Muslim). As well as these ascriptive similarities, Jordan and Kuwait also share a history of elected parliaments, constitutionalism, and self-identification as democratic states. In the context of Middle East domestic politics, the political leaderships in Kuwait and Jordan have historically cited their democratic nature in a bid for more external political legitimacy; and, by regional standards, political debate in these Arab countries is robust. In this way, Jordan and Kuwait are at the leading edge of political experimentation in the region and have much to offer as models for other regional liberalizers such as Bahrain, Yemen, Egypt, Morocco, Tunisia, and Oman.

Second, since policy outcome – the degree to which the private sector and the state coordinate on policy reform – is a dependent variable, this book also examines how each business community represented private-sector interests to the state. The role of business associations in each case provides a generalizable comparative base. In each case, and indeed throughout the Arab world, business was the alpha wolf of societal organizers. Chambers of commerce were established long before state independence, and by the 1970s these institutions were the largest (as measured by membership) domestic social organizations in the region. Both the Jordanian and Kuwaiti chambers were founded on the Anglo-American interest-group model, as opposed to the more corporatist continental model; however, these demarcations between public and private have never been absolute. Neither association was founded as a reaction to a rival labor organization. Both have held free elections for leadership every four years since their founding, and each is financially autonomous from direct state authority. On these points, a key difference is apparent with business associations in Egypt, Saudi Arabia, and Syria, where state sponsorship and management have been prevalent since political independence. However, as liberalization and greater private-sector initiative are pursued throughout the Arab world, it is the Kuwaiti and Jordanian business associations that are sought out as models to emulate.[9] A question remains, however: why focus on formal institutions when informal business–state clientelism may prevail?

While it is true that business lobbying in the developing world is often assumed to take the form of individual rent-seeking, increasingly state officials prefer an aggregated voice. Dealing with an official representative not only provides legitimacy; it also saves the cost of canvassing individual firms and sectors. Surviving fiscal shocks and pursuing reform require flexibility and responsiveness, capabilities an institutional actor can provide. Especially in countries where state capacities are underdeveloped, "how the state and other coordinating mechanisms (e.g., markets, networks, associations) coalesce and are related to particular social systems of production are important determinants of economic performance."[10] In the modern Middle East, business–state coordination is one of those mechanisms. Increasingly, in circumstances of protracted market uncertainty and fiscal volatility, institutional interaction is the preference. Moreover, as countries of the Middle East face rapidly shifting pressures from market globalization, what Philippe Schmitter terms the "continuous representation" of business associations can provide state officials with timely, clear signals on private-sector interests.[11] Certainly, clientelism has not lost its uses and business representation has hardly come to dominate the reform agenda in every country; however, greater

---

[9] The Egyptian Businessman's Association was modeled after the Jordanian version. In Syria, it is no secret that businessmen would like to freely elect the executive board of their main chamber in Damascus. The success of Syrian merchants in Jordan's chamber is not lost on the Damascene merchants. In the late 1990s, Syrian merchants made some progress in persuading state officials to elect at least a portion of the executive board. Consequently, in 1997 a vocal critic of government economic policies became president of the Damascus Chamber of Commerce.

[10] J. Roger Hollingsworth, "New Perspectives on the Spatial Dimensions of Economic Coordination: Tensions Between Globalization and Social Systems of Production," *Review of International Political Economy*, 5, 3 (September 1998), p. 487.

[11] Philippe C. Schmitter and Wolfgang Streeck, "The Organization of Business Interests: Studying the Associative Action of Business in Advanced Industrial Societies," Max-Planck-Institut für Gesellschaftsforschung, Discussion Paper 99/1 (March 1999); see also Richard F. Doner and Ben Ross Schneider, "The New Institutional Economics, Business Associations, and Development," International Institute of Labor Studies, Discussion Paper Series N 110 (2000), p. 19.

analysis is required of the changing dynamics of all aspects of public–private interaction.

Finally, in a broader political sense, Arab business associations, by virtue of their comparative autonomy and long history of intra-electoral competition, have at times played the role of proxy political party. In Latin America, for instance, "the social classes that formed the historic base for parties have fragmented into specialized sectoral and professional clienteles that have sought new forms of collective expression."[12] In most Middle Eastern countries, strong political parties were not institutional precursors to social organizations; rather, weak or non-existent party systems existed alongside the more established and more capable professional associations (al-Niqabat al-Mihaniyya), especially business associations. Thus, a focus on organized business grants insight into broader questions of changing patterns of state–society relations and the role interest associations may play in future political transitions.

An additional issue of concern is the treatment of business (or any social actor) as monolithic rather than disaggregating its interests and actions.[13] This study does not assume business as a monolith, nor is its purpose to address the business–state nexus from every vantage. A focus on the associational representation of business over time provides but one window into how a business community changes, how elites evolve, and why interests translate into action the way they do. Jeffry Frieden has termed this the "demand-side" approach to business politics. When interpreted together with the supply side, "This synthesis accepts that private interests are crucial inputs into policy-making and that the institutional context within which these interests are processed also has a substantial impact on outcomes."[14] For this study, then, the terms "organized business" and "association" refer to the respective peak chambers of commerce. The terms "business community" and "business elites" will be explained in context to refer either to the rank and file of the chamber or to the leadership. Finally, this study does not focus upon small merchants or the large informal economies of the Middle East.[15]

---

[12] Philippe C. Schmitter, "Transitology: The Science of the Art of Democratization?," in Joseph Tulchin (ed.), The Consolidation of Democracy in Latin America (Boulder: Lynne Rienner, 1995), p. 24.

[13] See Robert Vitalis, When Capitalists Collide: Business Conflict and the End of Empire in Egypt (Berkeley: University of California Press, 1995).

[14] Jeffry A. Frieden, "A Pax on Both Their Houses: State, Society, and Social Science," Contention, 3, 3 (Spring 1994), p. 180.

[15] For the political roles small business plays in widely differing contexts, see Kenneth C. Shadlen, "Orphaned by Democracy: Small Business in Mexico," Comparative Politics (October 2002), pp. 43–62; and Luiz Martinez, The Algerian Civil War, 1990–1998 (New York: Columbia University Press, 2000).

Third, the timeframe of comparison hinges on similar boom-and-bust patterns. A number of Middle East comparativists[16] have successfully utilized this two-country approach, and this book attempts to follow in that tradition. Clearly, there are uses and limits to this or any comparative method;[17] however, by juxtaposing the crisis period with the earlier periods of state-building and commodity boom, the elements of similarity and difference in business–state relations rise to the top. While the countries of the Middle East may provide little variation for those pursuing questions of democratization and regime change, focused and historically informed comparisons of economic development and state–society relations reveal rich variation among the Middle Eastern cases. Economically, both countries are late-late developers that have depended to a great extent upon inflows of capital. Kuwait cashed in on its resource endowment, while Jordan cashed in on its geostrategic position and expatriate labor. Some of the massive oil revenues received by the Kuwaiti state were channeled back to Jordan through remittance income and development aid. Tremendous inflows of capital fueled economic boom in the 1960s and 1970s. This aspect of the analysis bears a resemblance to Kiren Chaudhry's comparison of Saudi Arabia (oil rents) and Yemen (aid and remittance income). For Chaudhry, the different types of rent flows lead to different institutional arrangements between business and state and ultimately to contrasting forms of state autonomy in each case.[18] Through a more sustained focus on the evolution of business in Jordan and Kuwait, the purpose of this study is to highlight the role played in the evolution of business–state relations in the periphery by other political and, particularly, institutional factors: specifically, the organization of business representation, the cohesion of business elites, and the challenge of political rivals.

What became known as the bust period, the 1980s and 1990s, is the pivotal point of the comparison. It is in the period after the boom that

---

[16] See, for example, Crystal, *Oil and Politics*; and Kiren Aziz Chaudhry, *The Price of Wealth: Economies and Institutions in the Middle East* (Ithaca: Cornell University Press, 1997).

[17] James Mahoney, "Strategies of Causal Inference in Small-*N* Analysis," *Sociological Methods & Research*, 28, 4 (May 2000), pp. 387–424. For Middle East comparativists, see Robert Vitalis's review of Kiren Chaudhry, *The Price of Wealth*, in *International Journal of Middle East Studies*, 31 (1999), pp. 659–661. Mahmood Mamdani also provides an account of the positives and negatives of the comparative political-economy approach; see "Beyond Settler and Native as Political Identities: Overcoming the Political Legacy of Colonialism," *Comparative Studies of Society and History*, 43, 4 (October 2001), pp. 651–664.

[18] Chaudhry, *The Price of Wealth*, pp. 23–30. Also, Chaudhry's case selection derives, in part, from Yemen's and Saudi Arabia's "extreme" natures as cases of dependency. The current study presents cases with characteristics more in common with lower- to middle-income developing countries (i.e., Jordan) and with upper-income oil exporters (Kuwait).

the divergent patterns of business–state relations become most evident. For the comparativist, times of financial crisis provide excellent opportunities to see what really matters in a country's politics, since it is in such periods that political responses are clearest.[19] Obviously the assumption is that the crises in the 1980s and 1990s are similar for both Jordan and Kuwait. Table 1.1 demonstrates the income aspect of the crises in terms of declining per capita GDP in the 1980s. While analysis will detail important contextual differences in the crises, pressure on each state to reform economically and court greater private-sector participation was comparable. Moreover, it was clear that the two states attempted to react similarly to the crisis but that each was institutionally unprepared to resolve the crisis. Both countries pursued political liberalization and economic reforms during the 1980s and 1990s. Declines in exogenous rents to each state brought depressed economic growth; thus both states have had to juggle the necessity of liberalizing economically and politically while maintaining centralized political control. Bracketing the business role in economic policy debate from its impact on political liberalization is clearly not possible. Therefore, using fiscal crisis as the comparative focus for Kuwait and Jordan broadens investigation into how business–state interaction on policy generates political externalities. The explanation for the comparative success of institutionally based business–state coordination in Kuwait in advancing economic reform and addressing chronic debt by the mid-1990s, in contrast to Jordan, also provides some insight into the stagnation and reversal of political liberalization in the same years. One conclusion from this study is that the changing relations between business and the state reflect the broader evolution of authoritarianism in the region.

Consequently, while this book compares two countries, it does so at the level of state–society relations: specifically, patterns and change in the institutional mediation between business and state over time. Social science theories focusing on business–state relations are well developed and have keenly shaped how we view state–society relations in the developing world. Comparative scholarship of the countries of the Middle East provides material to test and correct these theories.

A single logic, two approaches

A goal of this study is to provide theoretically informed insight into business–state relations in the Arab world and generate correctives to some of the prevailing approaches to business–state politics in the developing world in general. Two interpretations that derive from a common

---

[19] Gourevitch, *Politics in Hard Times*, p. 221.

intellectual heritage can be identified: theories arguing that business–state relations are shaped by dynamics at the state level and higher (termed structural/statist), and those that focus on the collective action of business from the bottom up (termed new institutional economics). Though structural approaches have succeeded in generating comparative work on Middle Eastern countries and the focus on institutions has broadened economic inquiry, both clusters of literature generalize about important aspects of the business–state relationship within a framework of neoclassical economics. Each approach relies on the assumption that the reaction of domestic business can be explained by reference to structured incentives. For structural/statist theorists those incentives are ultimately economic. For the more actor-centered, collective-action theorists, those incentives overlap with an organizational logic, yet are nevertheless grounded in material interests. In other words, each is an extension of the foundations of neoclassical economics into political analysis. One critique offered by this study is that, in approaching the subject from different directions but operating from the same assumptions, the micro and macro arguments commit the same original sin.

This book seeks to advance the institutional revisions of political economy by arguing that assumptions about incentive and choice in business–state relations need to be relaxed and that systematic analysis is needed of the historical-institutional legacy of those relations and the political context of social actors. This is not a retreat into contextually driven arguments or the culturally constructed nature of social relations, but is driven by the conviction that responses to structural incentives are shaped by previous political struggles over regime coalitions, historical junctures, and institutional capacities during crisis. Consequently, this analysis of business representation and business–state relations in late-late developers takes as its start Karl Polanyi's famous claim that "man's economy, as a rule, is submerged in his social relationships."[20] Long before the advent of market capitalism, the Arab historian Ibn Khaldun struck a similar note in writing about the importance of rank among merchants:

The person who has no rank whatever, even though he may have property, acquires a fortune only in proportion to the property he owns in accordance with the efforts he himself makes. Most merchants are in this position. Therefore [merchants] who have rank are far better off [than other merchants].[21]

---

[20] Karl Polanyi, *The Great Transformation* (New York: Reinhart & Co., 1944), p. 46. See also Simon A. Herbert, "Organizations and Markets," *Journal of Economic Perspectives*, 5 (Spring 1991), pp. 25–44; Peter Evans, *Embedded Autonomy: States and Industrial Transformation* (Princeton: Princeton University Press, 1995); and Mark Granovetter, "Economic Action and Social Structure: The Problem of Embeddedness," *American Journal of Sociology*, 91, 3 (November 1985), pp. 481–510.

[21] Ibn Khaldun, *The Muqaddimah: An Introduction to History*, trans. by Franz Rosenthal, 2 vols. (New York: Pantheon Books, 1958), vol. II, p. 327.

Echoing Khaldun's logic, I aim not to dispense with the logics that underpin macro- and micro-structural approaches but rather to augment each. Insofar as an explanation of divergent crisis outcomes in Kuwait and Jordan requires systematic attention to each actor, business and state, and to both levels, structural approaches offer a degree of insight. What comes into focus at the macro end of the equation are states shaped by similar exogenous economic forces and administrative capacities that are similarly limited in their ability to enact reform during fiscal crisis. At the micro level, we see comparable private-sector elites working through (and around) functionally similar organizational representatives to shape state policy. At this point, what is left is form but no content. The key to variance can be found at the meso level. Here what comes into focus is a different political terrain facing business and state, and respective business representations with different capacities to coordinate with state officials. This book will trace these differences to the political legacies of state formation and to the trajectories of institutional evolution on the part of business representation. The historical narrative will seek, as much as possible, to recount struggles between (and among) business leaders and state officials and identify crucial turning points all within the larger political and economic dynamics that define late development in the Arab world.

The path-dependent flavor of this argument follows other comparative work on sectorally dependent states.[22] A common theme is the diversity of political outcomes and alignments despite the presence of similar external economic incentives. This study extends this analysis in a new direction by seeking comparative evidence of what drives business–state relations over time and how institutions of business representation evolved in tandem. Key shifts in those relations and in the capacities of business to participate in policy negotiation are prominent factors explaining crisis outcomes. What has been amply demonstrated in the earlier literature is that sectorally dependent African and Middle Eastern states exhibit similar administrative weaknesses in the face of persistent economic crisis. What has been absent is the societal side of this problem, that is, how states attempt to overcome administrative weaknesses by encouraging (and managing) policy involvement by the private sector, and how, in

---

[22] See Crystal, *Oil and Politics*; Chaudhry, *The Price of Wealth*; Dirk Vandewalle, *Libya Since Independence: Oil and State-Building* (Ithaca: Cornell University Press, 1998); Gregory F. Gause, *Oil Monarchies: Domestic and Security Challenges in the Arab Gulf States* (New York: Council on Foreign Relations, 1994); Mary Ann Tétreault, *Stories of Democracy: Politics and Society in Contemporary Kuwait* (New York: Columbia University Press, 2000); and Michael Herb, *All in the Family: Absolutism, Revolution, and Democracy in the Middle Eastern Monarchies* (Albany: SUNY Press, 1999).

turn, the private sector attempts to gain more voice during periods of crisis. The next section expands upon these claims by reviewing flaws of the structural/statist and the institutional-actor approaches to business–state relations in the developing world.

Rents and sectors in the Middle East

The rentier approach in the field of Middle East politics and what is known as the sectoral approach[23] in comparative politics best exemplify the top-down macro perspective on business–state relations in the developing world. This cluster of literature has been influential in shaping not just academic but also policy perspectives of what business is in the developing world and how it interacts with state officials. Since rentier and sectoral outlooks derive from the neoclassical tradition in the field of political economy, both approaches share similar assumptions about what drives private- and public-sector actions – economic incentives – and what should result. Also crucial to this literature is the idea that developing states are positioned as intervening variables and are thus constrained by exogenous factors. In other words, external economic shifts determine state capacities and interests that in turn shape the politics and position of business. Hence, the term "structural/statist" best describes this cluster of literature. Given the fact that most Arab states, including Jordan and Kuwait, are highly dependent upon external revenue, structural/statist accounts are central to many analyses of domestic politics in the region.[24] Reviewing three crucial questions of the structural/statist argument demonstrates how these basic assumptions are expressed and ultimately why they fall short. First, what are sectors and rents and how do they shape state capacities and interests? Second, what does this dynamic mean for social actors, particularly business and its relations with political

[23] This study will focus on the works of Michael Shafer (*Winners and Losers: How Sectors Shape the Developmental Prospects of States* [Ithaca: Cornell University Press, 1994]) and Terry Lynn Karl (*The Paradox of Plenty: Oil Booms and Petro-States* [Berkeley: University of California Press, 1997]). For the broader literature, which does not explicitly address the Middle East, see Ronald Rogowski, *Commerce and Coalitions: How Trade Affects Domestic Political Alignments* (Princeton: Princeton University Press, 1989); Jeffry Frieden, *Debt, Development, and Democracy: Modern Political Economy and Latin America, 1965–1985* (Princeton: Princeton University Press, 1991); and Jeffry Frieden and Ronald Rogowski, "The Impact of the International Economy on National Policies: An Analytic Overview," in Robert Keohane and Helen Milner (eds.), *Internationalization and Domestic Politics* (Cambridge, UK: Cambridge University Press, 1996), pp. 25–47.

[24] This dependence is reflected typically in the level of external revenue in government budgets, but it is also expressed in the dependence on commodity exports. In 1999, for instance, all Middle Eastern and North African countries, save Israel and Turkey, had on average nearly half of their exports in the form of commodity export: Hoekman and Messerlin, *Harnessing Trade*, p. 45.

authority? Third, what do structural/statist approaches suggest should be the outcome of fiscal and economic crisis?

Rent's modern definition is commonly attributed to Adam Smith, who distinguished between rents and profit:

Rent, it is to be observed, therefore, enters into the composition of the price of commodities in a different way from wages and profit. High or low wages and profit, are the causes of high or low price; high or low rent is the effect of it. It is because high or low wages and profit must be paid, in order to bring a particular commodity to market, that its price is high or low. But it is because its price is high or low; a great deal more, or very little more, or no more, than what is sufficient to pay those wages and profit, that it affords a high rent, or a low rent, or no rent at all.[25]

The importance of rents to modern political life in the Middle East comes into play when the fiscal resources of the state and society are considered. For a state, typical rents are derived from oil revenues, mining, transit fees, customs duties, and so on. For economic actors, rents comprise exclusive access to markets, production subsidies, or participation in trade protocol regimes (such as the old Iraqi–Jordanian oil/trade agreement). Therefore, the basic tenet of rentier-state theory – one that I argue is incomplete – holds that the character of resources available to a state or society fundamentally shapes politics in that country.[26]

Joseph Schumpeter argued that the nature of a state's resources should be a focal point for social and political analysis. "Public finances are one of the best starting points for an investigation of society, especially though not exclusively of its political life."[27] In considering state revenues, the key distinction is between revenues generated from the domestic economy versus revenue received from external sources. Revenue extracted internally refers of course to various forms of taxation (though most specifically direct taxation over indirect), and the progress of taxation has been closely linked to the development of the democratic state in the West.[28] External rents include foreign aid, oil, and various types of transit fees (in the case

[25] Adam Smith, *An Inquiry into the Nature and Causes of the Wealth of Nations*, edited by Edwin Cannan (Methuen & Co., 1904; Library of Economics and Liberty, 1 March 2002, http://www.econlib.org/library/Smith/smWN5.html).

[26] Giacomo Luciani, "Allocative vs. Production States: A Theoretical Framework," in Luciani (ed.), *The Arab State* (Berkeley: University of California Press, 1990), pp. 65–84.

[27] Joseph Schumpeter, "The Crisis of the Tax State," in Alan T. Peacock (ed.), *International Economic Papers*, No. 4 (London: Macmillan, 1954), p. 7.

[28] Charles Tilly, "War Making and State Making as Organized Crime," in Peter Evans, Dietrich Rueschemeyer, and Theda Skocpol (eds.), *Bringing the State Back In* (Cambridge: Cambridge University Press, 1985), pp. 169–191; Margaret Levi, *Of Revenue and Rule* (Berkeley: University of California Press, 1988); and Robert Bates and Da-Hsiang Donald Lien, "A Note on Taxation, Development and Representative Government," *Politics & Society*, 14, 1 (1985), pp. 53–70.

of the Suez canal, for instance). When a state derives most of its revenue from such external sources, it is termed a rentier state. Luciani offers two measures that distinguish between rentier and non-rentier states: state revenue in the form of rents above or below a 40 percent level, and whether or not state expenditure comprises a significant proportion of the gross domestic product (GDP).[29]

The first measure determines whether a state is primarily "exoteric," that is, deriving most of its revenue from outside its state borders, while the second determines whether a state is "allocative," that is, a state whose domestic fiscal activity primarily comprises distribution. Most of the pure rentiers (with percentages above 80 percent of state revenue in the form of rents) are found in the Gulf; Kuwait is a prime example. Other states outside the region, however, have been considered rentiers. At times, Venezuela, Nigeria, Norway, and some African countries dependent on foreign aid and commodity export can be considered good examples. When rent levels are significant, but do not form the majority of revenue (around the 40 percent revenue mark), the effect on the state is equally important, and these have been termed "semi-rentier" states.[30] Jordan is a prime example in this category, as are Egypt, Syria, Yemen, and other developing world states in periods of heavy reliance on foreign grants. So, Kuwait is properly defined as a rentier state and Jordan as a semi-rentier, though both are clearly allocative states, with usually over 50 percent of GDP composed of state expenditure.

Rents in the form of worker remittances flow to a country's society instead of directly into state coffers. Technically, this is not unearned income, as is the case with oil, but the effects of remittances on the domestic economy and polities are similar. In the Middle East, remittances have traditionally taken the form of Jordanian, Egyptian, Syrian, and other Arab nationals working in the Gulf states and sending their earnings back home. Thus, Jordan and Kuwait have historically shared more than just regional location; they have been dependent upon one another. Though remittance income does not go to the state directly (there may be forms of transfer taxation, but most transfers are informal and not well tracked), some of the effects of remittances follow closely those of state rents. Similar to state distribution, external worker finances flood the local economy, boosting internal consumption. Consequently, there is more money chasing fewer domestic investment opportunities.

---

[29] Luciani, "Allocative vs. Production States." It should be noted that Luciani offers no general reason for these thresholds in his definitions.

[30] Rex Brynen, "Economic Crisis and Post-Rentier Democratization in the Arab World: The Case of Jordan," *Canadian Journal of Political Science*, 25, 1 (March 1992); Hazem Beblawi, "The Rentier State in the Arab World," in Luciani, *The Arab State*, pp. 85–98.

Table 1.2 *Comparative government revenues: oil, remittances, and foreign grants*

	Jordan		Kuwait
	Remittances (million US$)	Aid (% total revenue)	Oil (% total revenue)
1963			92
1964			93
1965			92
1966			84
1967			91
1968			91
1969			87
1970	n.a.	48	92
1971	n.a.	39	92
1972	n.a.	44	93
1973	44.7	40	97
1974	74.8	39	97
1975	166.7	47	96
1976	390.4	32	95
1977	443.7	36	93
1978	469.6	24	97
1979	540.6	45	95
1980	714.6	40	92
1981	929.4	33	90
1982	975.5	30	92
1983	1,110.0	28	91
1984	1,237.0	16	89
1985	1,021.0	22	86
1986	1,184.0	16	88
1987	939.0	15	86
1988	894.0	16	91
1989	623.0	24	90
1990	500.0	14	77
1991	450.0	16	88
1992	800.0	8	84
1993	n.a.	14	85
1994	n.a.	13	86
1995	n.a.	12	85
1996	n.a.	14	97
1997	n.a.	14	95
1998	n.a.	11	97
1999	n.a.	11	90
2000	n.a.	14	n.a.

Sources: Central Bank of Jordan, *Yearly Statistical Series (1964–1993)* (Amman: Central Bank of Jordan, 1994); Kuwait, Ministry of Planning, *Statistical Abstract in 25 Years* (Kuwait City: Central Statistical Office, 1990); *Central Bank of Kuwait, Quarterly Statistical Bulletin* (April–June 1995); International Monetary Fund, *International Financial Statistics Yearbook* (various years); World Bank, *World Tables 1995* (Baltimore: Johns Hopkins University Press, 1995).

Outside the study of the Middle East, economically based arguments for development and political reform, commonly termed sectoral approaches, follow a similar path. According to Chaudhry, these approaches amount to an extension of "neoclassical trade theory."[31] Two recent works by Michael Shafer and Terry Lynn Karl, while not based on Middle East cases, nonetheless make explicit arguments aimed at the region by focusing on the political effects of a country's dominant economic sector. Both scholars closely follow Schumpeter's emphasis on a state's fiscal sociology. Karl put it this way: "Simply stated, the revenues a state collects, how it collects them, and the uses to which it puts them define its nature."[32] However, the sectoral approach goes beyond solely the state-revenue focus to theorize about the political effects of an entire economy's revenue source.

Michael Shafer, in his book *Winners and Losers: How Sectors Shape the Developmental Prospects of States*, develops an argument about the effect sectoral makeup has on a state's ability to launch economic restructuring. Sectors are defined as "a type of economic activity (mining, industrial, plantation crop production, peasant cash crop production, or light manufacturing) that constitutes an enduring, coherent whole defined by a distinctive combination of four variables – capital intensity, economies of scale, production flexibility, and asset/factor flexibility."[33] The attributes of the leading sectors, and how they are tied to the international economy, determine a state's developmental trajectory. Two ideal-type political economies, low/low and high/high, are given. High/high types exhibit high capital intensity, high economies of scale, high production inflexibility, and high asset/factor inflexibility, while low/low exhibit the opposite. The oil states of the Middle East are, for Shafer, "the best available approximation of the high/high ideal type," that is high in the sense of capital intensity, economies of scale, and production inflexibility.[34] Indeed, the sectoral profile of most Arab states tends toward the high/high ideal-type. In contrast to these political economies, low/low political economies have higher degrees of flexibility and hence are able to restructure better (in the face of international shifts) than inflexible high/high types. The result is a forceful argument echoing a near-structural determinism:

---

[31] Kiren Chaudhry, "Prices, Politics, Institutions: Oil Exporters in the International Economy," *Business and Politics*, 1, 3 (1999), pp. 317–342.

[32] Karl, *The Paradox of Plenty*, p. 13.

[33] Shafer, *Winners and Losers*, p. 10. "Production flexibility is the ability to meet short-term market shifts by varying output levels or product mix. Asset/factor flexibility refers to the sector-specificity of facilities, supporting infrastructure, and workforce skills" (*ibid.*).

[34] *Ibid.*, p. 233.

sectors have an optimal, or at least typical, *economic* organization and pose distinct economic challenges to all producers and states, and . . . states with similar sectoral bases face similar *political* constraints when they address these challenges, do so from similar institutional positions, and arrive at similar policy outcomes.[35]

Terry Lynn Karl's "structured-contingency" approach, though less deterministic in tone, still views excessive sectoral reliance as "pre-structuring" a state's decisionmaking and implementation capacities. Like Shafer, Karl expects incentives found in every petro-state to yield similar political economies. Consequently, the sectoral and rentier approaches agree that state interests and structures are conditioned by macro-economic variables. Evidence for these approaches can be drawn from the boom era of Arab economic development.

The jump in oil prices and other forms of external revenue in the 1960s and 1970s resulted in a dramatic growth of state ministries throughout the Middle East. The old mercantilist Spanish quip, "why make what you can buy,"[36] became translated in the Arab experience into "why work, when you can work for the state?" Ministries not only proliferated to embrace every conceivable policy area, but they also added countless numbers of civil servants beyond any reasonable bureaucratic need.[37] Economic planning lost any genuine application and most policymaking gravitated toward the Ministry of Finance, the primary rent collector. The state as the locus of economic activity through public employment became the primary distributor of capital in the economy.[38] Rates of direct taxation were negligible. Through a number of transfer schemes, the primary functions of state ministries became distribution over extraction or regulation.[39] What we are left with, then, is a weighted institutional structure where "'state interests' are uniquely identified with perpetuating the state's traditional fiscal base by advancing the existing development model and fostering social interests that will support state policy."[40]

In much the same way that state structure conforms to sectoral and revenue needs, social forces – particularly business – are expected to

---

[35] *Ibid.*, p. 22.

[36] David S. Landes, *The Wealth and Poverty of Nations: Why Some Are So Rich and Some So Poor* (New York: W. W. Norton, 1998).

[37] This should not imply a discount of the social benefits of public-sector expansion which included the employment of women and the reduction of income gaps in the region.

[38] Jacques Delacroix, "The Distributive State in the World System," *Studies in Comparative International Development*, 15 (1980), pp. 3–22.

[39] A virtue of this aspect of the structural/statist argument is its clear isolation of a connection between revenue/sectoral reliance and neo-patrimonialism, above a cultural or tribal explanation.

[40] Karl, *The Paradox of Plenty*, p. 224.

follow suit. The rentier literature is quite developed in this respect. As the rentier state becomes the locus of economic activity through public employment, it also becomes the primary distributor of capital in the economy. Large-scale real estate purchases, public investments in private corporations, robust subsidy programs, and other welfare projects are common among rentiers. Jacques Delacroix terms this the "distributive state."[41] In turn, the society of a rentier state is shaped by the availability of persistent state rents.

Interaction with state ministries becomes very intense within a rentier society. Whether people are working for the state, receiving some form of payment from the state, or bargaining for state permissions, political authority becomes inordinately a central target of much activity in society. These features of interaction contribute to what Hazem Beblawi terms the "rentier mentality" of societies in many Arab states. Citizenship is no longer built on reciprocal interaction with political authority but on rewards from state managers, severing the link between production and reward. Over 400 years before Smith's famous distinction between rents and profit, Ibn Khaldun chastised "weak-minded persons" who seek to "discover property under the surface of the earth and make some profit from it." While Ibn Khaldun was literally writing of treasure-hunting, the link between reward and non-productivity was clear in the intentions he ascribed to such endeavors: "When such a person cannot earn enough in a natural way, his only way out is to wish that at one stroke, without any effort, he might find sufficient money to pay for the (luxury) habits in which he has become caught."[42]

Since social actors are at the receiving end of state distribution, second-order rents often permeate economic relations in society.[43] A good deal of private-sector activity is geared toward securing a piece of state largesse in the form of subsidies, state contracts, or tax exemption. A number of businessmen become what Samuel Popkin terms "easy riders." They compete with one another, but it is a competition aimed at further political access that does not result in more efficient production or increased quality.[44] In the modern Arab economy these businessmen are termed al-kafil, sponsors or agents for foreign imports in which the agent receives a percentage of profits essentially for signing his name to various documents.[45]

[41] Delacroix, "The Distributive State in the World System."
[42] Ibn Khaldun, *The Muqaddimah*, vol. II, pp. 319–321.
[43] Beblawi, "The Rentier State in the Arab World," pp. 89–91.
[44] Samuel L. Popkin, "Public Choice and Peasant Organization," in Robert H. Bates (ed.), *Toward a Political Economy of Development: A Rational Choice Perspective* (Berkeley: University of California Press, 1988), p. 268.
[45] Beblawi, "The Rentier State in the Arab World," p. 92.

Consequently, the economic profile of rentier states is seen to privilege short-term, highly liquid investments such as real estate and stock markets over longer-term, fixed assets such as private infrastructure or industry, the so-called Dutch Disease. The implications for business and its representation are clear. Institutional autonomy is sacrificed for pursuit of state largesse. Given that much state distribution to business is exclusive (real estate, public contracts, and the like), incentives for the pursuit of individual rent-seeking should trump collective action.[46] Those business associations or representations that do exist are considered hollow. The sectoral approach modifies this rather negative portrayal in an interesting way.

The sectoral approach argues not that state revenue interests shape social actors but rather that sectoral makeup shapes the organization and interests of business directly. In countries where business is overwhelmingly tied to a few inflexible sectors (such as services and the public sector throughout the Arab world), distinct patterns of collective action will emerge.[47] Shafer and Karl argue that this compels formation of uniquely organized interest groups for two reasons. First, a smaller business community clustered around one or two dominant sectors brings into play Mancur Olson's idea that the existence of fewer firms makes collective action easier.[48] Second, when these sectors are booming and the pie is enlarging, the reduction of zero-sum social conflict streamlines access and lobbying strategies. Viewed in this light, business representation is deemed to be neither autonomous nor in possession of varied institutional capacities.[49] It is in all respects simply an extension of dominant sectoral interests in much the same way that rentier theorists see society as reflection of the state bureaucracy.[50] In sum, though the sectoral and rentier approaches arrive by slightly different routes, their portrait of business in the Middle East, and indeed most of the developing world, is rather negative and uniform from the perspective of the structural/statist approach. Beyond making "cries for help that are unanimous, loud, and anguished,"[51] domestic business is hardly autonomous and is afflicted

---

[46] The conception of a rentier state being a "flabby state," large but lacking in capabilities, it is often argued, extends to its society as well.

[47] Shafer, *Winners and Losers*, pp. 2–3.   [48] Cited *ibid.*, pp. 39–42.

[49] Revisions of this characterization still tend to paint a rather two-dimensional portrait of business. Chaudhry's comparative findings, for instance, cast business in the Arabian peninsula as either fully resistant (and successful in the case of Saudi Arabia) to government policy or fully supine and ineffective (as in the case of Yemen). In comparing approaches to democracy, Eva Bellin finds Arab business either resistant or agnostic: Eva Bellin, "Contingent Democrats, Industrialists, Labor, and Democratization in Late-Developing Countries," *World Politics*, 52, 2 (January 2000), pp. 175–205.

[50] Karl, *The Paradox of Plenty*, pp. 54–57.   [51] Shafer, *Winners and Losers*, p. 33.

with a rentier psychology. The private sector is, in the final analysis, a state client. Where formal representative associations do exist, they are deemed to be shells designed to pursue state largesse. The final element in the rentier/sectoral argument extends this argument to predict what political ramifications (specific to business–state relations) should emerge once the revenue base of the state changes. Or, in other words, what should happen once rents and exogenous resources decline, as was the case in the 1980s and 1990s?

Scholars advancing the rentier-state approach in the 1980s and early 1990s converged toward a clear view of what should occur once rents declined. Under fiscal pressure, the once-aloof rentier state must turn to domestic extraction to avoid crippling debt and austerity. Having developed little extractive capacity and fearful of social backlash, the post-rentier state is hard pressed to respond. In parallel, the drop in rents means a drop in payoffs to social groups. Issues of distribution, taxation, and representation are intertwined. Adherents to rentier theory expressed the rational in terms Albert Hirschman laid out in *Exit, Voice, and Loyalty*. When faced with a revenue-seeking state, an economic agent can either exercise "exit" (capital becomes mobile) or "give voice" (demand representation). A state wishing to minimize the number of exits will inevitably entertain more voice, thus expanding representation.[52] The post-rentier state displays conditions ripe for democratization and reform;[53] or, as Luciani put it, "a strong current in favor of democracy inevitably arises."[54] Lisa Anderson was more direct: "a clear trend was discernible, particularly in countries whose access to reliable sources of external funding was declining. With great trepidation, governments were being forced to face the unpleasant prospect of holding themselves accountable to taxpayers."[55]

If one compares relative contributions to GDP, the intuitive nature of the argument can be quantified to some extent. Thomas Stauffer offers a method of calculating the non-oil, non-aid component of a country's GDP.[56] The idea is to strip contributions from oil and aid out of the revenue and expenditure components. Stauffer argues that this gives a more accurate picture of an economy's productive growth (income that is reproducible) versus simply the expansion of an economy (which is generally

---

[52] Albert O. Hirschman, *Exit, Voice, and Loyalty: Responses to Decline in Firms, Organizations, and States* (Cambridge, MA: Harvard University Press, 1970).

[53] Brynen, "Economic Crisis and Post-Rentier Democratization."

[54] Luciani, "Allocative vs. Production States," p. 75.

[55] Lisa Anderson, "Remaking the Middle East: The Prospects for Democracy and Stability," *Ethics and International Affairs*, 6 (1992), p. 171.

[56] Thomas Stauffer, "The Dynamics of Petroleum Dependency: Growth in an Oil Rentier State," *Finance and Industry*, 2 (1981).

Table 1.3 *Adjusted GDP: non-oil/aid GDP*

| | Total GDP | | Adjusted GDP (% actual) | |
	Jordan (million Jordanian dinars)	Kuwait (million Kuwaiti dinars)	Jordan	Kuwait
1970	212	1,026	137.80 (65)	393.14 (38)
1975	379	3,485	192.19 (51)	n.a.
1980	1,151	7,755	736.88 (64)	3,015.66 (39)
1985	2,020	6,450	1,676.50 (83)	2,319.88 (36)
1990	2,668	5,328	2,363.87 (89)	133.59 (3)
1995	4,191	7,214	3,833.44 (91)	n.a.

Sources: International Monetary Fund, *International Financial Statistics Yearbook,* various years; Central Bank of Jordan, *Yearly Statistical Series (1964–1993)* (Amman: Central Bank of Jordan, October 1994); Kuwait, Ministry of Planning, *Statistical Abstract in 25 Years* (Kuwait City: Central Statistical Office, 1990).

Calculation:
CONVENTIONAL GDP
minus tax and royalty income from oil or foreign aid grants
minus oil/aid-financed domestic government expenditures
equals
NON-OIL/AID GDP

not productive). Table 1.3 provides these calculations and comparisons for Kuwait and Jordan over time.

The results, while only rough approximations, provide a picture of the relative importance of the private sector to overall economic activity in each country. That Jordan's private sector contributes far more than its Kuwaiti counterpart supports the conventional conclusion that business is more "important" in Jordan and predictably is in a better structural position to resist or drive policy. Certainly, it could be expected that as private contributions increase, the democratization logic might come into force. Since political outcomes have not reflected what the numbers predict, rentier theory has much to answer for.[57]

While Shafer and Karl's sectoral approach avoids the democratization issue, it nevertheless concludes that dependent states should display

---

[57] Criticism has also latched on to the failed connection between democratization and taxation. For instance, John Waterbury has argued that taxation has increased among the Middle Eastern states, yet democratization has not: Waterbury, "Democracy Without Democrats? The Potential for Political Liberalization in the Middle East," in Ghassan Salamé (ed.), *Democracy Without Democrats? The Renewal of Politics in the Muslim World* (London: I. B. Tauris, 1994), pp. 29–30. The question then becomes whether the distinction between direct and indirect taxation has an effect. At another level, the debate is clouded by the fact that some economic information (especially government revenue and expenditure) is highly uneven and simply suspect.

similar pathologies and regime pressures. Their judgement is that the structural legacies of oil export and rent reliance make it nearly impossible for the state to alter its development trajectory away from external sources. Given the size of oil reserves and the continuing strategic importance of the region, this prediction is rather mild. On the one hand, much variation – short of macro developmental shifts – remains, and requires explanation. Some states respond more effectively to crisis than others, setting the stage for divergent political patterns of winners and losers. On the other hand, recalling Shafer's claim that similar state institutional designs yield "similar policy outcomes," there seems little room for deviation.[58] Crisis policy outcomes are, therefore, overdetermined: inflexible institutions are unable (and unwilling) to effect policy change while oil-dependent social actors effectively resist any nascent moves for reform. Crisis begets stagnation. Karl goes further by suggesting that such stagnation leads to regime decay and decline. "Only prolonged fiscal crisis is likely to provoke change, and adjustment, when it comes, will be especially abrupt and severe." For the oil exporters of the Middle East, the expectation is a "deleterious combination of economic deterioration and political decay."[59]

In sum, the rentier and sectoral approaches essentially view fiscal crisis politics as an unfolding logic of increased business autonomy and policy leverage. Connecting the dots from revenue/sectoral dependency to state structure to business interests, one sees a clear model but little accuracy. A recent volume on business–state relations in the developing world concludes that, with these structural approaches, "If the political interaction between state and private actors is modeled at all, it tends to take a spare, game-theoretic form."[60] For instance, outcomes in the Middle East have hardly been so neat over the last two decades of fiscal crisis. In Kuwait, one of the world's most sectorally dependent states, the past decades have witnessed not democratization or regime instability but the evolution of intense business–state coordination aiming at economic reform and a blocking of deeper political liberalization. Working from structural/statist assumptions, one should expect, if anything, a more dependent business community that is of little assistance to the state. At a minimum, we should expect divided business resistance to reform. In contrast, consider the counterintuitive outcome in Jordan. With a less sectorally and rent-dependent state, we should expect greater business–state coordination on reform than in Kuwait. In addition, the comparative weakness of

[58] Shafer, *Winners and Losers*, p. 22.   [59] Karl, *The Paradox of Plenty*, p. 241.
[60] Stephan Haggard, Sylvia Maxfield, and Ben Ross Schneider, "Theories of Business and Business–State Relations," in Maxfield and Schneider (eds.), *Business and the State in Developing Countries* (Ithaca: Cornell University Press, 1997), p. 37.

business advocacy in Jordan violates the assumptions that support structural/statist logics. External shocks, such as exogenous price shifts, do not axiomatically translate into set political action among domestic groups. For the issue of business–state relations, the task is to chart – *pre-crisis* – how those relations were constructed during state formation, what past political struggles entailed, how business elites came to represent their interests, and what institutional capacities evolved.

The micro approach: collective action by business

Since the claim against structural/statist approaches calls, in part, for a closer examination of how business evolves and how it represents its interests to the state, a treatment of theories concerned with associational action is needed. What is known as the new institutional economics (NIE) has generated an influential field of social science inquiry into how institutions discipline markets. Like sectoral and rentier approaches, the NIE has been termed a form of "expanded neoclassical economics."[61] Collectively, while this scholarship privileges analysis of choice in the marketplace, of how prices shape behavior, and of how interests determine institutions, it has contributed to a reform of the classical paradigm by shifting investigation toward the importance of transaction costs, principal/agent relations, and collective action.[62] Consequently, as this body of literature examines organized business and business–state relations, it comes to share some of the same key assumptions of the macro approach.

The economists Douglass North and Mancur Olson are perhaps the most influential representatives of the institutional turn in economics. To simplify greatly, their core contribution has been that institutions and institutional arrangements fundamentally shape choice in the marketplace through their influence on transaction costs, principal/agent relations, and collective action. Consequently, institutions are created to solve concrete problems, regulate exchange, provide more information, set guidelines, or ensure contract enforcement. How institutions do this and where they come from have become the focus of much follow-on research. Institutions in this case are defined as rules or norms governing

---

[61] Christopher Clague, "The Institutional Economics and Economic Development," in Clague (ed.), *Institutions and Economic Development: Growth and Governance in Less-Developed and Post-Socialist Countries* (Baltimore: Johns Hopkins University Press, 1997), p. 16.
[62] Doner and Schneider, "The New Institutional Economics, Business Associations, and Development," p. 6.

behavior.[63] This definition is crucial because it avoids consideration of other structures, associations, and parties, for instance, as constituting institutions.[64] To the extent that organized interests involve themselves in decisions about market governance, this is seen to lead to suboptimal outcomes and economic distortion. As a consequence, professional and business associations have come to be viewed in a negative light by many new institutional economists, political scientists, and World Bank officials. Moreover, this perspective downplays how institutions and associations might form and develop in response to more than simply market problems.

In attempting to build a grand theory to explain the rise and fall of national economies, Olson develops the hypothesis that, to the extent that distributional coalitions proliferate in a national economy, productive investment and growth will be gradually reduced and market failure will result. Foremost among these cartels for Olson are organized representatives of business. Drawing on his original thesis explaining collective action, Olson argues that business will come together to act collectively if selective benefits result from group membership. These incentives could be information, political access, payoffs, and the like, but they share the character of being particular to the member. Translated into structural/statist reasoning, material interest drives collective action. To reintroduce the sectorally dependent state, one sees that Olson's bottom-up approach to business–state relations rests on the same abstract logic of material incentives evolving into political action. Business will organize to pursue rent from the sectorally dependent state. Following Shafer and Karl, once these resources decline, such distributive coalitions should provide obstacles to reform as particularist demands mount. In subsequent extensions of this logic, Olson did envision a way out. How associations are structured may alter the way business and state interact. Not all incentives for collective action are the same; hence, different types of associations may form, embodying different types of interaction with the state. Olson envisions two types: encompassing and non-encompassing. Olson advanced

---

[63] According to Lin and Nugent, institutions are defined as "a set of humanly devised behavioral rules that govern and shape the interactions of human beings, in part by helping them to form expectations of what other people will do": Justin Yifu Lin and Jeffrey B. Nugent, "Institutions and Economic Development," in J. Behrman and T. N. Srinivasan (eds.), *Handbook of Economic Development*, vol. IIIA (Amsterdam: North-Holland, 1995).

[64] Oliver Williamson, "The Institutions and Governance of Economic Development and Reform," in Williamson, *The Mechanisms of Governance* (New York: Oxford University Press, 1996), pp. 322–343. I am indebted to Richard F. Doner for discussions on the importance of this definitional distinction.

a tradeoff logic by arguing that "an encompassing association" (one representing all or most of the economy) would espouse a better policy view (benefiting the entire economy) than a more narrowly based association, but that the encompassing association would lack lobbying strength:

Peak associations, frequently, lack the unity needed to have any great influence on public policy, or even coherent and specific policies. Nonetheless, peak associations should on average take a somewhat less parochial view than the narrow associations of which they are composed.[65]

How associations are constructed thus provides the micro complement to the macro view. The micro approach fits neatly with the same assumptions and same conclusions generated by structural/statist arguments. The two approaches also run aground upon the same empirical shoreline. Just as structural logics fail to capture the variety of outcomes during crisis, Olson's logics have succumbed to a number of empirical problems since their elaboration. To quote Ronald Rogowski at length:

Since even narrow coalitions can act to achieve greater efficiency – productively rather than distributionally – Olson's theory must be modified. The evil consequences he predicts indeed ensue when distributional coalitions proliferate; but since Olson is wrong in relating distributional orientation only to size and proliferation only to age, we must try anew to analyze why coalitions will grow and why some others will pursue productivity, others only a bigger share.[66]

The same historical-institutional variables that correct structural/statist positions apply to the lower level as well. In Jordan and Kuwait, two functionally similar business representatives evolve. Gradually, however, the Jordanian association has become more encompassing than the Kuwaiti association; however, the way each interacted with the state during crisis inverts Olson's expectations. The more exclusive (in membership and internal representation) Kuwaiti association espoused the more catholic reform policies and interacted more smoothly with state officials, whereas in Jordan, the broader-based association consistently advanced particularist policy initiatives, failing to coordinate with state officials. By charting the political struggles that accompanied state formation in Kuwait and Jordan and by including consideration of organizational variables beyond simply encompassingness, the apparently counterintuitive outcomes make sense. As the economy is embedded in society, so too are associations of business representation.

[65] Mancur Olson, *The Rise and Decline of Nations* (New Haven: Yale University Press, 1982), p. 50 (emphasis in original).
[66] Ronald Rogowski, "Structure, Growth, and Power: Three Rationalist Accounts," in Bates, *Toward a Political Economy of Development*, p. 317.

One might be rightly suspicious of bringing Olson and North to the Middle East when their original arguments were based upon Western cases. Indeed, part of the critique here is that context and timing cannot be ignored. The influence of Olson's ideas regarding associations has spread far past the developed democracies to inform policy among developmental economists and practitioners. Before his death in 1998, Olson established the Center on Institutional Reform and the Informal Sector (CIRIS). With support from the United States Agency for International Development, CIRIS undertook a number of consulting projects in developing countries. Therefore, developing a systematic empirical grasp of where Olson's ideas fit and where they require adjustment affects our general knowledge of these institutions and specific policies in the developing world.

Contributions and framework

Only recently has it come to light that some of the most successful structural/statist theories about developing nations first emerged among Middle East specialists with the idea of the rentier state.[67] Since then, political scientists more concerned with generalization (Frieden, Rogowski, Shafer, and Karl) have elaborated cleaner models, with little attention to any of the Middle East cases that accompanied the initial scholarly interest. Accumulated comparative research has revealed evidence demonstrating significant variance among states ostensibly with similar sectoral and rent dependencies. Comparatively examining business–state relations is one means of expanding these debates and proposing new avenues for research.

Chapters 2 and 3 narrate the creation of business–state relations in Kuwait and Jordan before the crises of the 1980s and 1990s. How elites constructed their associations of representation, what domestic political struggles shaped the evolution of domestic business, and the strategies state officials adopted vis-à-vis organized business all condition crisis outcomes. Thus in chapter 4 I examine how, once the crisis took hold in the early 1980s, two variables arising from pre-crisis politics became most important in explaining divergent outcomes in Kuwait and Jordan: the

---

[67] For example, compare Hussein Mahdavy, "The Patterns and Problems of Economic Development in Rentier States," in M. A. Cook (ed.), *Studies in Economic History of the Middle East* (London: Oxford University Press, 1970), pp. 428–467, with Michael L. Ross, "Does Resource Wealth Cause Authoritarian Rule?," *World Politics*, 53 (April 2001), pp. 325–361. For how the Gulf cases figured into the founding of American political economy, see Robert Vitalis, "Black Gold, White Crude: An Essay on American Exceptionalism, Hierarchy, and Hegemony in the Gulf," *Diplomatic History*, 26, 2 (Spring 2002), p. 188.

institutional capacities and organization of business representation and the political calculus facing state elites during crisis. In each case, the important political calculus hinges on the relative strength of other social rivals for business privilege and state power, namely political Islam. Seen from this more empirically grounded vantage, we can then come to understand why similarly dependent states chart different crisis outcomes and why Olson's organizational logic is turned on its head. In addition, chapter 4 seeks to answer a looming question among studies of business–state relations in the developing world: what makes for productive coordination between business and state in some countries and not others?

In recent years the debate between scholars wedded to either state or market has, thankfully, matured. Each side recognizes neither force is sufficient, on its own, to deliver long-term productive growth. The recent work of Peter Evans has been perhaps the most influential in this regard. In an effort to explain the long-term success of the East Asian industrializers (South Korea, Singapore, and Taiwan), Evans has argued that a degree of state autonomy from leading social actors, such as business, is necessary at the onset of economic liberalization and restructuring. However, at the later stages of policy negotiation and implementation, a degree of "embeddedness" is required, that is, connections with social actors.[68] Evans terms this balance between connectedness and aloofness "embedded autonomy." What conditions allow this unique situation to prevail? According to Evans, the answer is found within the state. What he terms the Weberian characteristics of the typical Asian industrializer (non-political bureaucracy and extensive administrative and information capacities) allow these states both to maintain distance from business (thus avoiding an Olsonian world of collusion) and to fashion links with business when information, feedback, and implementation assistance are required. However, attempts to export these lessons outside East Asia have proven disheartening. Such "rational-legal" states are extremely rare in Africa and the Middle East. How then do we account for emerging patterns of business–state coordination and disjuncture in these circumstances? Because this study reverses the standard question of state autonomy by focusing on how business representation is formed and what its capacities are, the question of embedded autonomy can be approached from a new direction. Findings here stress the importance of capable business representation to the nature and success of the embeddedness project. It shows how structures of associational representation

---

[68] Peter Evans, "The State as Problem and Solution: Predation, Embedded Autonomy, and Structural Change," in Stephan Haggard and Robert R. Kaufman (eds.), *The Politics of Economic Adjustment: International Constraints, Distributive Politics, and the State* (Princeton: Princeton University Press, 1992), pp. 63–87.

shape institutional trajectory and capacities. Unlike Olson's organizational logic, however, associational capacities are not wholly the product of incentive structures but rather are artifacts of broader political and social struggles waged over time.

Building upon the historical patterns and what happens once rents decline, chapter 5 concludes by first revisiting rival accounts for these outcomes. In particular, the discussion engages a return to structural variables as well as more particular, contingent factors applicable in each case. The remainder of the concluding chapter branches out from these cases to assess why political liberalization has retreated while economic liberalization remains a priority. The answers proposed are tentative, as many of these processes are ongoing, not just in Kuwait and Jordan, but throughout the region. Nevertheless, it is clear that much of the policy optimism surrounding the return of Arab business is unwarranted. Neither in Kuwait nor in Jordan does business emerge as a force for greater political liberalization. Instead, efforts to refashion business–state interaction have figured into the evolving nature of authoritarianism in the Arab world. Certainly this is not the only ingredient in the mix,[69] but mounting evidence from the experience of other "liberalizing" countries suggests business–state patterns similar to those in Kuwait and Jordan.[70] Thus, it is not enough to conclude that with a change in external prices will come political change. What kind of change and in which direction cannot be answered from a vantage that asserts a connection between material interest, institutional formation, and political action. Accounting for crisis outcomes in the 1980s and 1990s requires a focus on the previous decades of state formation, institution-building, and regime consolidation. Likewise, the actual political struggles and lessons from these decades should form the foundation from which we speculate on the next phase.

[69] Jill Crystal, "Authoritarianism and Its Adversaries in the Arab World," *World Politics*, 46 (January 1994), pp. 262–289.
[70] For the case of Egypt, see Eberhard Kienle, *A Grand Delusion: Democracy and Economic Reform in Egypt* (London: I. B. Tauris, 2001).

2   Organizing first: business and political authority during state formation

Among equals: merchant–ruler relations and state creation in Kuwait

Most conceptions of the beginning of Kuwait involve the notion that its formation came with the first influx of Arabian peninsula tribes to the area. Actually, the historian Ahmad Mustafa Abu-Hakima gives the year 716 for the founding of Kuwait City.[1] The actual founders of what would become the political entity of Kuwait, the Bani Utub, did not arrive until the early eighteenth century, and were thus not the first inhabitants. They were, however, the most powerful. Gradually, families of this tribe built the basis for political rule in Kuwait by managing internal and external challenges. Consequently, Kuwait's future political and economic elites were cut from the same historical and social cloth.

Legend and the scant historical records that exist portray the Bani Utub as a loose grouping of tribal families who emigrated from the Arabian peninsula. After the Bani Utub settled in Kuwait, they took advantage of its natural port to develop trade links and build a small pearl-diving industry. As Jill Crystal has documented, the Bani Utub were believed to be composed of three principal family branches: al-Sabah, al-Khalifa, and al-Jalahimah. These families compromised among themselves to determine that the al-Sabahs would be responsible for political functions, the al-Khalifas for economic functions, and the al-Jalahimas for security affairs.[2] The year 1752 was the first recorded year of al-Sabah rule. In the 1760s, a dispute between the al-Sabahs and the al-Khalifas resulted in the latter's departure for Qatar. This event demonstrated two points. First, the ease of political mobility in the Gulf meant exit was a prime option when political or economic disagreements could not be solved.

---

[1] Ahmad Mustafa Abu-Hakima, *The Modern History of Kuwait* (London: Luzac, 1983).
[2] Jill Crystal, *Kuwait: The Transformation of an Oil State* (Boulder: Westview Press, 1992), pp. 8–9; Husain Khalaf al-Shaikh Khazal, *Tarikh al-Kuwait al-Siyasi 1962–1970* [The political history of Kuwait, 1962–1970], vol. I (Beirut: Matabu Dar al-Kutub, n.d.), p. 42.

Second, the departure of the al-Khalifas solidified al-Sabah political rule in Kuwait. From this period, no serious internal threats to al-Sabah rule would develop.

By the late eighteenth and early nineteenth centuries, a rough outline of the merchant community and its position in the overall social structure can be traced. First, among the Bani Utub, the largest merchants focused on the pearl-diving industry and on the boats needed to harvest and transport the pearls. As most observers have noted, the political importance of the pearl trade was not so much the evolution of a class consciousness, but the degree to which the al-Sabahs were dependent on the wealth produced. Bani Utub merchants, through the system of zakat (religious tax), provided much-needed financial support for the al-Sabahs, who, in this period, remained focused on relations with the bedouin tribes and the caravan trade. In their influential treatments of Kuwait, Crystal and Jacqueline Ismael also note that a second element of al-Sabah–merchant relations rested on the manpower resources merchants possessed. Laborers and slaves in the employ of Bani Utub merchants provided defense for Kuwait City in times of need. This financial and manpower support allowed the al-Sabahs to pursue foreign intrigues with greater freedom.[3] Close relations, therefore, developed between leading Bani Utub merchant families and the al-Sabahs.

Manpower and financial power gave Kuwaiti merchants an early sense of equality with the ruling al-Sabahs. From the perspective of Kuwait's merchants, social duties (commerce, defense, politics, and so on) were simply divided among the leading families; a hierarchy was not assumed in this division. Commerce was not viewed as subordinate to politics. Indeed, politics needed commerce. This particular Kuwaiti circumstance fit well with the historical Arab Muslim view of merchants: "Economic activity, the search for profit, trade, and consequently, production for the market are looked upon with no less favor by Muslim tradition than by the Koran itself."[4] Thus, well before British rule, Kuwait's merchants openly exercised influence commensurate with a perception of equality.[5]

Third, as a result of the Persian siege of Basra in 1775, merchants from this area began migrating to Kuwait.[6] Unlike the smaller middlemen

[3] Crystal, *Oil and Politics*, p. 21; Jacqueline S. Ismael, *Kuwait: Social Change in Historical Perspective* (Syracuse: Syracuse University Press, 1982).
[4] Maxime Rodinson, *Islam and Capitalism* (London: Penguin, 1974), p. 16.
[5] An example of this was the al-Nisf family. They represented the half of the al-Khalifa family (*nisf* means half in Arabic) that did not leave for Qatar. The al-Nisfs would not only be some of the founders of the Kuwait Chamber of Commerce and Industry, but they would maintain very close relations with the royal family.
[6] J. G. Lorimer, *Gazetteer of the Persian Gulf, Oman, and Central Arabia*, 2 vols. (Shannon: Irish University Press, 1970), vol. II, p. 146.

merchants of Kuwait City, these Basra émigrés pursued maritime trade relationships with regional centers as far away as India. Movement of these merchants tied Basra, already an important trading center, more tightly to Kuwait, helping to establish Kuwait City as a regional trading center. With these new merchants, a discernable merchant elite class took shape.

Some of the larger Sunni merchants from Basra combined with the largest of the Bani Utub merchants, coming to comprise what were loosely referred to as the *asil* (original) families. Though the number would gradually expand over time, the core of the *asil* included eight principal families: al-Sagr, al-Nisf, al-Ghanim, al-Hamad, al-Mudhaf, al-Khalid, al-Khourafi, and al-Marzouq.[7] Their early commercial interests went beyond the pearling industry to include commodity trading with Basra and the lower Gulf, eventually expanding to include date plantations in the areas around Basra. These families settled within the walls of the old city in the districts of Qiblah, Kayfan, and Hawalli (within the so-called first ring road) and, of the core eight families, members of all but one would sit on the first executive board of the Kuwait Chamber of Commerce and Industry in 1961. A second stratum of merchants, identified by Ismael, came from the middle and lower rungs of the Bani Utub "who dealt primarily with the transfer of subsistence products from external sources to the internal and desert markets."[8] A third, albeit in this period very small, merchant grouping was the Shi'a, mostly immigrants from Iran. They were considered below even the lower Bani Utub and generally performed economic activities (such as textile dyeing, water carrying, and later garbage collection) considered inferior to the more respectable activities of trade and finance.[9] Above these three divisions, the al-Sabahs themselves gradually took on merchant roles. Initially, the they took over land tracts within the old city, affording them not only wealth, but also an important source of patronage. At times, individuals in the ruling family fashioned business partnerships with merchant families (middle Bani Utub and later some Shi'a merchants) who in turn profited from al-Sabah foreign contacts. In times of economic downturn, these alliances would become points of antagonism with asil merchants.

---

[7] Several excellent studies confirm the identity of this core and overlap in identifying their histories: Ismael, *Kuwait: Social Change*; Nicolas Gavrielides, "Tribal Democracy: The Anatomy of Parliamentary Elections in Kuwait," in Linda Layne (ed.), *Elections in the Middle East: Implications of Recent Trends* (Boulder: Westview Press, 1987); and Abdul-Reda Assiri and Kamal Al-Monoufi, "Kuwait's Political Elite: The Cabinet," *Middle East Journal*, 42 (Winter 1988), pp. 48–58.

[8] Ismael, *Kuwait: Social Change*, p. 55.

[9] Interview with 'Isa Majid al-Shahin, Spokesman, Islamic Constitutional Movement, Kuwait City, 3 March 1996.

Mubarak the Great and political rule under the British

The modern history of Kuwait begins in 1896 with the rule of Mubarak the Great. Having come to power by killing his brother Shaikh Muhammed, Mubarak forged a new regional position for Kuwait and altered domestic political arrangements. At the close of the nineteenth century, Gulf politics involved competition among the Ottomans, the British, and the rising power, the al-Sa'uds. Mubarak sought to change Kuwait's precarious position among these rivals by securing protectorate status with the British. In 1899 under an agreement kept secret from Ottoman officials, Britain made Kuwait its protectorate and thus marked the beginning of the end of Ottoman ascendancy in the Gulf.[10] Shortly after the agreement, British obligations were tested. On two separate occasions, Britain sent ships and arms to dissuade Ottoman and al-Sa'ud incursions.[11] In 1904, Britain sent its first political regent, inaugurating a period (until 1961) of domestic British presence and influence.

The inception of a British presence in Kuwait did not mean colonial officials directly manipulated ruler–merchant relations. Kuwait itself was not an imperial object; rather, it was Kuwait's position in relation to Basra and the trade routes to India that was of British concern. The injection of British steamer trade certainly altered markets in the region by offering subsistence traders (Bani Utub) a steady source of supply while challenging larger Kuwait traders. However, it is an overstatement to assert, as Ismael does, that, "It was the new structure of colonial relations forged by the linkages with Britain that inhibited the development of productive forces in Kuwait and the region as a whole, initiating the historical process of the underdevelopment of not only Kuwait but the entire region." As Crystal notes, despite British trade and Mubarak's taxes, the larger Kuwait merchants did not abandon regional trade and continued ship trade with India and East Africa through World War II.[12] Moreover, it was Mubarak who sought to use British links to thwart his domestic rivals and to create new allies. The underdevelopment thesis, therefore, cannot explain specific patterns of merchant–ruler relations. What would be of more significance to the future of these relations were the political effects of British rule.[13]

---

[10] Frederick F. Anscombe, *The Ottoman Gulf: The Creation of Kuwait, Saudi Arabia, and Qatar* (New York: Columbia University Press, 1997), pp. 113–142.

[11] Crystal, *Oil and Politics*, p. 24.

[12] Ismael, *Kuwait: Social Change*, p. 56; Crystal, *Oil and Politics*, p. 26.

[13] This argument in the context of Africa is put forward by Mahmood Mamdani, "Beyond Settler and Native as Political Identities: Overcoming the Political Legacy of Colonialism," *Comparative Studies in Society and History*, 43, 4 (October 2001), pp. 651–664.

Mubarak's new relationship with Britain helped secure Kuwait's position between Ottoman and al-Sa'ud interests. The arrangement afforded domestic leverage to initiate three politically important domestic changes. First, protectorate status allowed Mubarak to limit future leadership successions to his side of the al-Sabah family, essentially cutting off his late brother's side. Though the British did not directly support this plan, they agreed to support his designated heir to the throne.[14] While al-Sabah rule had already been secured within Kuwait, this new support demonstrated that security regionally. Second, along with the initial agreement and all subsequent ones, the British gave Mubarak monetary payments, and guaranteed the safety of al-Sabah date plantations, an important source of family wealth, in southern Iraq.[15] These concessions yielded to Mubarak new sources of financial independence from asil merchants. Though the most overt characteristics of the rentier state came with the discovery of oil and its concessions in the 1930s, the protectorate relationship with Britain really marked the onset of the rentier state in Kuwait. Mary Ann Tétreault described this nascent rentierism: "Since the ruler [Mubarak] contributed little to the people of Kuwait, his wealth could be used for whatever purpose he wished, including to protect himself from them and to free himself from the necessity of behaving nicely in order to get their financial support."[16] British historical records from this period are replete with al-Sabah concerns for London's payments, their timing, and their level. Al-Sabah rule by reliance on domestic revenue was a thing of the past and, thus, the leverage merchants held with the ruler was weakened. British colonialism, more than anything else, instructed Kuwait's merchant elites – the future founders of the Kuwait Chamber of Commerce and Industry (KCCI) – that they would have to develop new policy levers if they were to retain influence with the monarchy. Mubarak's enhanced financial independence allowed him to embark on a third important domestic change, nascent state-building.

State-building in Kuwait introduced important dynamics in the relationship between ruler and asil merchants. Shortly after Mubarak came to power, he instituted new taxes on merchant activities. An import tax, a pearling tax, a house tax, a pilgrimage tax, and even price controls were decreed by Mubarak. Prior to this time, customs taxes were voluntarily

---

[14] Mary Ann Tétreault, "Autonomy, Necessity, and the Small State: Ruling Kuwait in the Twentieth Century," *International Organization*, 45, 4 (Autumn 1991), p. 573.

[15] *Records of Kuwait, 1899–1961*, edited by Alan deLancy Rush, 8 vols. (London: Archive International, 1989), vol. I, p. 149; and Alan Rush, *Al-Sabah: Genealogy and History of Kuwait's Ruling Family, 1752–1986* (London: Ithaca Press, 1987), p. 175.

[16] Tétreault, "Ruling Kuwait," p. 574.

contributed by leading merchants, but now taxation became a duty.[17] Ostensibly, this revenue was needed to fund Mubarak's external political intrigues, but Ismael ascribes a second reason to the taxes.

By the early twentieth century, British steamships had begun to dominate commodity trade within the Gulf and between India and the Gulf. The British competed with larger Bani Utub merchants and with the merchants tied to the Basra trade. Ismael argues that Mubarak saw this as an opportunity and used some of the tax revenue to extend easy loans to the middle and smaller Bani Utub merchants, who were becoming more and more dependent on British supplies to support their retail trade.[18] The favoring of Bani Utub merchants marked the first instance, but not the last, of ruler involvement in merchant affairs. Since asil merchants were perceived as domestic competition, weakening their position or enhancing the position (and loyalty) of other merchant groups would help minimize that threat. In 1909, the issue came to a head.

Wishing to strengthen his control over the important pearling industry, Mubarak declared a ban on diving for the season. This was the final straw. Leading pearl merchants along with other traders left Kuwait for Bahrain and Basra, taking with them significant capital and manpower. Still dependent on that revenue and bowing to the popular support the dissidents generated, Mubarak gave in and promised to reduce some of the taxes if the merchants returned.[19] Most of the merchants did return, but the effect on ruler–merchant relations was profound. According to Crystal: "The act of secession ended one era and began another for the merchants. It was both the last time the merchants would use secession as a political weapon and first of several times in the twentieth century that they would organize politically in opposition to the Shaikh."[20] The rule of Mubarak and his relationship with the British helped give merchant politics a distinctive oppositional flavor. Mubarak's involvement in the business and politics of asil merchants was the first expression of a subsequent trend in which rulers would try to influence merchant affairs to enhance their own political position. In response, merchants would, in their own way, oppose al-Sabah interests from time to time. Moreover, this opposition would evolve into a proto-Arab nationalism, especially in the pre-independence period, with the British as a target of elite merchant disdain. So, though many merchants fled Kuwait in 1909, they

[17] Paul Harrison, "Economic and Social Conditions in East Arabia," *Muslim World*, 14 (1924).
[18] Ismael, *Kuwait: Social Change*, pp. 54–59.
[19] *Records of Kuwait*, vol. I, pp. 542–551; Crystal, *Oil and Politics*, pp. 24–25.
[20] Crystal, *Oil and Politics*, p. 25.

gladly came back and consistently spoke of their loyalty to Kuwait and to the al-Sabahs.[21]

Merchant politics in the interwar years

In 1915 Shaikh Jabir, son of Mubarak, succeeded his father. Jabir (r1915–1917) was succeeded by his brother, Salim (r1917–1921). Events of domestic political importance were few during their reigns. However, during the reign of Shaikh Ahmed (r1921–1950), two events of note occurred: the organization of merchant opposition, and the discovery of oil.

World War I and its aftermath was a period of great profits for Kuwait's merchant elites. British steamers were called away for the war effort, reopening much of the regional trade to Kuwaiti traders.[22] The enhanced financial position of leading merchants, combined with the animosity generated under Mubarak's authoritarian rule, laid the foundation for a merchant backlash. With the sudden death of Salim in 1921, *asil* merchants saw their chance. Twelve merchants formed al-Majlis al-Istishari (Consultative Council) in order to establish a merchant voice in the decision of succession. Of the following ten members, descendants of five would form the first two executive boards of the KCCI (see table 1 in the appendix): Hamad 'Abdullah al-Sagr (whose son would be first KCCI president), Hilal bin Fajhan al-Mutairi, Shaikh Yousef bin 'Isa al-Qinai', Al-Sayyid 'Abdalrahman 'Aziz al-Rushaid, Ahmed Ibn Saleh al-Humadi, Marzouq al-Da'ud al-Badr, Khalef bin Shahen al-Ghanim, 'Ahmed al-Fahd al-Khaled, Mishan al-Khudayyr al-Khaled, and Ibrahim ibn Mudhif.[23] The council proposed three al-Sabah candidates to succeed Salim as emir. One of the candidates, 'Ahmed al-Jabir, became emir and agreed to work with the council in determining future policies for Kuwait.[24] After only two months, the council disintegrated due to "internal strife and indecision."[25] Though it accomplished little concrete change, the council signaled the future organizational and political

---

[21] *Records of Kuwait*, vol. I, p. 548.

[22] This was also a period of significant smuggling, especially to and from India. Much lore and legend was created during this period with leading merchants running wartime blockades and enduring foreign prison. Families like the al-Sagrs, al-Marzouqs, al-Khaleds, and al-Ghanims became well known in this period as shrewd regional traders and important financiers. Today, some of the older members of these families are still fluent in Hindi, Swahili, Persian, and English, the languages of Gulf trade in the early twentieth century (interview with Wael al-Sagr, Kuwait City, 6 April 1996; and *Records of Kuwait*, vol. IV, pp. 440–441 and pp. 428–429).

[23] Ismael, *Kuwait: Social Change*, p. 71.   [24] *Records of Kuwait*, vol. II, pp. 71–76.

[25] Crystal, *Oil and Politics*, p. 42.

prowess of Kuwait's merchant elites. Just as the failed 1905 Revolution foreshadowed the successful Russian Revolution of 1917, so too did the 1921 council foreshadow the more significant 1938 Majlis movement.

The 1938 Majlis movement followed profound interwar economic dislocations, which significantly affected Kuwait's merchant community. Like the 1921 council, the aim of the Majlis movement was political, that is, it reflected a merchant desire to gain leverage with the al-Sabahs. The ramifications of the movement were far-reaching and cemented a series of merchant organizational precedents that eventually culminated in the KCCI in 1961. The period leading up to the Majlis movement included other important merchant organizations. In 1932, the emir approved creation of the Kuwait City Municipality, which had a broad mandate in health and social affairs. Though the emir appointed the head of the municipality, the executive board was composed almost entirely of merchants and was elected every two years. A similar organization, the Education Council, was created by merchants in 1936 to manage Kuwait's growing school system. As Crystal argues, these two merchant-controlled institutions were important because they afforded merchants opportunities in electoral politics and collective action. As precursors to post-independence merchant organization, these bodies were important in another respect.

The way *asil* merchants organized among themselves to manage institutional leadership was notable. Essentially, candidate lists for the municipality board were drawn up by the executive board itself, a method that ensured that the same elite merchants and their allies would retain the leadership. As with the kind of elections that the KCCI would experience, "the elections were hotly contested. Election irregularities were common enough to elicit complaints, yet limited enough to preserve a high level of support among the merchants."[26] Even at this early stage, merchant leaders mastered the maintainance of elite coherence and continuity within an important social institution. In addition, the municipality was financially independent, operating from revenue generated from business taxes (some voluntary).[27] Therefore, those that ran the municipality ensured their own leadership continuity as well as securing municipality finances. In the short term, as Crystal notes, this reliance on maintaining intra-merchant coherence would handicap merchant aims during the Majlis movement, when efforts to forge a broader coalition against the al-Sabahs failed.[28] In the long run, however, these organizational attributes,

[26] *Ibid.*, p. 46.
[27] *Ibid.*; and Najat Abddalqadir al-Jasim, *Baladiyyat al-Kuwait fi Khamsin'aman* [Fifty years of the Kuwait Municipality] (Kuwait City: Kuwait Municipality, 1980).
[28] Crystal, *Oil and Politics*, p. 50.

exclusive representation and financial independence, would be adopted at the formation of the merchants' Chamber of Commerce.

The world economic problems of the 1920s did not spare the Gulf. In 1923 Ibn Sa'ud banned the tribes of the Najd from trading in Kuwait. In 1929 the pearl market collapsed for the last time. Though small and middle traders formed the majority of those whose interests were damaged, many *asil* merchants did not escape the downturn.[29] Despite these economic pressures, widespread government corruption and the perception that the al-Sabahs were dominating the businesses that were left pushed the merchants toward action. In 1938, leading merchants met secretly to draw up a list of reform demands. Though historical sources and interviews indicate that the meetings were secret, if modern-day Kuwait is any guide, it would be difficult to imagine any such gathering as truly secret, especially from the ruling family. In this way, the Majlis movement is also instructive of the kind of not-so-secret dealings that take place between the merchants and the state. Each side remains aware of the other's position. This transparency is one good reason why, despite the continued presence of an organized, powerful opposition in Kuwait, there has rarely been political violence. Each side is spared extreme surprises. As a result of these meetings, two sides quickly coalesced.

On the side of the opposition were fourteen members elected to the al-Majlis al-Umaa al-Tashri'i (the People's Legislative Council).[30] As in 1921, these were uniformly Sunni, elite merchants. Of fourteen, six members' families would sit on the first two executive boards of the KCCI: al-Ghanim, al-Sagr, al-Marzouq (two), al-Badr, and al-Khalid. These merchant families were backed by dissident members of the royal family led by 'Abdallah Salim, who had wanted to be emir ahead of Sheikh 'Ahmad. To bolster their position, the opposition distributed leaflets listing popular demands for improvements in health care, education, and so on.[31] On the side of Emir Ahmed were the majority of the ruling family, some Sunni merchants, and the bulk of Kuwait's Shi'a community.[32] The pro-Sabah forces also reacted quickly by arresting some of the most

[29] Ismael, *Kuwait: Social Change*, p. 73.

[30] Like the 1921 council, the election was tightly circumscribed. The original merchants, who had met in secret, drew up a list of candidates comprising 150 leading merchants, and voted among themselves for the fourteen. See Crystal, *Oil and Politics*, pp. 47–48.

[31] *Ibid.*, p. 47.

[32] *Records of Kuwait*, vol. II, p. 219. In Kuwaiti history, the Majlis movement is a watershed event used to gauge where prominent families fall regarding sentiments toward the ruling family. Some Sunni family members from the al-Marzouq and al-Khalid branches sided with the emir. Leading Shi'a families also tended to side with the ruler. As a result, like religious minorities throughout the Middle East, the Shi'a of Kuwait came to be perceived by the general population as being pro-government.

outspoken merchant elites, an act that frightened some merchants into fleeing to Iraq. Eventually, after a petition by the merchants calling for fulfillment of the 1921 pledges, Emir Ahmed agreed to elections for the new National Assembly. According to a report from the British political resident, the emir asked opposition representatives what the outcome would be if he refused their petition; their response, hinting at earlier exit strategies, was, "In that case, we bid you farewell."[33] The leading families met, drew up a list of candidates and elected the fourteen representatives. They then asked 'Abdallah Salim to be speaker of the assembly. This was a significant political victory by the merchant opposition, and they used it to form Kuwait's first political party, the National Bloc. The party sponsored speeches, events, and rallies to express their nascent nationalist message and voice opposition to Ahmed's policies. But the real task was to use the assembly to enact policy change. This sparked conflict.

Though the first assembly lasted only six months, its legislative record was impressive. It quickly passed a basic law, establishing assembly jurisdiction over a wide range of state activities, including health, finance, education, public works, and foreign treaties.[34] Reforms of existing laws were equally impressive and succeeded in gaining widespread popular support. Monopolies were ended, taxes reduced, schools built, corrupt officials dismissed, price controls introduced, and a new police force established.[35] By October 1938, the council began collecting and distributing state revenues. It further extracted a promise from the emir to turn over the oil-concession revenue by December. Ahmed quickly saw the implications and dissolved the assembly on 17 December. A standoff ensued, some opposition figures were arrested – including a head of the al-Ghanim family – and other merchants fled Kuwait. One of the leading dissidents, 'Abdallah al-Sagr never returned to Kuwait, dying in exile in India. The assembly did continue, but its members were appointed by the emir, and its oppositional flavor thus was diluted. In sum, trends surrounding the 1938 Majlis movement reinforced two important facets of merchant–ruler relations.

First, as one of the most important domestic political events in Kuwait's pre-independence history, the Majlis movement again attested to the general lack of British interference within Kuwait. Though asil merchants petitioned for British assistance,[36] the British avoided direct involvement. Merchant–ruler politics and the future trajectory of the KCCI cannot,

---

[33] *Records of Kuwait*, vol. II, p. 146.   [34] *Ibid.*, pp. 152–154.
[35] *Ibid.*, pp. 208–209; and Crystal, *Oil and Politics*, p. 48.
[36] Merchants also looked to Iraq for assistance against the al-Sabahs but received only rhetorical support. The al-Sabahs also sought support from the British against the *asil* merchants but were generally ignored as well: *Records of Kuwait*, vol. II, p. 172.

therefore, be ascribed solely to patterns of colonial rule. Ironically, one effect of Britain's aloofness was to enhance anti-British sentiment among the *asil* merchants and strengthen their nascent Arab nationalism. Indeed, as Crystal notes, *asil* merchants were among the first Arabs to establish a committee for assisting Palestinians against the British.[37] Second, historical sources confirm that the Majlis failed because *asil* merchants were unable to attract a wider base of popular support, particularly among the Shi'a, the Bedouin, and the smaller and middle merchants.[38] This inability was a direct result of the way the *asil* families controlled the election and nomination processes. Though the merchant opposition would try repeatedly in the future to widen their base, the success and subsequent failure of the Majlis demonstrated that they privileged the control of private institutions over a wider social appeal. In other words, just like the 1921 council, the Education Councils, and the municipality, the Majlis experience reinforced the value of elite cohesion and control over a more inclusive strategy that *might have* won greater political support. A list of Kuwait's most prominent citizens, prepared by the British resident in 1941, provides an interesting window into that elite. The *asil* merchants who became members of the first executive board of the KCCI (or their fathers) are included on that list, as shown in table 2.1.

Though oil revenues did not compose the majority of Kuwait finances in the pre-World War II period, changes were already on the horizon. In 1938, the Kuwait Oil Company struck oil in the Burgan field, one of the largest in the world. Kuwait would never be the same.

Oil and new business–state relations

Though many in the Third World today rue the effects oil rent has had on their societies and government, when oil was first discovered there were few who did not herald its possibilities. Oil fundamentally altered domestic politics in Kuwait. This section focuses on two relevant effects of oil rent: the expansion of the state, and the forging of a new relationship between the state and merchants. These effects were key elements of the environment in which asil merchants established the KCCI in 1961.

In 1950 Shaikh 'Abdallah (r1950–1965) ascended to the throne, after the death of Shaikh Ahmed. It will be remembered that Abdallah was the *asil* merchants' royal ally in the struggle over the 1938 Majlis. Goodwill between the two sides remained, and this helped ease the transition to a purely rentier/oil economy. The transition was fueled by an annual

[37] Crystal, *Oil and Politics*, p. 52.
[38] *Ibid.*, pp. 52–55; and *Records of Kuwait*, vol. II, pp. 219–221.

Table 2.1 *Prominent Kuwait merchants, 1941*

Name	Remarks	Future affiliation W/ KCCI Board
• Ahmed al-Bahr	General merchant	[1961 board, with another al-Bahr]
• Abdullah al-Sagr	Ship owner, in exile from 1938	[son, 'Abdulaziz, 1961 President]
• Abdulmohsen Khourafi	Ship owner	[M. Khourafi, 1961 board]
• Khaled A. al-Hamad	Ship owner	[1961 board]
• Fahad Marzouq	Ship owner	[1961 board]
• Fahad al-Fulaij & Bros.	Ship owners with a business house in Karachi	[Y. Fulaij, 1961 Vice President]
• Nisf al-Nisf	Ship owner, member of the Advisory board	[M. Yousef al-Nisf, 1961 board]
• Ahmed M. al-Ghanim	AIOC's agent and a leading merchant, contractor, ship owner	[two al-Ghanims on 1961 board]

Source: Records of Kuwait, Alan deLancy Rush (ed.) (London: Archive International, 1989–), vol. II, pp. 311–315.
Notes: The author's comments appear in square brackets in the final column. There are some spelling discrepancies from the original text, so they have been amended to match those given by members of the executive board. AIOC was a company – probably foreign – not identified in the records.

increase of 33 percent in crude oil output from 1950 to 1954.[39] In 1952 and 1953 oil revenues to the state doubled.[40] Much of this increase was due to a 50 percent tax levied on the British-owned Kuwait Oil Company (KOC) in 1951. Whereas customs taxes and British payments had composed the majority of state revenue prior to oil, the overwhelming bulk of state revenues became oil concessions almost overnight. Naturally, 'Abdallah's first task was to see to his family.

The emir instituted regular oil payments to prominent al-Sabah shaikhs and expanded the state positions al-Sabahs occupied. Close family members were given control of important ministries, particularly finance and security.[41] Increased financial resources fed a frenzied spate of land speculation as al-Sabah family members staked out large land claims outside Kuwait City. By the end of the 1950s, 'Abdallah succeeded in quelling al-Sabah family squabbles over the oil revenues and avoided excessive British influence in the process. A direct effect of this revenue distribution was the expansion of the Kuwaiti state.

[39] S. M. Al-Sabah, *Development Planning in an Oil Economy and the Role of the Woman: The Case of Kuwait* (London: Eastlords Publishing, 1983), p. 71.
[40] Tétreault, "Ruling Kuwait," p. 578.   [41] Crystal, *Oil and Politics*, pp. 68–73.

As government ministries were expanded or established at the behest of the ruling family members, public employment jumped accordingly. While concrete statistics on government employment are uneven during the 1950s, what is available suggests that a large-scale shift of the labor force toward public-sector employment began in the 1950s.[42] A traditional merchant strength had been its labor force and the manpower it could provide to the al-Sabahs in times of need. While this resource had been declining throughout the 1930s and 1940s, it disappeared in the 1950s. The expansion of state ministries also began undercutting merchant institutions and merchant access to the decisionmaking processes.

The elected municipality board, which had served as an *asil* merchant enclave since 1932, was replaced with an appointed board of shaikhs. As royal family members took control of government ministries, merchant committees within those bodies, designed to provide policy input, were disbanded.[43] In 1952, 'Abdallah established the Development Board to carry out economic planning and project coordination. In practice, the board began taking over many of the planning functions previously within the purview of the municipality.[44] Merchant presence on this board was tightly circumscribed in favor of prominent shaikhs. Eventually, the merchants protested to 'Abdallah, who responded with the formation of the High Executive Committee. However, royal family members dominated this committee too:

It is indeed unfortunate that the Ruler has not permitted a number of leading citizens to become members of the High Committee . . . The Citizens are wealthy and naturally wish to conserve and enjoy their wealth. Under the present system the extent to which they can press their claims without some danger is limited.[45]

The tactic of establishing powerless or unrepresentative state policy bodies would become a favorite response to protest in the future. It further convinced *asil* merchants of the uselessness of depending on the state for institutional access to policymaking. Conversely, state expansion and the

[42] Kuwait, Ministry of Planning, *Statistical Abstract in 25 Years* (Kuwait City: Central Statistical Office, 1990), pp. 91–92; M. W. Khouja and P. G. Sadler, *The Economy of Kuwait: Development and Role in International Finance* (London: Macmillan Press, 1979), pp. 39–45.

[43] Crystal, *Oil and Politics*, p. 73.

[44] Khouja and Sadler, *The Economy of Kuwait*, pp. 30–31. The Development Board became the Planning Board in the 1960s. Eventually, this would evolve into the Ministry of Planning, still in existence today.

[45] Official from the British Bank of the Middle East, cited in Crystal, *Oil and Politics*, pp. 73–74.

concomitant isolation of merchant influence were not without reward: namely, a new and more profitable relationship between merchants and ruler.

Because 'Abdallah had paid off all of his family's debts to *asil* merchants in the 1950s, he was able to lower customs duties significantly, and instead imposed a tax on all foreign firms doing business in Kuwait.[46] Formal levers of rent distribution were then institutionalized within the state. There were four principal means: (1) ordinary expenditures – wages to civil servants and goods and services in support; (2) development expenditures – public investment and spending on infrastructure; (3) expenditures on land – state purchases of land or low rent of public land; and (4) investment in new shareholding companies that combined public and private ownership.

Wages to civil servants were a rather straightforward means to tie larger sections of the Kuwait population to the al-Sabahs. This distribution did little to enhance the position of asil merchants. Instead, it actually weakened public support for the merchants in the long run. The latter three means, however, were tailor-made to buy off merchant elites.

Development projects in the 1950s were typical for a newly developing state: they were large-scale, ill-coordinated, and very profitable for the few.[47] 'Abdallah, through the Development Board, saw to it that lucrative infrastructure projects were steered to local developers representing favored merchants.[48] Construction boomed, and it quickly became the leading economic sector in the 1950s.[49] British firms that had previously bid on many of these projects were banned from further participation. By 1960, Law No. 15, the Commercial Companies Law, was established, stipulating that any foreign business involvement in Kuwait must have a 51 percent Kuwaiti partner. Though the awarding of these projects was lucrative for many *asil* merchants, the process was *ad hoc* and depended on the good will of 'Abdallah.[50]

In the same *ad hoc* fashion, the land-acquisition process enriched many. Vast tracts of land both within and outside Kuwait City were purchased from *asil* merchants at inflated prices. These outlays accounted for a massive distribution of the new oil wealth. From 1957 to 1966, the land-acquisition program accounted for over US $1 billion in public spending,

---

[46] *Middle East Economist*, February 1956, p. 29, and July/August 1959, p. 111.

[47] An excellent review of this period as it happened is contained in a British Foreign Office Report, *Records of Kuwait*, vol. IV, pp. 768–775.

[48] *Middle East Economist*, July 1957, p. 109; and Ismael, *Kuwait: Social Change*, pp. 133–134.

[49] *Middle East Economist*, July/August 1959, p. 111.   [50] *Records of Kuwait*, vol. IV, p. 774.

averaging more than 50 percent of state expenditures annually.[51] Often land purchases by the state were rented back to the merchant at well below market prices. The industrial park at Shuwaikh was one such example. The Port of Shuwaikh[52] is located on land originally owned by the al-Ghanims and al-Sagrs. Much of the land was sold to the state at a tremendous profit. To develop the industrial park, the state rented the land back to the same families at very low rates. The merchants divided the tracts, and rented these parcels to retailers at very high prices.[53] Thus, on both ends, the merchants made significant profits with state help. By comparison, it is useful to note that these types of subsidies and expansion of state employment are not unique to Kuwait, or to the developing world. US federal subsidies for cattle farmers have enriched many in the American Mid-West.[54] Moreover, in Harlem, New York, a recent study found that 43 percent of jobs there were held by people directly employed by the government.[55] The vital difference is the volume in respect to the rest of the economy. Kuwaiti oil revenues tied the overwhelming majority of the economy to the distribution of rents.

Despite the amount of investment tied to the other distribution means, public investment in merchant-initiated companies was probably the most beneficial to merchants in the long run. In the 1950s, leading merchant families established a number of companies in which the state invested significant start-up equity. Those companies included Kuwait Airways, Gulf Fisheries, Kuwait Cinema, Kuwait Oil Tankers Company, Flour Mills Company, Kuwait Hotels Company, National Industries Company, and Kuwait Transportation Company.[56] The establishment of these companies enriched *asil* merchants in two ways: first, government shares in these companies averaged around 50 percent in the 1950s and 1960s,[57] a stake which ensured state control over executive board

[51] Ragaei El Mallakh, "Planning in a Capital Surplus Economy," *Land Economics*, 42, 4 (November 1966), p. 427.

[52] There are two main ports in Kuwait, Shuwaikh in the north and Shubai in the south. Shuwaikh handles the cargo traffic, while Shubai handles most of the crude and refined oil export.

[53] Interview with Dr. Muhammed A. Al-'Awadi, Department of Business Administration, University of Kuwait, Kuwait City, 3 December 1995.

[54] The state of Wyoming is probably the best example of a bust rentier state in the United States. In 1998, despite having the second-largest average unearned income in the country (mostly in the form of cattle subsidies and mining receipts), Wyoming ranked at the bottom of nearly every major economic indicator: *The Economist*, 18 July 1998, p. 29.

[55] Fred Siegel, *The Future Once Happened Here: New York, DC, LA, and the Fate of America's Big Cities* (New York: Free Press, 1997), p. 236.

[56] *Records of Kuwait*, vol. IV, p. 235.

[57] E. A. V. de Candole, "Kuwait Today," *Journal of the Royal Central Asian Society*, 29 September 1964, pp. 35–36; and Ragaei El Mallakh, *Economic Development and Regional Cooperation: Kuwait* (Chicago: University of Chicago Press, 1968), p. 86.

appointments.[58] Second, since public investment in these companies was consistent and guaranteed, the value of merchant equity in them was greatly inflated over the years. Therefore, on the one hand, increased rents and state expansion increased al-Sabah autonomy, thereby decreasing merchant policy involvement, while on the other hand this wealth was channeled to *asil* merchants, making them very rich. There clearly had been a deal struck between the two parties.

Crystal's work was the first to detail this bargain and its impact. In return for 'Abdallah's largesse, *asil* merchants essentially opted out of the type of political involvement that had caused royal family concern in 1938. In addition, 'Abdallah and his successors kept family members out of excessive involvement, more or less, in the domestic economy, a significant merchant complaint in 1938. Another element of the literature on the Gulf states stresses that the character of the private sector was altered as a result of massive and rapid capital inflows. What is key to keep in mind, however, is that, while much changed, the private sector in the Gulf, especially Kuwait, was not created from oil.

With capital flooding into the local economy, *asil* merchants were able to establish themselves at the pinnacle of the domestic economy. One principal means was through agency licenses. By the 1950s, Kuwait already had one of the highest percapita incomes in the world. Naturally, this favored consumption of imported luxury goods.[59] Western exporters wishing to exploit this market had to secure domestic Kuwait representative agents (locally known as *al-kasool*) in order to access local distribution and retail networks. These were tremendously profitable deals for the agent, who received a percentage of sales in return for essentially no more than signing his name. The agency economy was one of the first manifestations of the secondary rentier economy, and elite merchants were well placed to take advantage of the process. By this period, most *asil* merchants maintained business contacts in Europe and North America. They gave many of their sons foreign educations and spent the summer months in Europe. Dealing with foreign companies was an activity in

---

[58] As an example, one of the most important of these entities was the National Bank of Kuwait (NBK), founded in 1952. This was the first bank established in Kuwait, and Emir Abdalla supported it with an interest-free loan. The bank's founders, however, represented the cream of the *asil* merchant families: al-Bahar, al-Sayer, al-Hamad, al-Sagr, al-Khaled, and al-Khourafi. Since the 1950s, the NBK has served as one of the most important sources of merchant capital, and it has established itself as one of the most profitable and respected independent banks in the Middle East (National Bank of Kuwait, *Annual Report, 1995*; interview with Nassar Al-Sair, Deputy Chairman of the Board, NBK, Kuwait City, 16 December 1995; and *Records of Kuwait*, vol. III, pp. 505–510).

[59] *Records of Kuwait*, vol. IV, pp. 780–781.

which they had extensive experience. In the 1950s these elites quickly secured many of the leading Western commercial producers. The al-Ghanims, for instance, represented General Motors, British Airways, and Frigidaire, while the al-Sagrs became the agents for Ford Motor Company and the Pepsi-Cola Company. In addition to the revenue resulting from performing agent services, the process helped entrench a unique hierarchy among traders and retailers within Kuwait. Though its impact will be discussed later, the oligarchic control of agency licenses gave asil merchants considerable power over other commercial/retail interests in Kuwait.

Political independence and the founding of the Kuwait Chamber of Commerce and Industry

In June 1961, Kuwait gained its independence from Britain. Though the KCCI was organized in 1959, it was not formally established until 1961 with the election of fifteen board executives. The 1960s was a complex environment for the KCCI's first decade of existence. Business downturns in 1961, 1965, and 1969–70 contrasted with increased inflows of oil rents. Development was fast-paced. Lobbying by business elites through the KCCI and coordination with state officials figured prominently in Kuwait's efforts to draft and implement laws governing economic policy. Political standoffs and opposition moves also affected the KCCI's position vis-à-vis the state. A cabinet crisis in 1962 and the first elections to the National Assembly in January 1963 solidified the KCCI as not only a business center, but a political institution as well.

The first Arab Chamber of Commerce was established in the nineteenth century in Aleppo, Syria. Jordan's chamber was founded in 1923. Why did it take Kuwait's merchants, ostensibly well organized and motivated, so long to form their own chamber? Kuwait's merchants had already established organizational affiliations and loyalties, as evidenced by the Majlis movement and institutions such as the municipality. However, in the 1950s expanding state powers in some cases weakened these institutions, and in others merchants were simply pushed out by the al-Sabahs and their allies. Political independence marked an appropriate time for the birth of the KCCI, the founding of which was in part a response to the weakening of merchant-controlled institutions in the 1950s.

Discussions among *asil* merchants in 1959 generated an informal organization of future chamber leaders, 'Abdulaziz al-Sagr, Hamoud al-Zaid al-Khaled, and Muhammed Yousef al-Nisf. In 1960, the first elections were held for the executive board. Records from this period are incomplete, but the membership of this first electorate clearly resembled the asil voters in the 1921 council, the 1938 Majlis, and the municipality elections. Like its institutional precedents, the KCCI was tightly organized and firmly controlled by its leaders. The first annual report of the KCCI described three salient elements of the KCCI's formation: by-laws of chamber operations, representation, and chamber financing.

First, by-laws were established to govern the chamber's internal activities and executive board elections. Future state laws would influence these by-laws, but their initial form was significant and enduring. Like many Arab chambers, KCCI by-laws were essentially modeled on the Anglo-American corporate model, as opposed to the continental European form. Internal organization, in other words, was a prerogative of chamber organizers, with no state involvement or appointment. The KCCI was an autonomous organization. The by-laws stipulated that the primary purposes of the chamber were:

Registration of merchants, industrialists, companies and establishments, and updating all information related to them according to the latest changes and modifications . . . Endorsing the authenticity of the merchants, industrialists, or their representatives' signatures . . . Receiving commercial complaints whether from the members of the chamber or their counterparts and acting toward settling the commercial disputes and pursuing members' rights . . . Receiving commercial, industrial, and investment delegations and circulating the news to interested members (companies, establishments, or individuals) for preparing meeting schedules, together with a special informative file for each delegation . . . The chamber voluntarily presents its viewpoints and proposals about all matters related to economic affairs, whether in the form of legal drafts, decrees, or regulations.[60]

Second, the by-laws also established voting rules. Rules on who could vote were simple: the entity voting was actually the company or license registered with the chamber; therefore, the signatory of the registration was the specific voter. Since each registration with the chamber had one vote, subsidiaries and branches of companies once registered could also vote (see table A.3 in appendix). The registered entity must have been a member for at least one year and have paid all registration fees. Rules governing who could run for the executive board stipulated only that the person be twenty-five years old if a university graduate, thirty years old if not a university graduate, and a member in good standing for one year.

Third, KCCI finances were drawn primarily from membership fees, which were dependent upon the type of registration (agency or

---

[60] Kuwait Chamber of Commerce and Industry, *Al-Qanun wa al-Nizam, Ghurfat Tijarat wa Sana'at al-Kuwait* [By-laws and rules of the Kuwait Chamber of Commerce and Industry], 1993.

joint-stock company, for example) and amount of capital. Already, however, the first board signaled its intent to invest KCCI finances to generate revenue independent of membership fees. As well, the first members of staff of the KCCI were drawn from the offices and companies of executive board members. The establishment of the KCCI was a collective effort by *asil* merchants.[61]

These by-laws produced a business leadership that, in Olson's terms, was non-encompassing. Membership in the association was essentially voluntary and thus the membership did not comprise all strata of the business community. The structure of representation within the association was also non-inclusive. Since each registered entity could vote, the largest and most diversified businesses would actually have multiple votes. Clearly, this is the type of association which Olson's logic would wish to avoid, given its exclusive nature and propensity to represent particular as opposed to general business interests. For Kuwaiti businessmen of the time, the aim was not to create a private club *per se*, rather to create an institution that would be autonomous from state control. By-laws to ensure elite leadership control were one means toward that end. Consequently, the establishment of the KCCI gave *asil* merchants a ready and secure institutional base from which to participate in the politics of the new state.

The cabinet crisis and the National Assembly

The fifteen elected board members (see table A.1 in appendix) were the leading *asil* merchants, all of whom had extensive experience dealing with state officials and the royal family. 'Abdulaziz al-Sagr, the first president and youngest son of the chairman of the 1921 council, emerged as the most dynamic of the young merchants. Al-Sagr's politically astute leadership gave KCCI policy advocacy a distinct advantage. Moreover, the institutional cohesion of the KCCI provided an early political base for al-Sagr's activities.

As the first president of the KCCI, al-Sagr was an excellent choice. Not only was he from one of the leading *asil* families with a rich political history, but his personality would help earn allies outside the merchant community. His leadership was a key idiosyncratic variable in the KCCI's success over the years. Discussions with Kuwaitis about al-Sagr typically characterize him as something akin to George Washington; his opposition

---

[61] KCCI, *Al-Taqrir al-Sanawiyy, Ghurfat Tijarat wa Sana'at al-Kuwait, 1961* [Annual report 1961, Kuwait Chamber of Commerce and Industry]; KCCI, *Al-Qanun wa al-Nizam, Ghurfat Tijarat wa Sana'at al-Kuwait.*

to al-Sabah policies is well known, but his loyalty to Kuwait is unquestioned. British officials identified al-Sagr's profile early on, commenting: "Abdul Aziz al-Sagr always talks with moderation and authority."[62] Al-Sagr's position within Kuwait's first cabinet and first parliament carved a prominent role for the KCCI.

In 1962 the emir formed the first Kuwait cabinet. The only non-royal family members were three KCCI board members: al-Sagr (Ministry of Public Health), al-Nisf (Ministry of Social Affairs and Labor), and al-Khaled (Ministry of Justice). There were two interconnecting disputes that led to the cabinet crisis. First, some opposition elements in the new National Assembly objected to the presence of merchants in the cabinet as a violation of Article 131 of the constitution banning government service while operating a private business. These elements were also joined by al-Sabah loyalists upset about the loss of positions on the cabinet. Second, *asil* merchants close to KCCI leadership claimed that al-Sagr had received a pledge from the emir to appoint four merchants to the cabinet.[63] Therefore, while some parliamentarians protested over the appointments, al-Sagr and his colleagues protested over the unfulfilled pledge. KCCI merchants had little popular support in this case. The emir, overseas at the time, returned to accept his cabinet's resignation and appoint replacements for the merchants.[64] For the KCCI leadership, this was the final straw in a series of events depriving them of public institutional representation and leadership. It made the presence and success of the chamber even more important; it was their only institution and a venue in which they could mediate their competing interests and communicate them to the state.[65] There would be future appointments of KCCI members and allies to cabinets and public companies, to be sure, but these were rightly viewed by *asil* merchants as transitory state gifts.[66] Such appointments could come and go, but the KCCI was independent and reliable. The National Assembly presented another participatory challenge to the business leadership.

In January 1963, Kuwait held its first elections for the al-Majlis al-Umma, or National Assembly. Following in the footsteps of the Majlis movement, political debate in the National Assembly was lively. Al-Sabah intentions were clearly to use the new venue to secure allies and isolate opponents. For the opposition in general, and the KCCI leadership

[62] *Records of Kuwait*, vol. III, p. 284.
[63] Interview, Yousef bin Nisf, Kuwait City, 9 April 1996.
[64] Crystal, *Oil and Politics*, pp. 86–87.   [65] Interview, bin Nisf.
[66] In the remaining cabinets of the 1960s, there were roughly five postings of KCCI members or allies. The importance of these postings to KCCI influence will be discussed later.

specifically, the assembly allowed a new venue for pressure and policy participation. The task was to press this access and expand it whenever possible. *Asil* merchants, primarily responsible for the genesis of the first Majlis, would play an important role in the early assemblies.

The powers of the assembly in newly independent Kuwait were different from the 1938 Majlis. While the 1938 Majlis generated and passed legislation on to the emir for approval, the National Assembly could only accept, amend, or reject legislation submitted by the prime minister. Parliament was thus a consultative body, not a legislative one. It was nonetheless important, because lobby efforts to influence laws could take place on two levels: first within the prime minister's cabinet and then, if legislation was passed on to the assembly, within assembly committees. The political opposition would test these limits over time, but the essence of consultation instead of legislation endured. The Kuwaiti constitution restricted voting to male citizens and divided the country into ten electoral districts, each electing five members to the assembly (for the period 1963 to 1975).[67] Three of the original ten districts (Hawalli, Qiblah, and Kayfan) could be described as mostly merchant, but the rest contained mixed populations (*asil* merchants, Bedouin, Shi'a, and so on). This districting afforded KCCI elites solid representation across seats.

Accordingly, the KCCI leadership enjoyed two advantages in early assembly elections. First, campaigns to the assembly traditionally took place through the *diwaniyya*, a traditional men's forum for discussing political and social issues. Since the Kuwaiti constitution bans political parties, candidates or groups of candidates generate support by hosting or visiting prominent *diwaniyya* sessions to discuss their positions. KCCI candidates (executive board members or affiliated individuals) hosted interconnecting sessions in their voting districts to encourage block voting. In other districts, lone KCCI-affiliated candidates benefited from covert funding from other merchant districts to enhance their *diwaniyya* campaigns. The cohesiveness of this strategy was aided by the institutional anchor the KCCI provided. Executive board members had gone through their own elections; hence, a smoothly working hierarchy was already in place. This organizational strength was augmented by not-so-covert financial incentives for voters. In the American South, local politicians have traditionally termed this practice "walk-around money," and in Kuwait it is a common practice among most Kuwaiti political groups, especially business. Second, KCCI elites benefited because of the lingering perception of them as the national opposition in the wake

[67] Gavrielides, "Tribal Democracy," p. 165.

of the 1938 Majlis. Other groups (Shi'a, Islamist, and Bedouin) had yet to strengthen their own organizational and political bases. Consequently, assemblies of the 1960s and early 1970s marked the high point of business influence in the only elected assembly in the region.[68]

In the first assembly (1963–67), there were twenty-two KCCI members or allies elected out of a total of fifty total representatives.[69] Four of the twenty-two were KCCI board members, including 'Abdulaziz al-Sagr, who was elected as the first speaker of the parliament. Though political parties were illegal in Kuwait, the merchants allied themselves behind a front of Nasserite nationalists (the National Bloc) headed by Ahmed al-Khatib. The real force, however, was al-Sagr, whose role as president of the KCCI, former cabinet member, and speaker of the parliament tied mainstream opposition in Kuwait to the elites of the KCCI. However, by 1967 another crisis erupted, signaling the beginning of the decline of KCCI power in parliament.

From the parliament's inception, merchant opposition focused on three demands: National Assembly elections without government pressure (i.e., ending covert funding for government loyalists), reduction of the number of voting districts from ten to two, and cancellation of Article 131 of the constitution banning government service while engaging in private business. In the year leading up to the second parliamentary elections, al-Sagr and the merchant opposition openly campaigned for these reforms and boycotted government functions. In those elections, the merchants and their allies lost ten seats. In January 1967, al-Sagr resigned as speaker of the parliament.[70] This would be the last government or parliament position he would occupy.

Business cohesion and relations with the state in the 1960s

In the first decade of its existence, the KCCI solidified its own internal cohesion by institutionalizing commercial relations among *asil* elites. This organization strengthened the KCCI as a foundation through which *asil* merchants could express opinions on national economic policy and influence the country's founding economic laws. According to the standard structural/statist approach, business organizes to influence policy or to

---

[68] In 1963, Qatar experimented with a short-lived elected municipal council, but it would not be until the 1980s and 1990s that other Gulf Arab states seriously considered such elected bodies: Louay Bahry, "Elections in Qatar: A Window of Democracy Opens in the Gulf," *Middle East Policy*, 6, 4 (June 1999).

[69] Calculations taken from data provided in Gavrielides, "Tribal Democracy."

[70] *The Arabian Peninsula and Jordan, Economist Intelligence Unit (EIU), Quarterly Economic Reviews*, No. 1, 1968, pp. 7–8 (as the title of this periodical underwent changes, all versions are subsequently referred to as *EIU*).

access rents. Given the size and arrival time of oil rents, one is tempted to interpret the early organization of Kuwaiti business as an embodiment of rent-seeking. This section presents evidence challenging the assumption that business organization derives solely from sectoral attributes. While business organization as a means to influence policy and secure rents characterizes some of the evolution of business–state relations, such a focus ultimately leads one down an analytical dead end. Interactions between business elites and the state in the 1960s were an extension of the wider social and political struggle that had marked Kuwait's pre-independence years. Hence, the use of the KCCI to influence economic policy in the 1960s and the role of the institution as a political and social anchor during rapid state expansion are two sides of the same coin.

Intra-merchant coordination through the KCCI was manifest in two principal areas. First, as mentioned previously, in the 1950s and especially in the 1960s imports to Kuwait rapidly expanded as consumer demand blossomed. From 1955 to 1960 imports more than doubled from 33.7 million Kuwaiti dinars (KD) to KD 86.4 million.[71] A British consular dispatch in 1961 described this situation:

> Kuwait has to import for its living every item . . . People have plenty of money to spend and while they can buy luxuries only once in a while the necessities of life have to be purchased everyday. The result is that luxuries are comparatively cheap, the margin of profit charged varying from 25 to 100 percent.[72]

Merchant elites at the KCCI grasped the potential for profits. In its first year of existence, the KCCI moved quickly to centralize trade around the executive board. KCCI board members organized licensing and importation monopolies among themselves around classes of goods, arranging which foreign producer would be represented by which Kuwait merchant.[73] Though the KCCI's legal involvement in approving import licenses would not come until the 1964 Importation Law, by 1961 the KCCI already played a significant role regulating imports into Kuwait.

A second type of internal collusion involved bids for state contracts. After British firms were expelled in the 1950s, state work projects went exclusively to Kuwait contractors and their foreign partners. Just as agreements among KCCI elites organized imports, similar arrangements clearly influenced public contracts. Merchant elites divided the work depending on the type of contract – i.e., road building, port facilities,

---

[71] Khouja and Sadler, *The Economy of Kuwait*, p. 51.

[72] *Records of Kuwait*, vol. IV, p. 781.

[73] *Ibid.*, p. 784; and interview with Jassem Al-Sadoun, Kuwait City, 5 March 1996.

public buildings, and so on.[74] Again, like import regulations, the KCCI's legal management of public project licenses would be established later in the 1960s. While public works and import collusion may have hampered economic competition, the point is that this collusion facilitated leadership cohesion at a key point in the KCCI's early history. The success of KCCI leadership cohesion was reflected in the ease with which the KCCI took over cases of merchant arbitration in the early 1960s. Kuwait's legal system was still in its infancy; consequently, there were few institutionalized procedures to adjudicate merchant disputes. The KCCI Arbitration Committee filled this void by ruling on such cases.[75] It proved so successful that the state rarely interceded in such cases from that point onward. In a period in which Kuwait's founding economic laws were being debated, the potential for conflicting merchant interests within the chamber had been alleviated. By compromising among themselves, KCCI leaders were better able to lobby collectively on the coming economic legislation.

Clearly, then, early business coordination was targeted at securing rents. However, this cannot be divorced from business's political struggles in the 1961 cabinet and resistance to the widening reach of the state's power. Instead of more direct confrontations, the basic theme in the 1960s comprised efforts to avoid the unregulated public spending and development decisions of the 1950s. The embarrassing departure of al-Sagr from the assembly, following as it did the string of institutional defeats in the 1950s, convinced KCCI leaders to carry the struggle to economic policy-making. The overall strategy was to increase state supervision and legal regulation over economic issues, while at the same time restricting state budgetary growth. This situation supports the argument that markets are built on a degree of state control/regulation and precipitate struggles between rulers and merchants.[76] Thus, in an odd twist, Kuwait's leading capitalists in the 1960s were actually lobbying for more, not less, regulation in the new rentier economy. Creation of the country's first economic laws presented a number of opportunities.

Historical details of the KCCI's first lobbying efforts are not complete. It is evident, however, that the aim of KCCI leaders was not to repeat development patterns of the 1950s. British records from the period frequently recount complaints by leading merchants (and the British

---

[74] British consular complaints about this process were common. See *Records of Kuwait*, vol. IV, p. 621.

[75] *Ibid.*, p. 786.

[76] Kiren Aziz Chaudhry develops this line of argument in "The Myth of the Market and Late Developers," *Politics & Society*, 21 (September 1993), pp. 245–274.

advisors) over wasteful development spending and arbitrary development decisions.[77] The supplanting of merchant-dominated institutions (i.e., the Development Board) in the 1950s allowed state centralization of the development schemes and the distribution of oil revenues. Centralization lessened societal input into decisionmaking. Through arbitrary, unplanned development spending, royal family members benefited greatly, allowing some an entrance into private business, a violation of the unwritten pact between ruler and merchant. Moreover, uncontrolled spending threatened to create new merchants to rival *asil* power. Consequently, leading merchants concluded that "keeping the arbitrary power of the [royal] family in check . . . provid[ed] the administrative stability which they recognize as being necessary for their prosperity."[78] By lobbying to influence Kuwait's new economic laws and pushing for better planning, KCCI leaders took the opportunity to submit state development decisions to a bureaucratic and political routine they could better influence.

A string of economic laws passed by the National Assembly and implemented in the 1960s (the Companies Law No. 15/1960, the Commercial Agency and Commercial Representatives Law No. 68/1964, the Law Governing Public Tenders No. 37/1964, and the Industrial Law No. 6/1964) revealed the effort both to entrench *asil* market dominance and to gain administrative access to policymaking. Individually and collectively, these laws directly benefited KCCI elites in several ways.

The establishment of commercial entities was restricted to Kuwait nationals. Foreign partnership was allowed but it could not exceed 49 percent of total capital. This in effect sealed off the Kuwait market from foreign domination and allowed monopoly arrangements hammered out within the KCCI to endure. Any entity wishing to import goods into Kuwait or bid on lucrative state contracts had to register annually with the KCCI. In line with similar mechanisms in other developing countries, the state was effectively extending public regulatory powers to a private institution; this was, in other words, a form of quasi-corporatism. It was an important step toward the goal of regularizing development spending and economic activity within Kuwait. By playing a role within the licensing framework for profitable sectors (trading and public works), the KCCI could better track and manage market competition. Licenses could either be quickly processed or delayed. While this was not an absolute power (final approval came from the Ministry of Commerce and Industry), it greatly aided monopoly arrangements among *asil* merchants. Furthermore, the regulation meant that every year the largest traders and

---

[77] *Records of Kuwait*, vol. IV, pp. 67, 161, 646–647, and 664–665.   [78] *Ibid.*, p. 64.

businessmen in Kuwait would join the KCCI. State law, thus, reinforced the exclusivity of the KCCI.

The Industrial Law specifically established a precedent that would greatly facilitate business's policy access in the future: an Industrial Development Committee was created within the Ministry of Commerce and Industry. This committee had nine members, three of whom were appointed by the KCCI. Its tasks were to review applications for industrial companies and, more importantly, award various tax breaks and incentives to start-up industries. By securing representation on this committee, the KCCI had succeeded in further regularizing state–business relations while gaining an important legal conduit for information.[79]

While these changes were important at the ministerial level, economic policy remained the final prerogative of the prime minister and his Council of Ministers. When KCCI elites were appointed as ministers, the KCCI could benefit from such access, but this was *ad hoc* and clearly used by the ruling al-Sabahs as a tool of reward and punishment. To lessen the dependency of this arrangement, al-Sagr and his top board members (Fulaij, al-Nisf, and al-Khourafi) directly pressed the emir to establish a more institutionalized planning body.[80] After independence, the KCCI therefore became an early supporter of a revamped Planning Board.

In 1962 the emir announced the formation of such a Planning Board, which, in addition to various ministers, included four members appointed by the KCCI (but approved by the prime minister). In line with KCCI prerogatives, then, "the planning process itself became institutionalized to ensure social stability through rationalization of the allocation of oil revenues."[81] Though the mandate of the board was "the formulation of the general economic and social policy, and the establishment of development programs and supervision of their implementation," planning in Kuwait never really became entrenched. Budgets were reviewed and suggestions made, but in the heady days of the 1970s planning goals, marked by five- year plans (which didn't always cover five years, but were used to indicate targets), were far surpassed by oil rents and their political application. Still, a regularized board at the level of the prime minister with KCCI participation set an important precedent. While the Planning Board may not have been a decisive arbiter of economic policy, it was an institutionalized venue for the KCCI to exchange information with state officials. For its part, the KCCI took the board seriously and assigned only its highest-ranking leaders to it. Consequently, a mission from the

---

[79] *The Official Gazette* (Kuwait), various years.   [80] Interview, bin Nisf.
[81] Ismael, *Kuwait: Social Change*, p. 134.

International Bank for Reconstruction and Development to Kuwait in the early 1960s concluded that "private-sector members [of the Planning Board] are very influential."[82] In considering these merchant efforts to reverse their earlier setbacks and curb arbitrary state power, several caveats are necessary.

First, there are strong indications that state preferences regarding the Planning Board and the new laws were not substantially different from those of the KCCI. The core issue was greater accountability (and access) in economic policy versus greater flexibility on the part of the ruling family to continue to dispense economic patronage. But new economic laws were needed, and the extent to which the KCCI achieved set bureaucratized routines in economic development cannot be said to have either altered the locus of economic decisionmaking or significantly impaired the state's fiscal independence. So, on the one hand, *asil* merchants had actually regressed from the near-success they had in 1938. On the other hand, however, given the *ad hoc* nature of economic development in the 1950s and the financial realities of a rentier state, the KCCI had made progress by influencing the creation of a bureaucratized economic decisionmaking machine in the 1960s. These were important lobbying successes despite the fact that there was no overt state opposition to be overcome.

Second, the role of parliament vis-à-vis business–state relations was generally insignificant. Merchant control of the parliament was at its height in the 1960s, but there were few legislative fights over domestic economic policy in that decade. Merchant opposition figures instead pursued more populist issues regarding oil concession deals, Arab nationalism, and foreign relations. Interviews with individuals politically active at the time suggest it was apparent that the majority of the initial business–state interactions took place through informal meetings among state leaders, the emir, and KCCI leaders such as al-Sagr. However, once structures such as the Planning Board and the ministerial committees were in place, a greater emphasis was placed on the KCCI's institutionalized access as a venue for lobbying.

Third, as the KCCI began to assume its institutional identity in the 1960s, it initiated annual economic reports, which became an important mechanism for future policy advocacy. Because the chamber quickly created and staffed an Information and Research Department – fed by information acquired through its access – it could produce professional studies and economic analyses. By 1968, annual economic reports issued through the KCCI in the name of al-Sagr became important bellwethers

---

[82] International Bank for Reconstruction and Development, *The Economic Development of Kuwait: Mission Report* (Baltimore: Johns Hopkins University Press, 1965), p. 99.

for the status of Kuwait's economy.[83] These reports were sophisticated means through which the KCCI voiced its approval or disapproval of state policies, coupled with suggestions for policy changes. The elite profile of al-Sagr and his board supported by the organizational assets of the KCCI gave these reports their influence. In combination with annual reports from the National Bank of Kuwait (NBK, controlled by KCCI elites) and the eventual creation of the *Al-Qabas* newspaper in 1970 (also controlled by KCCI elites), the chamber sat at the center of an effective media network that complemented its other institutional capabilities.

A less promising birth: the British, the Hashemites, and the creation of business–state relations in Jordan

The historian Malcolm Yapp described the creation of Transjordan as a "less promising birth."[84] In contrast to Kuwait's steady evolution while playing off Ottoman and British interests against each other, Transjordan's evolution was punctuated to make way for a period under British Mandate with an imported monarchy. Just a few decades prior to this birth, much of the core of Jordan's merchant elite immigrated to Transjordan from the cities of Syria and Palestine. At about the same time as their Kuwaiti counterparts were creating municipal and education councils, Transjordanian elites established their own associational representation and crafted close relations with Hashemite and British authorities. The formation of the Jordanian state, like that of Kuwait, closely followed rentier patterns, but business–state relations differed to a noticeable degree. The British role was more intrusive than in Kuwait, and elite merchants did not share as close a political and social relationship with their monarchy.

"Strangers with capital":[85] *the first merchants*

Both Emir 'Abdullah Ibn Hussein and Jordan's first merchants were strangers to a new land. Merchants from Syria and Palestine moved to the cities of what would become known as Transjordan in the waning years of Ottoman rule. The establishment of the British Mandate in 1923 satisfied both British regional designs and 'Abdullah's desire for a throne.

---

[83] *EIU*, No. 1, 1968, p. 9.

[84] M. E. Yapp, *The Near East Since the First World War: A History to 1995* (London: Addison Wesley Longman, 1996), p. 140.

[85] Quote taken from a British observer describing merchant emigrants to the city of Salt in 1867, cited in Mustafa B. Hamarneh, *Social and Economic Transformation of Transjordan, 1921–1946* (Ph.D. Dissertation: Georgetown University, 1985), p. 95.

In place since the late nineteenth century, Jordan's merchant elite would found the Amman Chamber of Commerce (ACC) in 1923. Unpacking the political and social dynamics accompanying these events is crucial for understanding the trajectory of Jordan's business–state relations into the 1960s.

Prior to the British Mandate, Transjordan was considered a southern province of Syria. In comparison to its northern neighbor, the area of Transjordan was virtually pre-modern. Well-armed but poor semi-nomadic tribes dominated the region, making long-distance trade a risky and infrequent endeavor. Cities were small and underdeveloped. The largest in the nineteenth century was Salt (with around 20,000 inhabitants by 1920), followed by Irbid, Jerash, and Kerak.[86] The history of Jordan's modern merchant class began in the late nineteenth century with the extension of Ottoman garrisons and the Hijaz railway to the area.

Attracted by the increased security, merchants from Nablus and Damascus emigrated to Salt, Irbid, and eventually to Amman.[87] These families would form the core of Jordan's leading merchants. Among some of the earliest and most prominent were the 'Asfour and Manku families, who moved to Transjordan from Nablus in the middle of the century. Yousef 'Asfour would be the first president of the ACC, and Hamdi Manku would follow as an important board member. Al-Sa'udi, Battikhi, Shuqair, and Shurbaji, all Syrian merchant families, also moved to Transjordan and served on the first boards of the ACC (see table A.4 in appendix). Other future ACC leaders, Tabba and Bdair, established important trading concerns in Transjordan after fleeing political turmoil in Damascus.[88] Therefore, like the Kuwaiti *asil*, Jordan's initial business elite did not originate within the country. A key difference, however, was that the ruling Hashemites (originating from the Arabian peninsula) shared neither native roots nor origins similar to its business community. Kuwait's original three-way pact (political, security, and commerce) did not correspond to origin differences. Jordan's three-way distinction first became politically salient during the Mandate period. British indirect rule in the Middle East involved the recruitment of first Syrian and later Palestinian managers to staff Transjordan's colonial agencies. In

[86] Ma'an Abu Nowar, *The History of the Hashemite Kingdom of Jordan*, vol. I, *The Creation and Development of Transjordan: 1920–1929* (Oxford, UK: Ithaca Press, 1989), pp. 25–27.

[87] Until the 1930s, Amman was not considered among the major urban areas of Transjordan.

[88] Interview with Hamdi al-Tabba, 27 June 1995, Amman; interview with Mohammed 'Asfour, former president, ACC, 24 May 1995, Amman; and Abla Amawi, *State and Class in Transjordan: A Study of State Autonomy* (Ph.D. Dissertation: Georgetown University, 1993), pp. 390–394.

the 1930s, the British created a new military force for Transjordan, the Desert Mobile Force, led by John Glubb. This force shifted its recruiting from exclusively Palestinians to East Bank bedouins. From independence onward, first King Abdullah and then King Hussein expanded this pattern to incorporate East Bank elites and rank and file to staff state bureaucracies (and security services). As was the case in Southeast Asia – where in many countries the nominal nationality of a country served in the organs of the state, while immigrant Chinese and Indian merchants filled business roles – a clear distinction grew up between the nationalities performing business and state activities. The first became primarily Palestinian and Syrian in origin and the second East Bank in origin. The broader distinction between East Bankers and Palestinians is often advanced as a basic theme in Jordanian politics; however, the link between social origin and what is to be explained is usually left vague. One area where the link is more clear is in the institutional repercussions from the division.

Throughout its history (and for many social institutions in Jordan), the Amman Chamber of Commerce was perceived as a Syrian, and later Palestinian, rather than Jordanian institution. While this distinction would seem to be a disadvantage once state-building was underway, foreign origin was actually an advantage in some ways, as it was in Kuwait. These early merchants formed a close-knit community, in one respect, which facilitated interconnecting social and financial arrangements. Foreign origin drew these merchants together and made collective action easier. Though Jordan's elite merchants did not have the experience of early institution-building as in the case of Kuwait, Jordan's first merchants nevertheless demonstrated their cohesion by organizing informally. One such organization, Jami'at al-Thulatha (Society of Thursday), was composed of chamber leaders and was set up to facilitate discussions and action on political and economic issues.[89] Similar to merchant *diwaniyyas* in Kuwait, this society served to reinforce intramerchant communication and social ties. That much of the merchant community was of foreign origin also had economic effects. In a manner similar to the Kuwaiti merchants who had arrived from Basra and increased trade interregionally with their home area, Damascene and Palestinian merchants greatly expanded trade in Jordan by exploiting their home links. Because of their ties with regional trading centers, Jordan's position as a commercial center gradually increased. In addition to this trade, Transjordan's new merchants' methods of enriching themselves were similar to those of their Kuwaiti counterparts in another way.

[89] Amawi, *State and Class*, pp. 513–514.

As in Kuwait, land provided an important early source of merchant wealth in Jordan. This became most apparent in Kuwait and Jordan during the boom of the 1970s. As real estate prices soared, merchant land tracts in Amman and Kuwait City generated tremendous rent revenue.[90] However, even before the Mandate period, Jordan's first merchants built their wealth through land acquisitions. While trade in Transjordan was still in its infancy, Palestinian and Syrian merchants turned to money lending. When urban borrowers could not repay these loans, moneylending merchants simply took land in return. In the towns of Kerak and Salt, this process accounted for the expansion of merchant landholding in the period before and after the British Mandate.[91] These were the same merchants who created the Amman Chamber of Commerce in 1923, more than forty years before the establishment of its Kuwaiti counterpart.

Records regarding the establishment of the chamber are modest. However, there is sufficient evidence to support a good description of the early chambers. In August 1923 the new Transjordanian government completed the Law of the Chamber of Commerce, and in November elections were held for a ten-man executive board. The organizational features established at that time remained in effect until the early 1960s. In its organization and operation, early business representation was the domain of a small, tightly knit merchant elite.

The impetus for the founding of the ACC came from two directions. Newly established, 'Abdullah's Transjordanian government (staffed as it was by experienced Syrian and Palestinian civil servants) desired to move quickly toward seizing a greater role in the domestic economy. Following the chamber's founding, 'Abdullah formed the High Economic Committee within the prime minister's cabinet and created the Department of Customs and Excise.[92] Second, elite merchants wanted their own association as a means to organize and register their businesses. By the early 1920s, with the arrival of the Arab Bank and the Ottoman Bank, a financial system began to take shape. More capital available to finance trade expanded capacity. The city of Amman was a growing trade center in Transjordan by this time; hence, the chamber was headquartered there. Also, many of the leading merchants had already come to

[90] Patterns of land ownership demonstrate another interesting similarity between these cases. In Syria, Iraq, and Egypt, a landed elite pre-dated state formation, while in Jordan and Kuwait a landed elite was created through state development. See Gabriel Baer, "Land Tenure in the Hashemite Kingdom of Jordan," *Land Economics* (August 1957), pp. 194–195.

[91] Hamarneh, *Social and Economic Transformation*, pp. 87–88; and G. F. Walpole, "Land Problems in Transjordan," *Journal of the Royal Central Asian Society* (July 1947), pp. 59–60.

[92] Abu Nowar, *The History of the Hashemite Kingdom of Jordan*, pp. 228–229.

settle in Amman. In short, a critical mass had been reached to organize intra-merchant relations. Because many of these merchants came from Damascus, there was a desire to emulate that city's chamber and its organization of merchants. Finally, it was not difficult to agree on common institutional norms, since the elites shared similar origins and had a history of social and business dealings.[93]

Structure of business representation

As with the first Kuwaiti chamber, the institutional organization of the Amman Chamber of Commerce was important. While the post-independence legal parameters of the ACC would be made law in 1949, the organizational features were set in 1923. The important organizational attributes of the ACC followed the Anglo-American model. It was an independent institution relying on membership dues for its operating funds, and deciding upon its internal features was the prerogative of the members, not the state. Twice weekly, the executive board would meet to discuss mutual concerns and prepare joint positions to present to the government. However, there is no documentation revealing exact structures and their functions (e.g., the KCCI's arbitration board) within the chamber. According to interviews, the early chamber was rather undifferentiated, and given its small membership this seems logical.[94]

Voting and representation rules were exclusive. Membership was voluntary for merchants and hence, like the KCCI, the initial ACC was not, in Olsonian terms, an encompassing association. Those merchants who did join did so as individual members, and were divided into categories according to their available capital. *Mumtaz*, or excellent, was the highest level, followed by five other numerical rankings. *Mumtaz* through category 2 comprised the elite members. Association by-laws stipulated that only these categories could nominate, vote for, and run as candidates for the twelve-man executive board. Elite control was thus ensured. These merchants would essentially gather and agree among themselves (prior to the election) who would sit on the next board. These crucial regulations remained in effect until the early 1960s.[95]

---

[93] Various interviews confirmed this basic insight, lately discovered by theorists of collective action such as Mancur Olson.

[94] What can pieced together about this early period comes from Amawi, *State and Class*, pp. 401–404; and some chamber publications: ACC, *al-Kitab al-Dhahabi* [*The Golden Book: 50th Anniversary of the Amman Chamber of Commerce*] (Amman: Amman Chamber of Commerce, 1973); ACC, *Sijill Asma' al-Tujjar, 1923–1927* [Registration of merchants], ACC archives.

[95] Interview, Mamdouh Abu Hassan, former board member, ACC, Amman, 5 November 1996; and ACC, *al-Kitab al-Dhahabi*.

Despite the paucity of records, it is clear the early organization of the ACC paralleled that of its Kuwaiti counterpart in that elites were guaranteed control. This institutional foundation eased similar types of merchant interaction with the state and facilitated enduring internal compromise among merchant elites.

The Mandate period and growth of a rentier state

It was during the Mandate period (1923–1948) that modern Jordan was formed; this section examines merchant–ruler relations during that important period. Merchant elites at the ACC did forge close, influential relations with King 'Abdullah and attempted to affect economic policies during the Mandate. As well, since some Mandate policies facilitated growing trade within and through Transjordan, ACC elites were able to achieve a dominant position within the economy and solidify their control of the ACC. As in Kuwait, the influence of the Mandate on business–state relations is explained less well by the underdevelopment thesis, and better analyzed through focus on how rule was established. The difference with British rule in Transjordan was the introduction of rents to fund the colonial state at precisely the period in which expatriate merchants and 'Abdullah's court were crafting their relations.

The 1921 Mandate agreement between Britain and King 'Abdullah established the British role in Transjordan's domestic and foreign affairs. To support operations of the new state institutions and to support the British-controlled Arab Legion, Britain gave Transjordan annual "grants-in-aid." Throughout the Mandate period, this rent remained the single most important source of state revenue, usually accounting for 50 percent of total state revenues.[96] The grants also made for persistent issues of debate between resident British officials and 'Abdullah's government. Typically, resident officials complained about 'Abdullah's expenditures, but nevertheless requested more funds to cover the shortfall.[97] Thus, at its birth, Transjordan could be considered a rentier state. Though this

---

[96] Calculation taken from Laurie Brand, *Jordan's Inter-Arab Relations: The Political Economy of Alliance Making* (New York: Columbia University Press, 1994), p. 42. Reliable and consistent statistics until the 1960s are scarce. Unlike Kuwait, where oil rent calculations were rather straightforward (amount of oil bought multiplied by world price), aid in Jordan shifted by type and was variable from year to year. Military aid, for instance, was not included in aid calculations, and its presence certainly freed up revenue to be spent in other areas.

[97] Several British resident reports contained these complaints: *Records of Jordan 1919–1961*, edited by Jane Priestland (London: Archive Editions, 1996) vol. II, *1923–1926*, pp. 72–73; and J. B. Philby, "Trans-Jordan," *Journal of the Royal Central Asian Society*, 10, 11 (1923–24), pp. 307–308.

lessened the need to tax merchants, the grant system did stimulate other points of leverage that ACC elites used for their own benefit.

Specifically, since 'Abdullah was forced to spend carefully under the scrutiny of resident officials, he sought other revenue sources. Merchant elites at the ACC were well placed to respond. There are several documented occasions of leading merchants providing *ad hoc* funds to 'Abdullah.[98] In much the same way as Kuwaiti merchants supported the al-Sabahs in the years *before* the arrival of the British and the discovery of oil, Jordan's merchants used this *ad hoc* funding to forge close relations with 'Abdullah *during* British rule. One leading ACC board member, Subri Tabba, met daily with 'Abdullah and frequently approached him regarding commercial issues. At times, this raised British concern that the merchants were gaining too much leverage. Later in the Mandate period, this relationship did facilitate concessions from 'Abdullah's government that greatly enhanced the position of ACC board members. While British grants to the al-Sabahs in Kuwait were reciprocated with political loyalty (in opposition to Ottoman interests) and little else was required, in Transjordan the British role was more intrusive.

British grants were premised upon the adoption of land and tax reforms to create a domestic tax base. The intent was to replace various indirect Ottoman taxation systems with a more direct scheme. Beginning in 1927, the British conducted land surveys to develop data for the tax. In 1933, the government approved legislation on the land tax. It applied a uniform 6 percent tax on specific uses of land throughout Transjordan.[99] Summaries of records from the time reveal that some leading merchants anchored in the ACC strongly resisted the law, but to no avail.[100] This failure has led some observers to conclude that these new taxes confirmed the weakness of merchant influence on the economic policies of the British and 'Abdullah's government.[101] However, the outcome was more complex and speaks to how merchant and landowner lobbying actually achieved a compromise on the land tax. The overall tax burden to any individual "should not exceed the total amount of the three

[98] During the Syrian Revolt of 1927, ACC elites (Tabba and Bdair) organized relief supplies on behalf of Abdullah for the refugees (Abu Nowar, *The History of the Hashemite Kingdom of Jordan*, pp. 195–196); resident officials mentioned the presence of other *ad hoc* funds, but were unsure of their origin (*Records of Jordan*, vol. II, p. 102). Interviews with the grandchildren of these chamber leaders confirm that their forefathers frequently gave Abdullah "unpaid loans" for his personal use.

[99] A. Konikoff, *Transjordan: An Economic Survey* (Jerusalem: Economic Research Institute of the Jewish Agency for Palestine, 1946), pp. 88–90; and Walpole, "Land Problems in Transjordan."

[100] Amawi, *State and Class*, pp. 283–289.

[101] Hamarneh, *Social and Economic Transformation*, pp. 162–165.

replaced taxes [former Ottoman taxes that were being replaced by the land tax] by LP 10,000."[102] The law also benefited big merchants in the Amman area because – in addition to the recognition of land gains made decades earlier through money-lending – the registration and security of land meant mortgages were possible. Large merchants gained access to tracts of urban land by financing the mortgages of smaller landowners.[103] Also, a compromise was implicit since acceptance of the land tax resulted in a significant dilution of a new income tax passed the same year.

This income tax was levied against employee salaries but was premised upon merchants and shopkeepers providing detailed employee payment records. These records were simply not kept on any large scale. Foreshadowing the administrative weakness of the rentier state, the Ministry of Finance did not bother to compel or audit merchant submissions. As a result, the tax yielded only some LP 5,000 annually.[104] Given that the land tax resulted in only a 12 percent revenue increase by 1946,[105] the entire colonial project of enhancing direct tax revenue was not quite the victory over merchants it is commonly assumed to be. Compromise on the tax issues offers only indirect evidence of the growing influence of merchant elites and the ACC. By the late 1930s, local chambers had been established in the cities of Kerak, Ma'an, Ajlun, and Salt.[106] However, the Amman Chamber of Commerce remained the center for coordinating business activities and representing the country's merchants to central authorities.

The final phase of the Mandate period (1938–1948) ushered in a period of intense business–colonial state interaction. During World War II, ACC members were able to take advantage of new trade opportunities, enhance their chamber's economic role, and use the strengthened association to influence new government policies.

Trade opportunities in Jordan and the region increased significantly as a result of World War II. In 1941, British authorities established the Middle East Supply Centre (MESC) as a means to lessen wartime shortages across the region. This new trade regime designated Aqaba as a primary import point for goods going not only to Transjordan, but to Palestine during the British Mandate as well. This placed Amman's merchants in a pivotal position to manage the increased reexport trade with the cities of Jerusalem, Nablus, Hebron, and Bethlehem. This supraregional institution also placed in the hands of colonial authorities new

---

[102] *Official Gazette*, No. 384 (1 April 1933).
[103] Walpole, "Land Problems in Transjordan," pp. 58–59.
[104] Konikoff, *Transjordan*, pp. 91–92.   [105] Amawi, *State and Class*, p. 288.
[106] Harry Luke and Edward Kieth-Roach (eds.), *The Handbook of Palestine* (London: Macmillan and Co., 1934), p. 485.

powers to regulate the entire region's exports and imports. The MESC's trade regimes favored awarding semi-monopolistic import/export rights, in order to guarantee supplies.[107] The business elite, with their government contacts and regional trade links, were able to exploit the situation. The control of import/export for Transjordan was located within the Department of Customs, specifically with its British director, P. Livingstone. Executive board members of the ACC used their contacts with Livingstone and 'Abdullah to steer trade concessions toward themselves.[108] The profits were significant. In the year 1940/1941, reexports from Transjordan increased by five times. Abla Amawi terms the recipients of this windfall the "quota coterie":

The quota coterie all shared similar characteristics. They already had established trading links. They were well placed socially to take advantage of quota allocations. They had a head start in importing through the quota system. They were a cohesive group. They controlled the chamber of commerce.[109]

Of the thirty-one merchants Amawi identifies as belonging to the coterie, twenty-four sat on, or were related to members of, the executive board of the ACC from 1935 to 1943. By securing these trading rights, board members not only enriched themselves but augmented the capabilities and position of the chamber. According to interviews, Livingstone and government officials would suggest that foreign traders or organizations contact the chamber for lists of potential import/export partners.[110] Expressed in instrumental terms, chamber-provided information was a collective good that eased transaction costs (of forging external trade links) and benefited members' individual businesses. In return, board members opened facilities under chamber control to satisfy emergency storage needs for the government.[111] Members also used the chamber's political contacts to secure travel documents needed to fashion more extensive trading relationships. By the late 1940s the chamber had become the focal point for merchant self-regulation, business collective action, and intra-merchant dispute resolution.[112] Thus, in much the same way that British aloofness during World War II aided the enrichment and consolidation of the Kuwaiti merchant community, British action through the MESC shaped the fortunes and organization of Jordan's merchants. Paradoxically, these external dynamics also strengthened state power, as

[107] Martin Wilmington, *The Middle East Supply Center* (Albany: SUNY Press, 1971).
[108] Interviews, Abu Hassan and Tabba. Subri al-Tabba was an early and popular recipient of these concessions.
[109] Amawi, *State and Class*, p. 480.   [110] Interviews, Tabba and 'Asfour.
[111] *Al-Sadirat*, 7 July 1942, cited in Amawi, *State and Class*, p. 496.
[112] Amawi, *State and Class*, pp. 519–520.

steady flows of colonial grants helped forge the type of state autonomy that would reach full expression in the boom of the 1970s. Institutionally, the MESC also set forth a nascent form of import-substitution industrialization long before the newly independent Arab states would officially launch these policies.[113] Consequently, the final stages of Mandate rule and institutions in the Middle East are vital to understanding the building of state and economy throughout the region and the changing relationship between merchants and the fledgling Arab state. New struggles arose from these shifting dynamics.

Tempted by the tremendous increase in merchant capital from wartime trade, Mandate officials again sought to implement the failed income tax from the 1930s as a way of seizing a share of the wealth. ACC leadership, of course, was vehemently opposed to such direct taxation. President Subri Tabba of the ACC exercised his clout and directly appealed to Prime Minister Tawfiq Abu Huda. Tabba succeeded in delaying the tax for a year by collecting the proposed tax amount from ACC elites and turning it over the Ministry of Finance. Reports from the British resident suggested this action not only angered British officials but also heightened their fear that "the influence of the business classes, as purveyors of financial credit, over the individual councilors [Transjordanian members of the appointed legislative assembly] is wide."[114] In the next year, government efforts to institute the tax began again, as did ACC resistance.

To derail the law, ACC elites mounted an impressive collective action campaign, which included a general strike in November 1945 and organization of several petitions and delegations to colonial ministers and King 'Abdullah.[115] Despite these efforts, British advice and Transjordan's financial needs won out. The law was passed. Still, lingering fear of the ACC's clout forced British officials to suggest that the power of tax exemptions not be vested with the minister of finance, with whom business influence was suspected to be more effective, but with the prime minister. As a single, though noteworthy defeat, the income tax still confirmed the impressive development of the ACC throughout the period of World War II. With independence in 1948, the ACC faced a different type of political authority in a post-colonial world. Accordingly, as the new Jordanian state expanded its control of the domestic economy, the ACC expanded its efforts to shape that intervention.

[113] Robert Vitalis and Steven Heydemann, "War, Keynesianism, and Colonialism: Explaining State–Market Relations in the Postwar Middle East," in Steven Heydemann (ed.), *War, Institutions, and Social Change in the Middle East* (Berkeley: University of California Press, 2000), pp. 100–145.

[114] Cited in Amawi, *State and Class*, p. 517.   [115] *Ibid.*, p. 520.

State expansion from the time of independence and
merchant–state relations

In the 1950s and 1960s, rent in the form of Arab and American aid
came to replace British grants as the leading source of state revenue.
By the 1960s, state management of the economy was well underway.
The state introduced measures to create distributive government institutions, encourage import-substitution industrialization, and initiate public
investment in private companies. Experimentation with elected assemblies followed. Elements of these trends closely paralleled those in Kuwait
during the initial boom years in the 1960s. Beyond the similar structural
features, however, crucial divergence was taking place in this period. In
the early 1960s, ACC elites undertook organizational changes that had
far-reaching consequences for its capabilities and the political position of
the entire business community.

Jordan's political independence from Britain occurred in the context
of the first Arab–Israeli war. The birth of Israel and Jordan's subsequent
position as a frontline state made the threat of war constant. Regional
instability continually complicated Jordan's domestic political arrangements. Two implications followed. First, Jordan's geographical position
in the region (bordering Syria, Israel, and Iraq) made the kingdom important geostrategically. Whereas Kuwait cashed in on its oil endowment,
Jordan cashed in on its geostrategic endowment. By the mid-1950s,
British grants were replaced by direct and indirect aid from the United
States. From 1956 to 1966 the United States provided almost 50 percent
of Jordan's external revenue. In the period 1973 to 1985, other Arab states
provided over 80 percent of that aid.[116] Arab money, predominantly from
Kuwait and Saudi Arabia, rewarded Jordan's support of the Palestine
Liberation Organization and its role as a frontline state against Israel. In
the aftermath of the 1967 war, Arab states at the Khartoum Conference
pledged a renewal of and increase in Jordan's assistance. From 1959 to
1970, foreign aid as a percentage of GDP averaged 22 percent annually.[117]
While this level of aid did not approach the post-1972 boom, it was ade-
quate to support the core distributional aspects of a rentier state. Second,
the 1948 war and the periodic conflicts of the 1950s and 1960s pushed
hundreds of thousands of Palestinian refugees into Jordan. By 1950, the

[116] Fawzi Khatib, "Foreign Aid and Economic Development in Jordan: An Empirical Investigation," in Rodney Wilson (ed.), *Politics and the Economy in Jordan* (London: Routledge, 1991), p. 65.
[117] Khalil Hammad, "The Role of Foreign Aid in the Jordanian Economy, 1959–1983," in
Bichara Khader and Adnan Badran (eds.), *The Economic Development of Jordan* (London:
Croom Helm, 1987), p. 17.

population of the country was three times what it had been in 1947.[118] After the 1967 war another 250,000 to 300,000 refugees entered Jordan. While many settled in the West Bank, tens of thousands more headed for Amman. By the 1960s Amman was the commercial center for both sides of the Jordan River. These waves also provided an influx of new entrepreneurs and expanded the domestic market. With new merchants and consumers, the Palestinian character of the merchant community was confirmed.[119] This was reflected in the leadership of the ACC, with the presidency of Subri Tabba, of Syrian origin, giving way to the Palestinian presidency of Ibrahim Manku in the 1950s and 1960s. As the contours of the business community changed, state expansion and development of the 1950s and 1960s began to alter the relationship between state and business.

As in Kuwait, development of Jordan's state entailed construction of a larger bureaucracy and greater intervention in the domestic economy. The two most important economic ministries, the Ministry of Commerce and Industry and the Ministry of Finance, were established in the 1950s. The Ministry of Commerce and Industry controlled import licensing and approval of new business licenses (commercial and industrial). The Finance Ministry was the bureaucratic focal point for the two leading sources of state revenue: external aid and customs duties. Recruitment of civil servants expanded accordingly. Figures on precise employment in this period are rough, but a general picture emerges in which between 1961 and 1975 military employment (and related public security) tripled. In that same period, civilian employment increased by two-thirds.[120] The majority of the labor force remained anchored within the private sector (specifically the service sector); the greatest decline in employment predictably occurred within agriculture. These patterns mapped to the previously discussed distinctions between waves of Palestinian refugees entering the private sector, while East Bank Jordanians gravitated toward public-sector jobs.

To channel state capital into selected industrial ventures, the state established the Industrial Development Board in 1957. The board was superseded in 1965 by the Industrial Development Bank (IDB). In hand with the 1955 Law for the Encouragement of Investment, which offered tax incentives, the first state policies to induce industrialization were in place. Overall, these were moderate forms of intervention, since the initial

---

[118] *Ibid.*, p. 11.

[119] British situation report commenting on the new merchants, *Records of Jordan*, vol. VI, *1948–1950*, pp. 571–572.

[120] Michael P. Manzur, *Economic Growth and Development in Jordan* (Boulder: Westview Press, 1979), pp. 108–115.

capital of the IDB was only 3 million Jordanian dinars (JD).[121] The real focus of state intervention, as in Kuwait, was public investment in or creation of semi-public (or shareholding) companies. Joint-sector ownership was concentrated in what became known as the Big 5 companies. Four of these five were established in the 1950s. The Jordan Phosphate Mining Company began as a private corporation in the 1940s; by the mid-1960s the state had purchased over 60 percent of its shares. Similarly, the state took over the Arab Potash Company by purchasing a majority share. In 1956, the state established the Jordan Petroleum and Refinery Company (JPRC) as a joint-stock company with private investors. State investment and expansion of these companies progressed steadily, so that by the 1970s these firms accounted for a significant portion of employment and production in the kingdom. There was a political purpose to this large-scale intervention.[122]

While profits from these companies were an important source of public revenue, it is a mistake to assume state-led development flowed solely for economic reasons. A common analytical fallacy concerning late-late developers is the assumption that state investment was necessary solely because indigenous capitalists lacked either the capital or the skills to take up such projects. A confluence of factors better explains these initial statist strategies. While ideologies of the day and prior colonial patterns of market management undergirded the early developmental models, the focus here is upon an important domestic component of state investment: the cooptation of economic elites. Once the state secured majority shares in the Big 5, it could appoint most of their executive boards. For example, the first board of the JPRC included two important ACC leaders, Muhammed 'Ali Bdair and Ibrahim Manku. Positions on such boards gave elite merchants an advantage in acquiring government contracts and influencing future purchases. Additionally, shares held by either board members or private individuals increased in value as state investment increased. As in Kuwait, state investment in the economy often served the political exigencies of coalition building, something John Waterbury termed "side-payments."[123] A further similarity with the Kuwaiti experience was in the way the state used land to bind merchant elites to state largesse.

---

[121] Raphael Patai, *The Kingdom of Jordan* (Princeton: Princeton University Press, 1958), p. 109; *Middle East Economic Digest* (subsequently referred to as *MEED*), 2 July 1965, p. 305.

[122] For a comprehensive analysis of the Big 5, see Timothy Piro, *The Politics of Market Reform in Jordan* (Lanham, MD: Rowman & Littlefield, 1998).

[123] John Waterbury, *Exposed to Innumerable Delusions: Public Enterprise and State Power in Egypt, India, Mexico, and Turkey* (Cambridge, UK: Cambridge University Press, 1993).

Supported by American and British aid, the East Ghor Canal Project was launched in 1961. The goal was to irrigate thousands acres of Jordan Valley land to permit year-round cultivation. The project was almost identical to the Kuwaiti land-purchase program.[124] The state bought much of this valley land from merchants (many of whom were ACC board members who had amassed this land through mortgages) at well above market prices, and then distributed the irrigated land back to some of these same merchants as a method of selective cooptation.[125] As Amman grew, another process took shape whereby the state and the local municipality purchased land for city expansion from merchants at high rates.[126] Or, to spur development, municipal land was sold to merchants at well below market value. This positioned merchant elites to reap huge profits once the boom of the 1970s drove up real estate prices. For the merchants benefiting, the cost was, of course, political. In return, merchant elites would avoid any political positions overtly counter to the state and the monarchy. Loyalty was exchanged for profit. Timing was important because these merchant elites stood at the pinnacle of the growing Palestinian majority, in a country whose regime's political support rested upon East Bank notables. Future waves of Palestinian refugees would be influenced by these merchants' loyalties and attitudes. Despite the close similarity with Kuwait's famous merchant–state compromise, the issue of political loyalty demonstrates a key difference between Kuwait and Jordan: the role of business elites in the elected parliament.

Merchants in parliament

There were key parallels but also significant divergences between the parliamentary histories of the two countries. Due to protests by legislators wanting to expand their powers, Jordan's first assembly was dissolved in 1931. Legislator agitation for greater freedom also pushed King Abdullah in 1951 and King Hussein in 1956 to dissolve the assembly. In 1947, a new electoral law was completed allowing elections for the Majlis al-Umma (National Assembly or Lower Parliament) and royal appointments to the Majlis al-'Ayyan (the Upper Parliament). Similar to Kuwait's legislative body, the lower house was restricted to the approval, not the introduction, of bills. Constitutionally, final approval of any legislation rested with the prime minister and by extension the monarchy, which appointed the

---

[124] *Middle East Economist*, December 1961, p. 163.
[125] Many East Bank notables were also included in this process.
[126] Interview with Muhammed Tijani, former general manager of the ACC, Amman, 31 May 1995, 26 July 1995, 2 November 1996.

prime minister.[127] Also, like Kuwait, issues of debate in the 1950s and 1960s tended to coalesce around anti-British, Arab nationalist causes. Varying degrees of government interference in the election process took place in the 1950s and 1960s, but generally – as in Kuwait – the opposition was able to achieve some electoral success and engage in public policy debate.[128] The last election before the parliament was suspended in 1974 took place in 1967, two months before war with Israel. Despite these broad similarities, Jordan's experience with an elected parliament was different from Kuwait's in an important aspect.

Unlike in Kuwait, parties were legal in Jordan, but the Jordanian party system appeared far weaker than opposition groupings in Kuwait. While there are convincing external and systemic reasons for this weakness,[129] another important factor is that the merchant role in Jordan's parliaments was much less pronounced. After independence, the state created, essentially, separate districts for representation in the Lower House of parliament between the East and West Banks. This helped dilute any opposition by forcing it to straddle two different electoral areas. And since elections on the East Bank were organized to maximize the election of East Bank notables at the expense of urban-based Palestinians,[130] ACC elites located in Amman were at an additional disadvantage.[131] Consequently, in Kuwait (for a time at least) the opposition was the merchant elite, whereas in Jordan the opposition was composed of Baathist (anti-colonial, socialist party influenced by the Baath party in Iraq) and Arab nationalist parties. Few merchants were elected to the Lower House. Of the twenty elected members (eventually rising to sixty by the 1980s) in the first few parliaments, prominent ACC-affiliated merchants accounted for one or two seats at the most. One of those members, from 1951 to 1954, was Muhammed 'Ali Bdair, an important ACC board member and future president.[132] In the Upper House, however, early ACC presidents were regularly appointed by the monarchy, beginning with Subri Tabba

---

[127] Under Article 52 of the constitution, this can be, technically, overridden by the parliament.

[128] Philip J. Robins, "Politics and the 1986 Electoral Law in Jordan," in Rodney Wilson, *Politics and the Economy*, pp. 185–189; Linda Layne, "Tribesmen as Citizens: 'Primordial Ties' and Democracy in Rural Jordan," in Layne, *Elections in the Middle East*.

[129] Ellen M. Lust-Okar, "The Decline of Jordanian Political Parties: Myth or Reality?," *International Journal of Middle East Studies*, 33, a (November 2001), pp. 545–569.

[130] Aqil Hyder Hasan Abidi, *Jordan: A Political Study, 1948–1957* (London: Asia Publishing House, 1965), pp. 66–70.

[131] This was done by simply according more representational weight to rural southern areas where the Hashemite power base was concentrated.

[132] Interviews, Tijani and Abu Hassan; and Abidi, *Jordan*, p. 216.

in 1950.[133] While this presence was minor in comparison to Kuwait, it was sufficient for the ACC to achieve an important policy success – one that would organizationally cripple the association.

Institution-building and institutional change

Available records portray Jordan's business community of the 1950s and 1960s as cohesive and enjoying close contact with the state and the monarchy. The leading and most influential merchants of Jordan elected among themselves the president and executive board of the chamber. It was an informal process, with merchants in the richer categories (*mumtaz*, 1, and 2) meeting shortly before the election to decide who would serve on the next board. Disagreements were often resolved at these gatherings.[134] The puzzle in all this intra-merchant organization is why – in a period of increased wealth and excellent relations with political authority – would merchants bother with institution-building, a job that ostensibly took time away from one's own business. Structural/statist approaches offer two interpretations. In one view, business is considered structurally advantaged along the lines of Charles Lindblom's thesis that, in contrast to labor, it is easier for capitalists to organize. In the other, one may simply conclude that "the more the state intervenes in the economy, the greater the incentive for business to mobilize to influence that intervention."[135] However, if one examines the character of state intervention and considers that, in Middle Eastern and African cases, it often involves distribution of exclusive rents (that is, not public goods), then the structural incentive favors individual, particularist rent-seeking, not collective institution-building. The state's political goal is to distribute and manipulate resources so as to undercut any societal organizations that do not fall under state control. However, material factors are only one form of incentive shaping collective organization. A deeper understanding of this issue in Jordan and Kuwait can be found in Ibn Khaldun's conception of rank among merchants; that is, while material incentives of the time would favor individual merchant–state interaction, the social prestige and recognition gained through associational investment and leadership favor the collective.

The Syrian and Palestinian elites who made up Jordan's early merchant class were a tightly knit community. As that community expanded with the building of the economy and increased access to capital, participation

---

[133] *Records of Jordan*, vol. VI, p. 565.
[134] Various interviews with former ACC presidents and staff officials.
[135] Haggard, Maxfield, and Schneider, "Theories of Business and Business–State Relations," p. 50.

in autonomous business representation increased in social importance and prestige. In a time when the state was the locus of wealth distribution, and material gain could be garnered through government service, factors other than money could motivate. For businessmen especially, economic gain *per se* lost its social status, creating a situation in which election to the peak business association became, in itself, an important marker of social status.[136] A second, non-revenue-maximizing function of election to the chamber was in the recruitment and recognition of younger merchants. Recalling yet again Ibn Khaldun's observation about rank among merchants being achieved not solely through wealth, for new merchants wishing to be "known," election to the board of the ACC was a necessity.[137] In a period with a rapidly developing economy and state, young merchants wishing to move up the ladder required status. Running for and serving on the board demonstrated acceptance by the elite, facilitating contacts and partnerships. Conversely, standing elites used the nomination and election processes to socialize the new merchants, thereby turning the ACC into a venue for elite reproduction.

Three figures who exemplified this process were Subri Tabba, Muhammed 'Ali Bdair, and Ibrahim Manku. Tabba, originally from Damascus, had made tremendous profits through land and trade in the 1940s and 1950s. He served as ACC president in that same period and enjoyed not only national recognition but some international notoriety as well.[138] His relations with the monarchy ('Abdullah and Hussein) were so close that one of his daughters married into the royal family. After the young King Hussein ascended to the throne, Tabba played a role in helping the new king situate himself with Jordan's merchant community.[139] Also a Syrian by origin, Bdair was ACC president in the late 1940s, and again in the 1960s and 1970s. He also made a great deal of money in the 1940s and was considered among the top merchants in Jordan. Whereas Tabba enjoyed unique personal access to the monarchy, Bdeir was tremendously popular with the growing Palestinian merchant community. He was a gifted negotiator and was considered to be an extremely honest dealer,[140] a reputation that greatly assisted his election to parliament in 1951. Ibrahim Manku followed in the footsteps of his father, Hamdi Manku, in serving on the board. Manku represented a

---

[136] Mahdavy, "The Patterns and Problems of Economic Development in Rentier States"; and, recently, Hootan Shambayati, "The Rentier State, Interest Groups, and the Paradox of Autonomy," *Comparative Politics*, 26, 3 (April 1994), pp. 307–331.
[137] Interview, Abu Hassan.   [138] In the 1950s, *Life Magazine* ran a story on him.
[139] Interviews, Tabba and Abu Hassan.
[140] Interviews, Tijani and Sa'id Ma'atouq, former general secretary and board member, ACC, Amman, 13 November 1996.

return to Palestinian leadership of the chamber. He gained prominence by serving on the board and was viewed as a young up-and-comer when he was elected president in 1954. Under these presidencies, younger merchants from prominent families were groomed into service. Names such as 'Asfour, Toufan, Raghib, Abu Hassan, Nouri, and Barakat gained prominence through early service on the board (see table 4 in appendix). In turn, their presence reinforced the growing prestige and political access of the ACC. It was a confluence of these material and non-material factors that encouraged organizational changes within the ACC, alterations that would profoundly alter its future.

In 1955, ACC elites created the Federation of Jordanian Chambers of Commerce. By the 1950s there were some ten regional chambers in kingdom, so an umbrella association was needed to organize the national activities of these associations. The federation filled this need as "the peak business association to advocate policy and to participate [in formulating] state policy."[141] ACC elites ensured that their association would control the federation by stipulating that half of the executive board would comprise ACC board members (the remainder to be elected from the other chambers), and its director would be the president of the ACC.[142] In this way, ACC elites placed the kingdom's entire business community under their representation and guidance. Federation leadership and national lobbying were a direct extension of the ACC's executive board. This led to a second organizational change.

Beginning in 1951 when Bdair was elected to parliament, the ACC leadership began pressing the minister of commerce and industry to alter the licensing process for new businesses in Amman. The previous process only required new businesses to be registered with the municipal authority and with the ministry. Fees were charged and annual renewal was unnecessary. ACC leaders lobbied to have membership in the chamber made a prerequisite for licenses with the municipality and ministry. State preferences on the issue were not strong and, due to the positive relations between ACC president Tabba and then minister of commerce and industry, Sulaiman Sukkar, the ministry agreed. In parliament, Muhammed 'Ali Bdair attached a rider to the forthcoming Law of Professional Associations stating that "all businesses [in Amman] must first be in good standing with the Amman Chamber of Commerce before a license application to the ministry and municipality."[143] Once this law

---

[141] Federation of Jordanian Chambers of Commerce, *Organizational Structure* (Amman: Federation of Jordanian Chambers of Commerce, 1989).

[142] Interview with Amin Y. Husseini, Secretary-General, Federation of Jordanian Chambers of Commerce, Amman, 29 July 1995.

[143] *Official Gazette*, Law No. 21, 1961; and interview, Ma'atouq.

was passed in 1961, all of the Amman business community (the largest and most important in the kingdom) would be represented by the ACC, since membership was obligatory if one wanted a license.

This change made the ACC what Mancur Olson terms an "encompassing association," embracing all sectors of the economy and all sizes of merchants. Moreover, extension of regulatory power to this social association created a quasi-corporatist arrangement between the state and the chamber. While not a characteristic of the outright state creation or incorporation of a business association (as witnessed in Syria and Egypt, for instance),[144] the arrangement nevertheless exhibited some aspects of formal corporatism. For the state, allowing the chamber to be part of the licensing process fit well with the ongoing cooptation of private-sector elites. In the form of dues from members who were now obliged to join, the merchants' association became indirectly dependent upon state enforcement of obligatory membership. For the ACC, one clear reason for this encompassingness was revenue. In 1950 the chamber registered only 500 paying members, and since membership dues were its primary source of income, increasing membership scope was a logical step toward increasing operating revenue.[145] A second reason for encompassingness was the discretion it gave ACC officials. As in the Kuwaiti experience, by routing all business applications through the ACC, merchant elites achieved a much more expansive degree of market control. The delay or expedition of applications could be used as a tool to discipline individual members. The success of membership expansion set the stage for more intra-associational changes.

In 1960, ACC board members considered additional changes to the by-laws to accommodate the anticipated influx of new members. As an institution with a Palestinian majority, the chamber was sensitive to regional political repercussions emanating from the Arab–Israeli conflict. When waves of new refugees affected Jordan's domestic politics, institutions were not spared. Driven by a desire to be more inclusive of and "democratic" toward the new members, the executive board approved alterations to the chamber's by-laws in 1961.[146] Specifically, voting and nomination powers were extended to members in the lower categories,

---

[144] See Heydemann, *Authoritarianism in Syria*; and Tignor, *Capitalism and Nationalism at the End of Empire*.

[145] The change was not immediate, however. Municipal authorities did not respond quickly, and over the next decade ACC leaders had to continually press to make the prerequisite of membership in the chamber a matter of bureaucratic routine at the municipal level.

[146] Two individuals, Muhammed Tijani and Sa'id Ma'atouq, who served as officials of the chamber in this period, confirmed the intent of the by-law change. It fit the political mood of the day, which was dominated by popular support for the Palestinian cause in every Arab country and active guerrilla operations along the Israeli border.

3 and 4 (although not to those in category 5). Since the obligatory membership rules had not taken full effect, these categories did not yet make up the majority of members. Eventually, however, the voting majority shifted away from the top three, elite categories, toward category 3 and 4 members, the middle and small businessmen of the chamber. Both amendments, obligatory membership and voting rules, were enshrined in a reform to the original 1949 Law of the Chamber of Commerce. After chamber approval, the minister of commerce and industry and finally the prime minister agreed to the changes with no debate. The law was then passed to parliament for approval, and in 1961 Law No. 21 was passed.

Elites figured in a final institutional change in that same year. The 1958 executive board elections sparked the first real dispute among chamber elites. Ibrahim Manku, the incumbent, and Muhammed Bdair, the challenger, were both elected to the board in 1958, but neither won enough executive board votes to secure the presidency. Personality issues entered the debate, and neither man would relinquish his claim to the presidency. Conflict was exacerbated by the fact that, with the expected increase in the association's size, the presidency carried much greater prestige and power.[147] Eventually a compromise was reached, whereby from 1958 until 1962 Bdair and Manku alternated each year between the presidency and the vice-presidency. The compromise did not, however, alleviate the animosity between the two camps. In 1961, Bdair, backed by his faction, approached the minister of commerce and industry to gain approval for a Chamber of Industry. Despite arguments that Amman needed its own industry representative, observers at the time suggest that the move was personal, intended to create a rival elite institution to challenge Manku.[148] Manku and his supporters resisted the idea but did not consider it a serious challenge, since membership in the ACC remained obligatory: members of the industry chamber would have to belong to the ACC, and hence that is where the real power would reside.[149] State officials appeared to take no significant interest in the conflict at this point, but since a chamber of industry fit well with nascent state industrial policies, the minister of commerce and industry approved its creation. Consequently, a combination of ACC disregard and state

---

[147] Interview, Tijani; ACC, *al-Kitab al-Dhahabi*.

[148] This was confirmed only four years later, when Bdair returned to the ACC to begin his long tenure as president: interview with 'Ali Dajani, advisor to the Amman Chamber of Industry, Amman, 4 June 1995.

[149] The Chamber of Industry was set up along lines closely resembling the ACC of 1923. Membership was voluntary and voting was reserved for the upper echelons of members: Amman Chamber of Industry *Nizam Ghurfat Sana'at 'Amman* [By-laws of the Amman Chamber of Industry], 1961.

acquiescence helped create the Amman Chamber of Industry (ACI) in 1961.

Policy coordination and politics

Jordan's political independence introduced many of the same economic policy issues and opportunities that had been observed in Kuwait. In some cases, colonial institutions needed to be adapted and new economic legislation was required, while in others completely new institutions were necessary. Close business–state coordination marked these transitions.

Given the youth of Jordan's political and economic institutions in the 1950s and 1960s, the ACC was well placed to provide expert advice and information on proposed economic policies. For instance, the Central Bank of Jordan, the primary reservoir and compiler of domestic economic data, was not established until 1964. Prior to this period, the Department of Statistics in the Ministry of National Economy produced some data, but they were hardly comprehensive.[150] Business lobbying in this period, with one exception, was quite similar to that in Kuwait, in that the ACC reacted to government-proposed policies instead of proactively pushing a set agenda. This interaction was also primarily informal and personal. In some cases, regularized committee meetings with officials at the ministerial and prime ministerial levels were instituted, but these were exceptions. By the late 1960s, to augment such meetings, the chamber invited ministers to speak at its functions, or to attend its sponsored exhibitions. Important executive board members such as Manku, Bdair, 'Asfour, Malhus, and Tabba would use these encounters to schedule *ad hoc* meetings with either the prime minister or other relevant ministers to provide input on policy. In this period, use of parliament as a lobbying venue was minimal: amendments to legislation that were required were agreed upon previously in the informal meetings. The general-manager of the chamber from this period, Muhammed Tijani, described this situation:

Chamber officials were under the umbrella of the monarchy. They enjoyed not only the position of leading businessmen, but their position vis-à-vis the monarchy meant that the lower levels of government [ministers and deputies] knew that these men had the backing of the monarchy . . . so in return, their interests were served.

Some of the first successes at policy coordination were in shaping the founding economic laws of the kingdom. Generally, drafts of these laws

---

[150] Jordan, Ministry of National Economy, Department of Statistics, *Annual Statistical Report 1952* (Amman, 1953).

would be hammered out at the ministerial level where some chamber input could be achieved. From there, the draft went to the prime minister's office for legal review and then – as a matter of routine – the draft would be passed formally to the chamber's executive board for its suggestions.[151] Several laws underwent this process.

The Commercial Law and Companies Law set up the legal parameters of what types of companies could be formed and how they should be registered. This seriously affected the way leading merchants would have to restructure their firms, since most of them pre-dated independence. Data provided by the ACC were key in establishing the capital requirements for the joint-stock company and the reporting procedures, which were modest by design. The Trademarks and Merchandise Law (No. 19, 1953) and the Patents and Design Law (No. 22, 1953) updated a 1930 law on trademarks. Because of ACC contacts with foreign traders and members' import companies, ACC elites were able to provide details to ensure that the law complied with international standards. As well, the law provided for a trademarks committee to be set up within the Ministry of Commerce and Industry, on which the ACC had representation. The Labor Law (No. 21, 1960) was of obvious concern to the ACC. There was no significant labor movement in Jordan at that time, and consequently the ACC maintained a freer hand in influencing the law. However, this law, in contrast to those preceding it, required a greater amount of elite effort. ACC lobbying efforts centered on amending the draft law once it was received from the prime minister. Of primary concern was widening the definitions of employer and employee (so as to give merchant employers greater discretion in their application) and limiting negotiating obligations between employer and employee. The resulting law was consequently vague and open-ended in many respects. Evidence from interviews suggests that there were some sectors of the government in favor of a more detailed and stricter labor law. Nationalist opposition elements in parliament also supported this position; however, ACC elites were able to overcome these demands and succeeded in helping fashion a modified version.

The Encouragement of Investment Law (1955) allowed for tax breaks and tax holidays for selected projects. Also, as in Kuwait, ACC merchants successfully sought protection by limiting foreign ownership to 49 percent of any project. Details provided for a technical committee within the Ministry of Commerce and Industry to review applications by investors. The ACC was given four personnel appointments to the

---

[151] Various interviews. This routine was not legalized but was an artifact of the chamber's previous status.

committee, which met once a month. While this institutionalized access realized little meaningful leverage over future industrial and commercial projects, it did offer business representatives an important conduit of information about issues that affected their interests and, as in Kuwait, created institutional access that could be built upon in the future. The Arbitration Law (No. 18, 1953) legalized chamber requests to grant the association legal purview over merchant disputes. Reports suggest that lobbying for this law was driven by an ACC desire to regulate growing construction-sector disputes among members.[152]

Aside from legal reform, an issue of paramount concern to the ACC in this period was customs duties. Customs on imported goods accounted for the largest percentage of domestic tax revenue (direct and indirect) and required layers of bureaucratic procedure.[153] Officials at the Ministry of Commerce and Industry also used customs duties to protect favored domestic industries. Consequently, customs duties were regularly raised or expanded throughout the 1950s and 1960s.[154] Interviews with business leaders confirmed that, despite unified business resistance to the tax and, most importantly, to its regulation process, the state was willing to give little leeway on the issue. As a recourse, ACC leaders began pressing state officials to support the idea of an Arab Common Market. The idea had gained momentum in the early 1960s within the Arab League as a means to link the Arab economies. Within Arab countries, the Jordanian merchant class, led by the ACC, was one of the Common Market's main proponents.[155] Jordan's most important external markets lay in Syria and Iraq, and the proposed Common Market promised to help alleviate customs duties on imports from and exports to these markets. However, since the idea of a Common Market intersected with larger regional issues of Arab nationalism and Jordan's bilateral relations with countries like Iraq and Syria, the "state's initial position was neutral." To push the issue, ACC elites first coordinated with the Joint Arab Chambers of Commerce in Beirut to get its members to agree on reciprocal customs exemptions within the Common Market. ACC board members

---

[152] *Official Gazette* (Kuwait), various years; Ali Sharif Zu'bi and Sharif Ali Zu'bi (eds.), *Business Legislation and Incentives* (Amman: Allied Accountants, 1995); *Industry, Trade and Services* (Amman: Allied Accountants, 1995); Manzur, *Economic Growth*, pp. 222–227; Patai, *The Kingdom of Jordan*, pp. 108–110; various interviews.

[153] Central Bank of Jordan, *Yearly Statistical Series (1964–1993)* (Amman: Central Bank of Jordan, October 1994). Until the 1970s, customs amounted to less than 10 percent of the entire state revenue. Rates differed by the good and its origin, requiring government agents at the Port of Aqaba to inspect most imports.

[154] *Middle East Economist*, March 1960, p. 42.

[155] Interview with Burhan Dajani, Secretary General, General Union of Chambers of Commerce, Industry and Agriculture for Arab Countries, Amman, 6 June 1995.

then appealed directly to the monarchy "to bring Jordan on board."[156] Certainly regional political interests figured into Jordan's acceptance of the idea and the state took the negotiating lead, but it was ACC lobbying that first introduced the issue in Jordan and helped shape its eventual outcome. In 1964, agreement among Jordan, Syria, Egypt, and Iraq created the Arab Common Market. Though the Common Market never fulfilled its goals, Jordan's participation led to some goods escaping the customs regime and exempted some goods from further rate increases.[157] The proposal of an Arab Common Market, in addition to representing an important instance of business–state coordination, also initiated a relationship between business elites and Crown Prince Al-Hassan Bin Talal that was to blossom.

Crown Prince Hassan, King Hussein's brother, became a key conduit for ACC elites to influence the monarchy. While relations between ACC elites (the 'Asfours, Tabbas, Mankus, and Bdairs) and King Hussein were considered good, the king was not known for being concerned about economic issues. The crown prince, however, took a keen interest. In the 1960s, he established the Royal Scientific Society, an institution which convened an assembly of economic and social advisors, hosted seminars, and produced policy documents. Hassan periodically recruited ACC elites into the society, and made himself available to hear ACC ideas on economic issues.[158] In return, ACC elites routinely invited the crown prince to chamber-sponsored events and exhibitions.

Finally, in this period, the ACC successfully pressed state officials to allow its presence on important policy boards. Along with representation on the Investments Committee within the Ministry of Commerce and Industry, the Industrial Development Bank (IDB) was a good example of this access. ACC elites successfully convinced state officials that the best method to ensure private-sector responsiveness to the IDB would be to assign private-sector members permanently to its board of directors.[159] Three members would be appointed by the state, with the remaining six from the private sector. The ACC was given the responsibility, which it shared with the new Chamber of Industry, to appoint these members.[160] There were also *ad hoc* appointments of ACC members to the board of the National Planning Council to provide input into Jordan's economic

[156] Interview, Tijani.
[157] *MEED*, 10 August 1965, p. 378. More nefariously, some Jordanian importers and reexporters could use false papers of origin to circumvent the duties.
[158] Interview with Ahmed 'Obeidat, former prime minister, Amman, 5 June 1995.
[159] Interview 'Ali Dajani.
[160] Manzur, *Economic Growth*, p. 230; and Jordan, National Planning Council, *Jordan's Economic Plan, 1964–1970* (Amman, n.d.).

planning process, which included five-year plans covering targets, as did Kuwait's; the new Central Bank of Jordan was created to support deliberations on fiscal policy measures, along with the new Housing Bank Corporation to extend loans to the booming construction sector.

On the whole, for a new country with a small market, ACC coordination with state officials was impressive in this period. Elite cohesion and control of the institution facilitated regularized influential access with state decisionmakers. Despite the formation of the ACI, the Chamber of Commerce remained the most important representative of the private sector in Jordan, and the association was able to strengthen its pre-independence relationship with the new state. However, by the late 1960s, change was already evident. While institutional effects from the 1961 reorganizations were yet to be fully realized, changes in the fiscal situation of the state were underway. In the wake of the 1967 war, a sudden jump in external aid prompted the prime minister's cabinet to repeal a new income tax law.[161] Likewise, Jordan's first five-year economic plan was revamped once new external revenue sources became available. Subsequent economic planning would evidence this stop–start quality. Increased state fiscal autonomy would have a profound impact on business–state relations.

Conclusion

A more "substantive political-economy"[162] approach allows for a wider lens with which to view how colonial legacy and state formation shaped business–state relations in Kuwait and Jordan. Structural/statist approaches that zero in on rentier dependency and shifting material incentives tell only part of the story: they emphasize a causal link between access to external rents, state-led growth, and cooptation of the domestic private sector. Discounted are the historical and political struggles that pre-dated and accompanied commodity dependency and state formation. Political independence and accession to the capitalist system did not mark the beginning of Jordan and Kuwait, but introduced new dynamics into their histories. This vantage allows one to view both similarities and differences in the evolution of business–state relations.

First, the origins of Jordan's and Kuwait's business communities prior to European penetration were different. Though both communities came to their host countries from other lands, they figured into the founding of political authority differently. The Kuwaiti *asil* were an integral part of the social/tribal elite that founded the modern Kuwaiti state whereas,

---

[161] *MEED*, 2 November 1967.   [162] Chaudhry, "Prices, Politics, Institutions," p. 334.

at best, Transjordan's merchant elite could be considered simply partners of the Hashemites. Over the ensuing decades these differences in origin and relationship to ruling family would become more significant in shaping patterns of business–state interaction. Initial business–state relations in both countries were marked by conflict and cooperation, but in Kuwait the conflict was more politically and institutionally significant. The gradual sequestration of independent associations and councils since the 1938 Majlis movement directly resulted in the founding of the KCCI in 1961. There was little such political struggle accompanying creation of Jordan's peak business association in 1923. Integrating these political and social contexts with economic shifts precipitated by European penetration yields insight into elite investments in institutional representation, which a narrow structuralist/economic interpretation would not allow. The creation of revenue-autonomous states should lead to particularist rent-seeking and anti-associational incentives, but in the cases of Kuwait and Jordan did not. Instead, the political and social contexts of late development mean that "Under such circumstances even the businessman, even the classical daring and innovating entrepreneur, needs a more powerful stimulus than the prospect of high profits."[163]

Within the context of these dynamics, the impact of the British Mandate on merchant–ruler relations was crucial. While there is little evidence of direct British intervention in business affairs, provision of operating funds to colonial state authorities and intervention in regional trading decisively altered the fortunes of business and state. In each case, this intervention granted a degree of fiscal autonomy to colonial officials that would only increase after independence. Expanded trade opportunities and the management of trade during World War II significantly enriched both countries' merchants. These structural changes – the sudden influx of exogenous revenue, the expansion of the state, and the distribution of that wealth – were more than mere statistical artifacts; they were part of larger political and social changes that shaped subsequent political patterns. Experiences in state-building are rarely uniform. For instance, while early state-builders in Egypt and Saudi Arabia used external rents to destroy and replace their domestic capitalists, Jordanian and Kuwaiti officials sought to draw their business community closer to themselves. In Kuwait and Jordan, access to external resources (first during the

---

[163] Alexander Gerschenkron, "Economic Backwardness in Historical Perspective," in Gerschenkron, *Economic Backwardness in Historical Perspective* (Cambridge, MA: Harvard University Press, 1962), p. 24.

Mandate and then after independence) facilitated a pact between ruler and merchants. Enriched materially but stripped politically, merchants could be expected to discount associational organization in lieu of individual pursuit of state rents. In reality, the merchant–ruler pact actually created its own non-material, selective incentives for association formation. Kuwaiti and Jordanian merchants relied on their associations as the last remaining independent institutions that were situated not only to engage state agencies, but also to institutionalize social status and recruitment. Echoing Ronald Inglehart's thesis of high levels of development in Western Europe generating post-material values,[164] a similar, albeit more restricted, dynamic was at work in Kuwait and Jordan. The exclusive manner in which business representation was organized supports this interpretation.

The institutionalization of merchant representation, then, aided elite cohesion during the construction of what were ostensibly, at political birth, highly revenue-autonomous states. One can view the first policy initiatives and coordination efforts that came from this elite representation as motivated purely by rent-seeking, but responding to their concerns was the price to be paid to ensure merchant involvement. In other words, rent-seeking can display different features and can yield different outcomes depending on the political conditions.[165] Though state formation and economic development during the early to middle part of the twentieth century are commonly characterized as top-down,[166] the experience in Kuwait and Jordan suggests the process combined contestation and cooperation with business.[167] This evidence qualifies David Waldner's argument that "it is elites who make side-payments for their own political goals and not redistributive-seeking groups that demand them."[168] Thus, the involvement of business representation and business elites in the creation of Kuwait and Jordan's founding economic laws and institutions is at once both a form of rent-seeking and an element in state-building.

---

[164] Ronald Inglehart, *Culture Shift in Advanced Industrial Society* (Princeton: Princeton University Press, 1990).

[165] This revision of orthodox economic claims is widespread outside the study of Middle Eastern politics. See Mushtaq H. Khan and K. S. Jomo (eds.), *Rents, Rent-Seeking and Economic Development: Theory and Evidence in Asia* (Cambridge, UK: Cambridge University Press, 2000).

[166] Lisa Anderson, *The State and Social Transformation in Tunisia and Libya, 1830–1980* (Princeton: Princeton University Press, 1986).

[167] For similar themes regarding Syria and Saudi Arabia, see Heydemann, *Authoritarianism in Syria*; and Gwenn Okruhlik, "Rentier Wealth, Unruly Law, and the Rise of the Opposition: The Political Economy of Oil States," *Comparative Politics*, 31, 3 (April 1999), pp. 295–315.

[168] Waldner, *State Building and Late Development*, p. 164.

Finally, this chapter pinpoints an important institutional shift in Jordan that would recast the trajectory of business–state relations. The widening of the Amman Chamber of Commerce's representation structure (obligatory membership and expanded membership suffrage) combined with future influxes of new Palestinian merchants would produce unforeseen externalities.

3   Politics and profits

Good times in Kuwait

The 1970s rise in oil prices generated an unprecedented economic boom in Kuwait and throughout the Middle East. From 1960 to 1985, Middle East and North African countries outperformed all other regions in the developing world in terms of income growth and distribution.[1] The implications for business–state relations were equally profound. On the one hand, increased state investment in shareholding companies and the general increase in domestic demand significantly enriched merchant elites. Whereas the KCCI elite was already comparatively wealthy within their own country, the boom of the 1970s made them rich regionally and internationally. On the other hand, the monumental increase in state autonomy and distributional resources reduced the KCCI's policy leverage while increasing the leverage and profile of new business elements. By the mid-1970s, state officials and the monarchy ignored most KCCI attempts at policy input and altered distributional policies to enrich rivals to the traditional elite, thus building a wider network of supporters. The economic effect of these policies was creation of a fragile fiscal system that by 1982 was on the verge of collapse.

While Kuwait reaped oil riches in the 1960s, the boom of the 1970s was massive by comparison. In the latter half of the 1960s oil revenue to the state averaged about KD 270 million annually. In 1974, oil revenue had increased to over KD 2 billion.[2] The 1973 war and ensuing OPEC interventions helped keep oil prices high throughout the decade. In some policy areas, the windfall accelerated state initiatives of the 1960s; in others, the state launched wholly new endeavors. Many state actions during the boom *did* conform to structural/statist logics; however, an exclusive focus on structural shifts does not tell us how or why the new resources might affect business–state relations.

[1] World Bank, *Claiming the Future*, pp. 2–3.
[2] Kuwait, Ministry of Planning, *Statistical Abstract in 25 Years*.

A first expression of increased rent was what Crystal called "rapid, disorganized bureaucratic growth." As in the 1960s, the goal of government expansion was distributional; in the 1970s, though, the means were shifting. Land purchases, which had accounted for 30 percent of annual public expenditures in the 1960s, dropped to around 10 percent in the 1970s.[3] In their place, increases in public expenditures (from 1967 to 1977 government spending increased by an average of 26 percent annually) were routed into already robust public provision of health, education, and welfare. Kuwait came to lead the Gulf oil states in the development and extent of coverage of its welfare system. Public spending also went to expand the ranks of the civil service. More than 75 percent of Kuwaitis were employed in government service by the mid-1970s.[4] Politically, welfare distribution and government employment served to cement the ruling family's support. Economically, because much of the increase in external revenue was pumped into the economy, the state's position in the domestic economy grew. The proportion of private-sector employment correspondingly declined; as most Kuwaitis began working for the government, the private sector turned to imported foreign workers,[5] so that by 1977 only 12 percent of the private-sector workforce was Kuwaiti. While the merchants once represented a sizable portion of Kuwaiti society, they were now a minority.

The state's enhanced fiscal position allowed officials to support merchant elites while at the same time introducing a new goal, the creation of new business elements. The first steps in these processes were the nationalizations of the 1970s. In 1971 the government nationalized the natural gas industry in Kuwait. Following four years of negotiation and debate in parliament, the government took a 60 percent share in the Kuwait Oil Company (KOC) – the successor to the joint British Petroleum Gulf Oil company that had secured the first oil concession in Kuwait. By 1976, the state had taken full control. Next, the government nationalized the Kuwait National Petroleum Company (KNPC) in 1975; and in 1980 all of Kuwait's nationalized oil companies were placed under a holding company, the Kuwait Petroleum Company. Consolidation of the oil industry paralleled an expansion of state investment in the shareholding corporations. The magnitude of this investment is demonstrated by the fact that

[3] Hazem Beblawi, *The Arab Gulf Economy in a Turbulent Age* (New York: St. Martin's Press, 1984), p. 169.

[4] Ragaei El Mallakh, *Kuwait: Trade and Investment* (Boulder: Westview Press, 1979), pp. 79–80; Kuwait, Ministry of Planning, *Statistical Abstract in 25 Years*.

[5] By 1975, foreign workers composed 70 percent of the population of Kuwait: Anh Nga Longva, *Walls Built on Sand: Migration, Exclusion, and Society in Kuwait* (Boulder: Westview Press, 1997), pp. 27–28.

over a 10-year period (1968–1977), the authorized capital for Kuwait's joint-stock sector more than tripled. From the 1950s until 1968, eighteen such joint companies had been established, but from 1970 to 1977 alone twenty-two such companies were created.[6] The state made its public investment using two methods. The Ministry of Commerce and Industry first negotiated with the board of a company to expand its authorized capital. Once the size of the expansion was agreed upon, the ministry simply purchased the newly available shares. In 1976, the state took a 49 percent share in the Kuwait Oil Tanker Company (founded in 1957 by KCCI president al-Sagr) by doubling its authorized capital, and by 1979 the company was completely state-owned. In a similar manner, a 51 percent public share was secured in the National Industries Company in 1978.[7]

A second means of public investment was the purchase of existing stock shares. Kuwaiti citizens had been allowed to trade in shareholding companies through licensed local brokers since the 1960s, but in April 1977 a formal stock market was inaugurated. As a result of wild price fluctuations and market instability in late 1977 and 1978, the state directly purchased shares in many joint companies to support prices and guard liquidity. In some cases, previously private companies became public virtually overnight. For example, Kuwait Flour Mills, Gulf Insurance, and Gulf Cables all experienced sizable increases in public ownership after the stock fluctuations.[8] The macroeconomic result of this massive state intervention was the continued reduction of the private sector's contribution to the overall economy. By Hazem Beblawi's calculation, the share of non-oil GDP fell from 43 percent in 1970 to 30 percent in 1975.[9]

Endangering the pact: political industrialization, the stock market, and the new merchants

If the 1950s and 1960s were decades in which the monarchy sought to co-opt the merchant elite, the 1970s was a period in which the state attempted to create its own economic elite. The process eventually involved ruling family members entering private enterprises, a clear violation of the unspoken merchant–ruler pact of the 1960s. This undertaking occurred in two phases.

---

[6] Calculations made from data provided in Y. S. F. Al Sabah, *The Oil Economy of Kuwait* (London: Kegan Paul International, 1980), pp. 70–71.

[7] *EIU*, No. 5, 1977; No. 5, 1980.

[8] Stock purchases also took place through other state-owned companies – such as the Kuwait National Petroleum Company.

[9] Beblawi, *The Arab Gulf Economy*, p. 164.

In the first phase, the state in the early 1970s earnestly sought to implement the industrialization policies that had been inaugurated in the 1960s. Not satisfied with the progress of the Industrial Development Committee (created in 1965) or the lack of commercial bank lending to private industry, officials in the Ministry of Commerce and Industry and the prime minister's office emphasized import substitution in Kuwait's 1971–1976 economic plan.[10] To spur private-sector industrialization, more robust incentive and protection regimes were created, products of domestic industries were given purchase preference by government ministries, and industrial zones were created. To guide and supervise implementation, the prime minster created a committee with all relevant government ministers (but no KCCI representative).[11] To finance projects, in 1973 the state established the Industrial Development Bank of Kuwait (IBK) with the express mandate of providing start-up funding for domestic industries.[12] Undergirding these industrial policies was a not-so-subtle political project.

Through industrialization, state officials hoped to foster a business elite to rival the KCCI. By drawing younger Kuwaitis, Shi'a, and Bedouin into industrial ventures, the state intended to foster a sectorally distinct business elite not tied to the commercially rooted Sunni KCCI elite.[13] As a result, many of the "new merchants" who appeared in the 1980s got their start during this period. For example, the al-Wazzan group (a Shi'a family business with close ties to the monarchy) used industrial incentives to form a very successful sugar company in the mid-1970s.[14] Praise for the Kuwaiti industrialization program was common in the international press:

The wise policies followed by the Kuwaiti government in encouraging industry, and even manufacturing industries and artisan products, ha[ve] along with other factors triggered a trend of industrialization in Kuwait which is expected to take wider dimensions by virtue of the increasing tendency towards inter-Arab economic cooperation.[15]

By and large, however, the industrialization program was a failure. Private-sector manufacturing accounted for 3.6 percent of the GDP in

---

[10] *Financial Times*, 25 February 1977, p. 25.
[11] Ragaei El Mallakh and Jacob K. Atta, *The Absorptive Capacity of Kuwait* (Toronto: Lexington Books, 1981), pp. 94–97.
[12] The majority of IBK funding was public but there were also private investors. The bank raised further capital by issuing bonds, a direct response to the unwillingness of the commercial (private) banks to make industrial investments.
[13] Interviews: Jasem al-Sadoun, economic consultant, Kuwait City, 5 March 1996; Professor Hassan Johar, Kuwait City, 12 April 1996; and 'Isa Majid al-Shahin, Spokesman, Muslim Brotherhood, Kuwait City, 3 March 1996.
[14] *EIU*, No. 4, 1976, p. 20.   [15] *Arab World Weekly*, 4 February 1978, p. 11.

Table 3.1 *Sectoral comparison: percentage of GDP*

	1960–1973	1965–1973	1970–1981
Commerce sector[a]			
Jordan	35.8	35	35.1
Kuwait	n.a.	26.8[b]	27.7
Industrial sector			
Jordan	10.4[c]	11.19[c]	13.4[d]
Kuwait[e]	n.a.	3.6[b]	4.3

Source: World Bank, *World Tables*, various years.
[a] Includes construction, transport/communications, trade/finance.
[b] 1960–1970.
[c] Includes government mining.
[d] Government mining is excluded.
[e] Oil is excluded.

1970; by 1976 it had risen to only 5 percent. The private sector remained rooted in commerce, trade, and services.[16]

Near the close of the five-year plan, Dr. 'Ali Khalifah al-Sabah, undersecretary in the Ministry of Finance, admitted that the program had failed, recognizing that "a series of white elephants draining the economies of oil exporting countries under the guise of industrialization" was not Kuwait's goal.[17] Though the economic program was cut short, its political aim remained.

A second phase of the creation of a new business class followed on the heels of failed industrialization. It roughly corresponded to Prime Minister Crown Prince Shaikh Jaber taking the throne upon the death of Emir Salim al-Sabah in 1977. The second phase was less a direct policy and more a decentralized approach by the government to allow those "not formerly in the private sector to get their share."[18] Though incentives to lure investors into industry failed, those enticing them into the commerce and services sectors held out a better chance for success. For instance, in the mid-1970s the Ministry of Commerce and Industry relaxed its guidelines for approving new business licenses. It should be remembered from the 1961 cabinet crisis that the constitution in Kuwait precluded

---

[16] This commitment to commerce is commonly attributed to Kuwaiti tradition or preexisting cultural norms. Seen from another angle, the types of industries the state was encouraging (cement, pipes, construction materials) were precisely the same that other Arab states were pushing for their own economies. Given the prospect of market saturation and Kuwait's lack of industrial raw materials, private Kuwaiti investors of the day begin to appear more as rational actors than as tradition-bound traders.

[17] *EIU*, No. 4, 1976, p. 20.   [18] Interview, Johar.

civil servants from operating private-sector businesses. In relaxing its screening of new applications, the ministry, in effect, turned a blind eye to many civil servants setting up businesses.[19] Many of the new entrants focused on the booming construction and real estate sectors. Others used the ministry loophole to start what were referred to as *tij'ra al-qama* (the business of visas). The domestic need for foreign workers as housekeepers, maids, and so on led to a booming business for these services bringing in these workers. Charging the worker a fee for the visa procurement, and charging a finder's fee to the Kuwaiti employer, made for profitable side businesses for many civil servants. Larger-scale government incentives toward Islamists followed a similar logic.

Kuwait's Islamists are generally composed of three camps: the Muslim Brotherhood, moderately orthodox and tied to other Brotherhood parties in the Middle East; the *salafi* movement (from *salaf*, meaning ancestors), considered more strictly orthodox and generally concentrated in the Gulf region; and the Shi'a movement (the others are Sunni) represented by the *ma'atem* institutions (funerary societies).[20] Collectively, these groups came to define themselves in opposition to the type of leftist, Arab nationalism predominant among KCCI elites. One example of the Islamists' growing power was the 1977 creation of the state-approved Kuwait Finance House (KFH). State ministries took a 49 percent share in the bank and appointed four of the nine board members. This bank was run according to Islamic principles and was allowed a wide purview to operate in all economic spheres, from commercial banking to consumer lending. Moreover, it was exempted from normal Central Bank regulations and oversight. The KFH was immediately successful, receiving over 5,000 deposits in its first two months of operation.[21] It became a principal source of support for the growing Islamist movement in Kuwait. In hand with the KFH, the state approved and subsidized the formation of several non-profit, Islamic charitable societies that would draw funding from the KFH. Pre-dating the institutionalization of the Islamic non-profits was the Cooperative Movement, inaugurated in the 1960s and significantly enhanced in the late 1970s.

The cooperatives, essentially grocery store outlets, were established in every district in Kuwait. With government subsidies, the cooperatives sold basic goods at below or near market prices, and were governed by

---

[19] Often the registration of the business would be in the name of the civil servant's wife or son.

[20] Gause, *Oil Monarchies*, p. 85.

[21] *Business Week*, 6 November 1978, p. 83; *Middle East*, February 1983, pp. 72–73; and Kristin Smith, "Culture and Capital: The Political Economy of Islamic Finance in Kuwait," paper presented to annual meeting of Middle East Studies Association (November 2001).

an elected body from the district. For the first time in the mid-1970s, the state allowed cooperatives to import goods on their own. Later, state supervision of the cooperatives was further relaxed, allowing unregulated profit margins at a time of increasing consumer demand. Greater profitability made share purchases in the cooperatives more attractive for those living in the local districts. From 1973 to 1976 total sales almost tripled, and membership (that is, numbers of shareholders) increased from just under 30,000 to over 50,000.[22] In 1980 there were twenty-five cooperatives in Kuwait with over 100,000 shareholders. In purely economic terms, the cooperatives posed a growing threat to merchants' market share. In 1976 cooperatives accounted for only 10 percent of private consumption, but 50 percent of the total expenditure on foodstuffs.[23] Cooperatives' gradual move into direct importing did not bode well for the future of merchant interests. Politically and more immediately, however, Islamist groups (at first the *salafi*, then the Muslim Brotherhood) won control of some of these cooperatives through the local elections. Cooperatives proved valuable not only as electoral training grounds but also eventually as venues for revenue and patronage. Hence, by the late 1970s, state policies (or their calculated absence) had aided the consolidation of the core of an Islamist economic and political network. In 1977, the state brought to the fore a more potent tool of rival coalition construction: Kuwait's stock market.

In 1970 and again in 1971, the Ministry of Commerce and Industry issued resolutions designed to regulate the growing securities trade in shareholding companies. In 1972 the Bureau of Securities Exchange was created, with the principal aim of limiting trade to shares only in Kuwaiti companies. However, these measures were incomplete. Owing to the unregulated increase in the number of shareholding companies and the lack of restrictions on individual subscriptions, the market boomed in the early 1970s. Because investors could trade in real estate companies and land prices were soaring, small investors, not previously able to invest directly in land, were afforded tremendously profitable opportunities.[24] Oversubscription, heavy speculation, and soaring prices ensued. Fortunes were being made as "brokers with little knowledge of the markets . . . rose to prominent positions as dealers."[25] These fortunes, however, obscured ominous trends in the stock trade.

---

[22] Khouja and Sadler, *The Economy of Kuwait*, p. 131. The cooperatives also got their own associational representation in the 1970s: the Consumers' Co-operative Union.

[23] Kuwait, Ministry of Planning, *Statistical Abstract in 25 Years*, p. 336.

[24] Beblawi, *The Arab Gulf Economy*, pp. 194–199; and Fida Darwiche, *The Gulf Stock Exchange Crash: The Rise and Fall of the Souq Al-Manakh* (London: Croom Helm, 1986), pp. 5–9.

[25] Darwiche, *The Gulf Stock Exchange Crash*, p. 4.

First, a general lack of supervision encouraged forward trading in stocks. Small traders with little or no capital were able to purchase and trade shares with postdated checks. Checks were then exchanged in secondary and tertiary trades with other traders in the hope that future profits would make the checks good. This magnified the number of subscribers, investors, and profiteers. In 1974, the minister of commerce and industry issued a resolution banning such forward trading, but again lack of state enforcement allowed the practice to continue. Second, since disclosure guidelines were weak, there was little "meaningful relationship between stock prices and the underlying companies' financial and earning position."[26] Poorly informed, excessive speculation, especially in newly established companies with low stock prices, became the norm. Third, beginning in 1976, trade in the first offshore Gulf company began. Kuwaitis in partnership with other Gulf state nationals set up companies (often in the UAE, for example) and offered stocks in Kuwait. Since these companies were outside the purview of the state and because almost any earnings rate could be imputed to them, offshore trading opened another important venue for the new investor. Once more the Ministry of Commerce and Industry appeared to act by banning trade in non-Kuwaiti companies, but enforcement did not follow. Indeed, most government interventions fostered further incentives toward destructive speculation. The most obvious example came in 1975–1976 when the state purchased large numbers of shares to shore up falling prices. Instead, this actually flooded the market with excessive liquidity (in 1975, 24 percent above the normal market level, and 37 percent in 1976), leading to renewed speculation and the belief on the part of the investor that the state would forever ensure their investments.[27]

Finally, in 1977, the state created an official stock exchange and made the 1972 Bureau of Securities Exchange its executive. The new market traded securities in some forty Kuwaiti-based companies with a total value of KD 347 million. Of the initial stock issued, the government controlled around 24 percent.[28] To gain further control over the market, the Ministry of Commerce and Industry released a string of new guidelines in 1977. Since forward transactions had continued, the ministry sought to establish standards and manage them. A subsequent ministry ruling banned further establishment of shareholding companies in Kuwait and prohibited any increase in the capital of existing companies. These measures achieved some stability, but they also pushed the aggressive new

---

[26] Beblawi, *The Arab Gulf Economy*, p. 209.
[27] Darwiche, *The Gulf Stock Exchange Crash*, p. 57.
[28] Beblawi, *The Arab Gulf Economy*, p. 211.

investors into uncharted waters. Trade in the offshore companies offered a way around these restrictions. Thus, in 1979, the Souq al-Manakh opened its doors. Its purpose was to deal in stocks of the shareholding companies not registered in Kuwait. Despite the fact that the Manakh was illegal, "the government turned a blind eye."[29] The speculative activity and forward trading that eventually occurred outstripped even levels that the legal market had achieved.

Ramifications for business representation

Industrial incentives and a permissive regulatory environment helped to fashion the outlines of a new class of Kuwaiti entrepreneur. In some cases, these were civil service employees with side businesses; others were Shi'a and bedouin groups who had taken advantage of new market openings; and still others were simply gamblers with good connections. One US State Department cable, referring to the stock market and this period in general, put it this way:

The Stock market so enveloped Kuwaiti society that one could not sit down with a Kuwaiti for more than 30 seconds without the subject being raised . . . young aggressive Kuwaitis became billionaires in a matter of months; Kuwaiti women found an activity they could profit at and enjoy. Kuwaiti society – with the perceived blessing of the government – indulged in an orgy of greed that knew no bounds.[30]

To be sure, more Kuwaitis were in business. KCCI membership figures reflected the jump. From 1970 to 1975, membership increased by 40 percent, but these increases reflected mainly the obligatory registration of new businesses. Any first business license required chamber membership, but the new businesses tended to register only once, as only licenses for importing and bidding on public contracts required yearly renewal. With this in mind, the double-digit membership increases of the 1970s were composed mostly of those new merchants. In addition to swelling the ranks of the small and medium-sized businessmen, government policies also succeeded in laying the foundation for a new business elite. Some, like the al-Wazzan family, participated in some of the few industrial concerns that developed. Many more, such as Ahmed Du'aij, chief executive of the Kuwait Real Estate Investment Consortium, focused on real estate and construction.[31] None of these business groups approached the size and

[29] *Ibid.*, p. 233.
[30] Cited in Edward Jay Epstein, "Kuwait Embassy Cables," *Atlantic Monthly*, 251, 5 (May 1983).
[31] *The Times* (London), 12 July 1977.

diversity of the conglomerates of the KCCI elite, but many were gaining recognition, principally from the state. A former official in the prime minister's office in the 1970s, 'Isa Majid al-Shahin, recalls that

Lists for invitees to official functions at the prime minister's office began showing new names. The richest of the new businessmen began calling on the prime minister and showing up at meetings, whereas before only the Sunni elite of the chamber had been present.[32]

More extensive state control of shareholding companies meant new names also began appearing on the executive boards of some companies. Correspondingly, the cabinets of the 1970s saw an increase in new faces. Prominent Shi'a and non-*asil* Sunni representatives increased their share of cabinet posts from about 30 percent in 1965 to over 40 percent in 1975 (an increase of two to three posts), while KCCI representation dropped from 38 percent in 1965 to a steady 33 percent in the 1970s.[33] To a certain extent, much of this was tolerable for the KCCI leadership. Few of the new merchants were challenging elite economic concerns, and no immediate leadership challenge within the KCCI was apparent. However, KCCI elites were clearly aware of the direction and intent of state policy. "We knew that, by ignoring [market] excesses, the government was hoping to foster a rival merchant class."[34] The problem was that, although direct government industrialization policies had failed on their own, the more amorphous permissive policies that followed were difficult to pin down and move against. Previous merchant failure during the 1961 cabinet crisis and the exclusive nature of the KCCI offered business elites little opportunity to secure wider support to challenge state policies. Moreover, the boom in real estate and infrastructure investment greatly enriched the investment positions of the chamber leadership.[35]

"Grabbing at a wild horse": the breakdown of coordination

What had proven a coordinated business–state approach to economic issues in the 1960s became more contested in the 1970s. Structural

---

[32] Interview, al-Shahin.
[33] Assiri and Al-Monoufi, "Kuwait's Political Elite: The Cabinet." The change in these numbers may appear small, but in small and medium-sized developing nations even slight shifts in the composition of cabinets carry political meaning.
[34] Interview, 'Abdullah M. S. Beaijan, KCCI board member, Kuwait City, 26 March 1996.
[35] Imports soared in the 1970s, and as many KCCI elites maintained monopolies on the importation of some goods, they directly benefited from the increasing demand. For instance, in 1975 Kuwait had the highest per capita number of cars in the world; all these cars had to be imported, and each had to have import duties and agency fees paid: *MEED*, 8 August 1975, p. 14.

accounts correctly pinpoint how an expanding pie of rent distribution can bury policy disagreements between business and state. Redistribution tends to be accompanied by more conflict than distribution does. However, distribution during the boom did not bury political disputes between state and society,[36] nor did it reverse business elites' institutional achievements with the KCCI – in contrast to al-Sabah sequestration of the municipality in the 1950s. Still, it was evident that business's influence on the state and the ability of the KCCI to advance its agenda weakened dramatically in the 1970s. Attempts by the chamber to shape ongoing policy or broach new initiatives were, in the words of one informant, "like trying to grab at a wild horse in full gallop."

In the 1970s the chamber was quite active. It augmented its institutional capabilities by establishing a Public Relations Department and expanding its support staff and panels of advisors with experts from outside Kuwait.[37] The chamber moved to diversify its revenue base by investing more finances into real estate and development projects within Kuwait. In perhaps their shrewdest public relations move, KCCI elites started a national newspaper, Al-Qabas, in 1970. Four of the original investors in the newspaper – al-Sagr, al-Khourafi, al-Bahr, and al-Nisf – sat on the KCCI's board. With the paper, the KCCI had a respected media outlet through which to press its claims. For instance, the president's annual economic statement, which had gained notice in the 1960s, was published by Al-Qabas. The paper carried KCCI policy statements and draft proposals. One of the first issues tackled in this way was the rise in prices.

Tied to the tremendous inflow of capital beginning in 1972, prices skyrocketed in Kuwait City. Demand forced an increase of more than 50 percent in imports from 1974 to 1975.[38] Retail prices went up. The state and the Central Bank responded with a variety of measures that worried traditional business elites. In 1972 and again in 1974, the state declared retail price freezes on certain commodities. In some cases, the state took over the importation and subsidized distribution of basic commodities.[39] The Central Bank imposed a more stringent liquidity requirement on Kuwait's commercial banks to stem lending. Individually these policies did not strike at the heart of any KCCI interests, yet collectively they were ominous. Little consultation with KCCI officials took place on these measures. The KCCI responded in 1972 and again in 1976

[36] Okruhlik, "Rentier Wealth, Unruly Law, and the Rise of Opposition."
[37] Interview with Majid Jamal Al-Din, advisor, KCCI, Kuwait City, 6 December 1995.
[38] EIU, No. 5, 1980, p. 62.
[39] EIU, No. 2, 1972, p. 4; Middle East Economist, November 1975, p. 139.

with public proposals to lower costs. The core proposal was a free-trade zone in Kuwait. The KCCI hired a group of British consultants to study the idea and put forward recommendations on how it might be accomplished. With the report in hand, KCCI elites argued to state officials that the establishment of a customs-free zone at the Port of Shuwaikh would bring down the cost of imported items. Moreover, they asserted that Kuwait's entrepot trade stood to benefit by lowering the cost of goods reexported to Iraq and Iran.[40] The government did not act on the free-trade zone proposal. Despite the KCCI's ability to fund research into the project, the proposal was wholly ignored. In a second effort, KCCI elites proposed creation of an export promotion fund within the IDB to be funded with customs duties on imports. In this way, entrepot merchants could recover some of the import tax by having their reexports partially subsidized by the fund.[41] In this case, the Ministry of Commerce and Industry and the IDB agreed but never diverted any customs revenue to the new fund. The autonomy high rents fostered and the ensuing weak consultation and implementation were reflected in the appointment of civil servants as well.

An important point of policy leverage was the personal relationship between KCCI leaders and the minister of commerce and industry. Traditional consultation had developed between KCCI elites and the prime minister regarding the selection of each minister. That tradition broke down in 1975 with the appointment of 'Abdulwahhab Yousef al-Nafisi to the post. Though the precise nature of the disagreement was not documented, it was clear that al-Nafisi was not close to KCCI elites and was chosen over resistance from traditional merchants.[42] Previous appointments to the post had either been royal family members or individuals close to the KCCI. Al-Nafisi had not served in any previous cabinet, but his closeness to the monarchy won him four posts in state-controlled shareholding companies. He was also not associated with any of the core asil families, and some observers suggest that part of the conflict flowed from the fact that al-Nafisi was a virulent critic of al-Sagr's leftist, Arab nationalist politics.[43] Whatever the source of disagreement, al-Nafisi was an "outsider" to the KCCI, and he was appointed only over their resistance. By all accounts, the institutional relationship between the KCCI and the ministry suffered. Policy committees within the ministry held

---

[40] Interview, Al-Din.

[41] Interview, Dr. Muhammed A. al-'Awadi, Kuwait University, Kuwait City, June 1996.

[42] Interviews, Wael al-Sagr, son of 'Abdulaziz al-Sagr, Kuwait City, 6 April 1996; and al-Awadi.

[43] Various interviews. In Kuwait, few personal disputes are secret, but there is discretion in discussing them.

fewer meetings with KCCI officials. The personal animosity meant the minister rarely attended KCCI events, in contrast to previous ministers. Despite KCCI protests, al-Nafisi was appointed for another term in 1976 – the first non-Sabah reappointed to that ministry. Loss of this ministerial leverage had an impact on broader business–state relations.

Traditionally, the KCCI relied on the Ministry of Commerce and Industry to provide an institutional counterweight to the Ministry of Finance, where KCCI influence was weaker. Leadership at the Ministry of Commerce and Industry was traditionally deemed a pro-merchant voice among state agencies.[44] Intermittent recession in 1976 and 1977, coupled with a growing public budget, sparked bold comments by Minister of Finance Abdulrahman Salim al-'Atiqi[45] that Kuwait would have to consider "direct taxation in the range of 10–15 percent."[46] The Ministry of Finance did not consult KCCI elites on the proposal,[47] but the traditional supporter of KCCI positions, the Ministry of Commerce and Industry, put up no resistance to a tax that would have hit elites hard. In the end, nothing came of the tax proposal, but the lack of ministerial support left its impression. For the first time, the KCCI lacked an ally in the ministry.

Poor relations with the Ministry of Commerce and Industry could not have come at a worse time. In 1976 the emir dissolved parliament, which had been growing increasingly restive; in 1972, for example, opposition members, in rancorous debates, had threatened to withhold approval of the state budget. Crown Prince Jaber explained that "the defective application of democracy in Kuwait has reached a serious turning point . . . the deterioration of the situation represent[s] a threat to Kuwaiti security and stability."[48] The risk to Kuwait involved possible repercussions from Lebanon's civil war, and fear about potential reactions to that war

---

[44] This situation supports Joel Migdal's contention regarding the importance of "disaggregating the state" in order to view conflict within and among state bodies as a determinant of policy outcomes. The broader point that this study emphasizes, however, is the strength and organization of the social elite – like business – as a factor in the manipulation of rival segments of the state.

[45] Al-'Atiqi was another minister close to the monarchy and with whom the KCCI had open disagreements. When he was minister of oil in 1968, KCCI loyalists in parliament demanded his suspension: *Middle East Record*, vol. IV, 1968, edited by Daniel Dishon (Jerusalem: Israel Universities Press), p. 615.

[46] *EIU*, No. 1, 1978; *MEED*, 31 December 1976, p. 31; and *Arab World Weekly*, 3 February 1979, p. 11.

[47] Counterintuitively, this was an excellent example of the poor relations between state and business during the boom. There had been little fiscal need during the boom years for increased domestic revenue, and therefore the finance minister's statement reflected more the autonomy the Finance Ministry had achieved from organized business at the time than any genuine revenue need.

[48] Quoted in *Arab World Weekly*, 4 September 1976, p. 13.

among Kuwait's 300,000 Jordanian workers of Palestinian origin. On a deeper level, the monarchy was frustrated with the opposition in parliament. Preoccupied with oil-concession negotiations, the opposition had on several occasions refused to approve state plans regarding the oil industry.[49] Press crackdowns followed the suspension, undercutting one of the KCCI's newest outlets, the *Al-Qabas* newspaper. Cabinet reform after the suspension did result in the return of three KCCI loyalists, but conversely it was in this reshuffling that al-Nafisi was reappointed and a new post, that of Islamic affairs, was created.[50] Overall, loss of the parliamentary venue for demonstrating political loyalty injured the KCCI's ability to supply a *quid pro quo* in exchange for policy input. This led to the further centralization of economic decisionmaking and its insulation from organized business involvement.

With no chamber representation, a committee consisting of the ministers of finance, commerce/industry, oil, and planning took over the activities of parliament's Finance Committee.[51] Trends toward institutionalizing Islamist opposition and limiting KCCI leverage were foreshadowed in the elections immediately prior to dissolution. In the 1975 elections, half of those elected were new to parliament. Owing partly to state gerrymandering, the number of *asil* (KCCI loyalists) dropped from around twenty to fourteen, tribal elements realized two more seats, and Shi'a representation rose to twelve. The result was a curious alliance among tribal, Shi'a, and Sunni fundamentalists, whose voting block could ensure that the state was able to oppose any "legislation sponsored by the liberal urban merchants."[52] Thus, even before the suspension of parliament, KCCI leverage there had diminished. The cumulative effect of these weakened venues became obvious with unsuccessful lobbying over the stock market and the gradual entrance of ruling family members into the private sector.

As reviewed earlier, the growth and development of Kuwait's stock market required institutional crafting and policy implementation. Politically, the KCCI interpreted weak state regulation as a tool with which to create a politically loyal merchant elite. More specifically, by the late 1970s some of the KCCI leadership began to fear the economic repercussions of a runaway, unregulated stock market and the harm it could do to their own interests. Certainly the KCCI's failure to affect the state's decisionmaking arose in part from the fact that many KCCI elites benefited from the stock market; hence opinion on regulation was divided in

---

[49] *Arab World Weekly*, 5 August 1972, pp. 13–14.
[50] Crystal, *Oil and Politics*, p. 92.   [51] *EIU*, No. 4, 1976, p. 19.
[52] Gavrielides, "Tribal Democracy," p. 164; see also Crystal, *Oil and Politics*, pp. 91–92.

the early stages. Accordingly, the KCCI backed the initial institutional phases of the stock market in the early 1970s. KCCI board members sat on the first Bureau of Securities Exchange and continued to serve when it headed the formal creation of the stock market in 1977. Those same members directly benefited from government share purchases in companies in which they held stock. Access, however, did not translate into successful influence.

Even before the inauguration of the stock market, KCCI position papers reflected a growing concern. After four meetings with government officials, a panel of KCCI board members completed a comprehensive document detailing chamber proposals. Themes that were emphasized included greater supervision by state agencies and greater market transparency. First and foremost, the KCCI wanted more forceful regulation of the infamous forward transactions. "Circulating stocks by postponed payment caused an increase in speculation and a drop in prices; that is why this kind of circulation should be organized." The KCCI called for greater transparency by compelling shareholding companies to publish "quarterly bulletins about their financial situation." To address the problem of excessive liquidity, the KCCI proposed the Central Bank be empowered to float "treasury bonds or public debt bonds." Modeling the Bureau on the Security and Exchanges Commission in the United States, the KCCI further argued that the Bureau of Securities Exchange be able to "stop dealing in any stock, if there is enough certainty that the process increased or decreased due to rumors or planned contrivance." Though well researched and professional, the proposals reflected more than purely economic concerns. The writers went out of their way to stress the importance of the market to small investors and the positive benefits of "widening the market." In that vein, they even proposed that closed stock companies be allowed on the market to widen investment opportunities. However, the clear thrust of this document, and others that would follow, was to rein in the market, thereby curtailing the creation of a rival merchant class.[53]

Proposals for regulations appeared in *Al-Qabas*, and there were presentations within the Ministry of Commerce and Industry and within the Securities Exchange.[54] As the progress of offshore trading and the creation of the Souq al-Manakh demonstrated, the KCCI was unable to marshal any internal government support. There was certainly no sympathy at the top of the key economic ministries. Furthermore, involvement of government officials and some royals in the illegal trade meant that resistance

[53] KCCI, *Mudhakkara 'an Souq al-Ashum wa al-Nash'at al-'Iqariyy fi al-Kuwait* [Memorandum on the stock market and real estate activity in Kuwait], 1977.
[54] Various interviews.

to KCCI complaints was driven by powerful personal interests. Once the Souq al-Manakh came on the scene in 1979, an institutionalized, albeit illegal, market for trading in offshore companies was available. Chamber strategy switched from banning this trade toward bringing it under ministry control.

A now famous (in Kuwait, that is) chamber-sponsored conference in November 1981, shortly before the crash of the Souq al-Manakh, encapsulated this effort. The conference brought together government officials, KCCI leaders, and economists to discuss the markets. In a key address, al-Sagr laid out the KCCI's position. While admitting the "second stock market" served a useful purpose in Kuwait's economy, al-Sagr focused on the need for more information and state supervision. "I believe that the problem is very difficult but we can reduce its impact by providing accurate information, making studies, and by giving traders and small shareholders the information to know where to step and when to buy."[55] More specifically, al-Sagr called for the Manakh to be subsumed under the Ministry of Commerce and Industry, essentially bringing these companies into the official stock exchange and regulating forward transactions.[56] He concluded with an ominous warning: "This is so dangerous because these days are different than before; we are dealing with millions [of KD] and if any problem occurs, there will be a disaster."[57] In the end, no effective measures were taken.

The failures to rein in the stock market and limit state creation of rival merchants were demonstrative of the inability of business and state to coordinate on policy in the 1970s and of the KCCI to lobby for its interests effectively, but they were not the most serious for the KCCI leadership. Crystal's work reveals that, after the succession of Jaber Ahmed in 1977, more and more al-Sabah family members entered the business boom.[58] This directly threatened the unspoken deal between KCCI elites and the al-Sabahs and, because of ruling family political connections, undermined asil economic positions. Parliament's dissolution, and the lack of merchant protest about it, confirmed that KCCI involvement in all areas of political participation was not a given. With al-Sabahs entering business, reciprocity was withering away. Some ruling family members even used their access to win state contracts for front companies or pressed

[55] *Tatwir Souq al-Ashum fi al-Kuwait* [Development of the stock market in Kuwait], papers from KCCI-sponsored conference, Kuwait City, November 1981 (supplied by KCCI Research and Studies Department), pp. 292–293.

[56] By 1980, forward transactions were effectively controlled on the official stock market.

[57] *Tatwir Souq al-Ashum fi al-Kuwait*; see also Darwiche, *The Gulf Stock Exchange Crash*, pp. 62–63.

[58] Crystal, *Oil and Politics*, pp. 93–97.

the new emir to punish competing merchants.[59] While much al-Sabah involvement was covert, royals such as Shaikh Nassar al-Sabah al-Ahmed surfaced as well-known domestic investors.[60] KCCI engagement on this issue was naturally sensitive and open records are scarce. Indeed, given that the famous agreement was covert, protesting its violation had to be covert as well. Thus, the KCCI entered the 1980s reeling from challenges from both the state and the ruling family. Moreover, the previous decade had witnessed significant changes in the composition of the Kuwaiti private sector that hinted that future challenges would originate within the business community or in other sectors of Kuwaiti society.

Business and state under high rents in Jordan

The dramatic rise in oil prices and worker remittances generated an unprecedented economic boom in Jordan also. In a number of ways, the implications for business–state relations mirrored those in Kuwait. Increased state investment and expenditure coupled with greater consumer demand enriched the merchant elite. Conversely, state expansion and enhanced distributional capabilities weakened business's policy leverage. By the mid-1970s, state officials and the monarchy not only ignored business representation and policy initiatives from organized business but even enacted policies that directly endangered those interests. Therefore, as in the boom years in Kuwait, political patterns confirm a number of structural/statist expectations. However, the institutional changes that began to reshape business representation are overlooked in such interpretations. The dramatic change in the contours of the business community and how business representation reacted both figure prominently in the crises that would define the 1980s and 1990s.

War, rents, and state autonomy

Jordan entered the decade of the 1970s facing its most significant domestic crisis, the September civil war. Armed forces of the Palestine Liberation Organization (PLO) fought the Jordanian army in Amman and surrounding areas. Eventually, King Hussein prevailed, expelling PLO forces from Jordan. Politically, the conflict inexorably altered state and society.

On 15 September 1970, just two days before open hostilities broke out, the ACC held its executive board elections. A group of PLO-affiliated

[59] Tétreault, "Ruling Kuwait," p. 581.
[60] *The Times* (London), 4 November 1976; *Financial Times*, 25 February 1977, p. 23.

candidates ran against Muhammed 'Ali Bdair and his allies. The war and its issues tested the loyalty of the ACC to the Hashemite monarchy as it did for most social groups in Jordan. Despite the fact that the ACC was by 1970 a fully Palestinian institution, PLO candidates were completely defeated. The close historical relations between ACC elites and the state, the merchant desire for calm, and the latent fears of communist sympathies within the PLO influenced the defeat.[61] During the conflict and after, the ACC never issued a direct statement, but it was clear where their loyalty lay. For example, after hostilities the executive board formed a committee to assess the destruction caused by the fighting and present the data to state officials. Damage was significant. The war virtually shut down commerce, and most trade routes were closed, reducing GDP for the year by 15 percent.[62] Politically, the war provided an opportunity for the state to alter its role.

King Hussein's victory put in place new rules for domestic politics. Serious domestic challenges to the regime were quelled once and for all. Whenever regional instability did occur, the Jordanian army took up positions outside Palestinian refugee camps, but no serious internal military threat emerged after 1970. So, while latent fears of Palestinian encroachment persisted among East Bankers, an important test – the military one – had been overcome. Victory also set new parameters for future opposition movements (such as Islamist and tribal groups). Opposition within bounds was accepted , but the control of the monarchy was never in dispute.

In the aftermath of the war, the state centralized the processes of economic decisionmaking. As in Kuwait, technocrats in charge of policymaking gained greater insulation from the private sector. This was best exemplified in the creation of the Economic Security Committee (ESC) in 1970. Empowered through martial law protocols and originally designed to bar currency flight from Jordan during the civil war, the ESC was located within the prime minister's office and was composed of ministers from the leading economic ministries. Its first head was Crown Prince Hassan, and there were no private-sector or ACC representatives.[63] After the initial recovery period, the ESC became the body responsible for state sequestration. For instance, in 1975 the ESC invoked national security regulations to sequester private investors operating a large, nearly

---

[61] Interview, Abu Hassan.
[62] *Middle East and African Economist*, October 1971, p. 143; *MEED*, 12 July 1974, p. 785.
[63] *Arab World Weekly*, 25 June 1972, p. 15. Eventually, the sitting prime minister would summon and head the committee.

insolvent, bakery company.[64] Though the ESC was created to address issues of national economic security, it began to generate regulations cracking down on the press in the 1970s and 1980s. Much of this new decisionmaking was the legacy of Prime Minister Zaid Al-Rifa'i government in 1973. Al-Rifa'i brought in a younger generation of economic technocrats, including Muhammed Nouri Shafiq (Ministry of Finance), Kamal Abu Jabir (Economy), Mudar Badran (Education), and 'Umar al-Nablusi (Agriculture).[65] Certain ministries were empowered to participate in the economic policymaking that took place within the ESC: the renamed Ministry of Commerce and Industry (previously the Ministry of National Economy), the Ministry of Planning, and the Ministry of Finance (specifically, the Customs Department).[66] Ministers from each of these agencies composed the core of the ESC. Dramatic growth in the level of foreign aid meant that these institutional augmentations could be matched with increased fiscal capabilities.

Aid pledges from the 1967 Khartoum Summit, increases following the 1973 war, and reaffirmation at the 1978 Baghdad Conference kept external revenues as a percentage of total state revenue just under 50 percent for the first half of the 1970s (see table 1.2, p. 16).[67] As a portion of GDP, foreign aid averaged 30 percent from 1970 to 1980 (whereas in the 1960s the average was 22 percent), peaking at 40 percent in 1975.[68] If one includes internal/external debt and profits from state-owned enterprises (phosphate and potash mining) as forms of rent, then the percentage rises much higher.[69] Owing to rises in the world price in 1972, phosphates accounted for over half of the increase in industrial value added from 1972 to 1975; at the end of that period they constituted half of total commodity export value, and 16.3 percent of GDP (this last figure represents a quadrupling between 1973 and 1975).[70] The increase in

---

[64] Michael B. Sullivan, "Industrial Development in Jordan," in Khader and Badran, *The Economic Development of Jordan*, p. 136.

[65] Shmuel Bar, "The Jordanian Elite, Change and Continuity," in Asher Susser and Aryeh Shmuelevitz (eds.), *The Hashemites in the Modern Arab World* (London: Frank Cass, 1995), pp. 224–226.

[66] Interview with Riyad al-Khouri, Amman, June 1995; and Tayseer Abdel Jabber, Amman, 27 June 1995.

[67] At the Baghdad Conference, Arab leaders agreed that Jordan, as a frontline state, should be given on average $1.25 billion a year – an amount nearly equal to the public budget in 1978.

[68] Hammad, "The Role of Foreign Aid," p. 17.

[69] Phosphate and potash mining are slightly more labor-intensive than oil drilling. Moreover, since profits accrue directly to the state, they work like foreign aid in freeing the state from domestic revenue extraction.

[70] Central Bank of Jordan, *Yearly Statistical Series*; and Manzur, *Economic Growth*, p. 214.

government spending reflected almost precisely the increase in state revenue. From 1970 to 1975 absolute levels of aid increased by 184 percent while absolute state spending increased by 192 percent.[71] A good deal of the increase in spending went to the military,[72] but a significant amount also supported the state's increased share in the economy. This process in Jordan took place in ways that mirrored the Kuwaiti experience.

While Jordan's spending on social services was far less generous than Kuwait's, the government nevertheless embarked on major social programs in the 1970s. The state enacted minimal health and social security plans, boosted the minimum wage, expanded health facilities, and extended coverage of the educational system. In hand with greater military employment, state ministries also expanded their payrolls, bringing on thousands more East Bankers. By the mid-1970s, the state employed half of Jordan's workforce.[73] State revenue also found its way into the economy through new modes of distribution. The precedent of direct state investment in shareholding companies (i.e., the Big 5; see p. 69) was established in the 1960s. In the 1970s, new institutions to direct state investment were created, and public ownership of mixed companies increased.

State-financed, but structurally autonomous institutions,[74] such as the Social Security Corporation, the Postal Savings Fund, and, later in the 1980s, the Jordan Investment Corporation (JIC), established their own investment portfolios in shareholding companies. In addition, individual ministries were allowed to take out smaller shares in companies operating within sectors under their jurisdiction. Through this network of state appendages, what evolved were fewer wholly publicly owned companies and more varied participation in a number of companies. Outright public ownership was limited to utilities, the national airlines, and the Big 5 (tobacco and cigarettes, cement, phosphates, potash, and petroleum).[75] Dispersed public ownership gave Jordan the appearance of living up to its claim of being a free-market economy. Certainly in contrast to Egypt's formidable array of publicly owned enterprises, Jordan's thirty-one state

---

[71] Calculations taken from data in Central Bank of Jordan, *Yearly Statistical Series*.

[72] There were three salary hikes for the military from 1975 to 1980 alone: cited in Robert Satloff, *Troubles on the East Bank: Challenges to the Domestic Stability of Jordan* (New York: Praeger, 1986), p. 19.

[73] Roger Owen, "Government and Economy in Jordan: Progress, Problems and Prospects," in Patrick Seale (ed.), *The Shaping of an Arab Statesman: Sharif Abd al-Hamid Sharaf and the Modern Arab World* (New York: Quartet Books, 1983), p. 88.

[74] Meaning run by its own government-appointed executive board and not under the direct control of a specific government ministry.

[75] World Bank, *Jordan: Consolidating Economic Adjustment and Establishing the Base for Sustainable Growth*, vol. I (Washington, DC: World Bank, 24 August 1994), pp. 59–61.

companies (by the 1980s) appeared negligible by comparison. But when one considers the tremendous importance of mining to the domestic economy, these small numbers belie the consequence of the companies themselves, because these few state-owned companies were the ones performing the most significant economic activities. Moreover, by buying company shares in different sectors of the economy, the Jordanian state, like the Kuwaiti state, came to exercise wide influence in the composition and direction of ostensibly private companies in the 1970s. Therefore, total state employment (the state-owned sector plus some semi-private companies plus direct state employment) exceeded the 50 percent figure commonly attributed to Jordan.

Political industrialization and a basis for new merchants

Three policy directions provide evidence for the state's reach and its increasing insulation from parts of the private sector: import-substitution industrialization, liberal business licensing, and subsidized importation and distribution of commodities. Each policy fit the state's overall desire to fashion a new business elite, one geared more toward industry than commerce and marked by Hashemite political loyalties.

In line with the developmentalist ideologies of the day, Jordan's economic decisionmakers were enamored of the idea of turning Jordan's economy away from "non-productive" commerce toward more productive industrial enterprises. State guidance was a key ingredient. A core of economic advisors, mostly of East Bank origin and associated with the Royal Scientific Society (RSS), gained prominence in the 1970s by advocating these policies. Bassem Saket, a young advisor to Crown Prince Hassan, frequently commented that Jordan should curb imports and direct investment toward more fixed assets.[76] The RSS published a series of studies suggesting various import-substitution strategies to wean Jordan of its excessive reliance on trade.[77] These ideas were most evident in the expansion of the state's Big 5 industrial companies. Cement ($21.3 million), phosphates ($325 million), and potash ($420 million) all expanded their facilities and capacity through public funding and external aid.[78] The state's various five-year plans also stressed more straightforward incentives for private-sector industrial projects.

[76] *MEED*, 22 August 1980, p. 4; *EIU*, No. 1, 1980, p. 15.

[77] *Middle East*, September 1976, p. 54; *Middle East Reporter*, 14 September 1979, p. 8; Royal Scientific Society, Jordan, Economics Department, *The Economic Realities: Jordan 1976–1977* (Amman: Royal Scientific Society, March 1977).

[78] Jordan, Ministry of Planing, *Five-Year Plan for Economic and Social Development*, 1973–1976 and 1976–1980 (Amman: Ministry of Planning, 1973 and 1976); *EIU*, No. 5, 1978, p. 94.

Augmenting loans from the Industrial Development Bank, the 1972 Encouragement of Investment Law expanded the powers of the Investment Committee within the Ministry of Commerce and Industry to grant tax breaks for new industries. The ministry also shifted industry protection away from quantitative import restrictions toward greater reliance on tariffs. More targeted assistance came with the Small Industries and Handicrafts Fund established within the IDB in 1975.[79] Still, IDB loans amounted to only a moderate effort, totaling sixty-five industrial loans worth JD 2.6 million in 1976.[80] Of more importance quantitatively were government purchase preferences for local industries, as well as Central Bank policies. Beginning in 1973, the Central Bank called for Jordan's commercial banks to lend more toward "productive activities." Since commercial banks accounted for far more loans to the industrial sector than the IDB, this was an important direction. In 1974 the Central Bank placed ceilings on commercial lending but exempted industrial loans. Finally, through its varied investment routes, the state directly participated in newly established industries by purchasing shares. With the formation in 1977 of Jordan's stock market – the Amman Financial Market (AFM) – public investment in these shareholding industrial companies could be easily tracked. Thus, it was no surprise to find that, of the seventy-seven industrial companies currently registered on the AFM in the mid-1990s, twenty-five were established in the period 1970 to 1982, twice the number that were established in the period 1948 to 1970.[81] It is tempting to view these industrial policy initiatives as constituting a type of Gerschenkronian industrialization. A sectoral interpretation would then indentify any alterations in subsequent state–business interaction as flowing from the expected sectoral shifts. This, in fact, was not the case.

Central Bank lending regulations were barely enforced. The bulk of commercial lending remained biased toward the trade sector, with industrial lending only moving from about 8 percent of total lending in 1970 to 12 percent by 1975.[82] By the 1980s, state shares in the major industrial companies listed on the AFM averaged over 60 percent. Therefore, while private-sector investment in fixed assets did rise, most of those private investors retained the majority of their diverse portfolios within the services sector. Overall, then, industrial expansion, as measured by percentage of GDP, was slight (see table 3.1).

[79] Manzur, *Economic Growth*, pp. 223 and 231.   [80] *EIU*, No. 1, 1977, p. 16.

[81] Author's calculation taken from Amman Financial Market, *Jordanian Shareholding Companies Guide*, Issue 10 (1995). Industrial companies listed on the AFM are publicly traded and are the largest industrial concerns in the country. Most have more than ten employees.

[82] Central Bank of Jordan, *Yearly Statistical Series*.

How does one explain the failed effort? Certainly the small domestic market and the lack of an export regime account for some of the obstacles to greater private industrialization in the 1970s. However, there were others. Industrialization policies were not a product of the moment but flowed from a tradition of state-led policies instituted during the colonial period (i.e., the MESC). Just as these colonial policies had the effect of refashioning relations between business and central authorities by increasing the latter's autonomy, industrialization strategies of the 1970s were also tied to political rationales. Similar to the al-Sabahs, the Hashemites viewed industrialization as a means to draw politically loyal elements into the private sector. Contrasts with Palestinian-dominated private commerce were hard to miss. Many of the new government technocrats pushing Jordan's industrialization found themselves appointed to the boards of the Big 5 and other publicly invested industries: for example, Saket at Jordan Cement Factories; Abu Hassan at Jordan Ceramics; and 'Ayyoub at Aluminium Industries. This pattern was quite consistent with that in other Arab countries (Egypt, Iraq, and Algeria) where policies aimed at *infitah* (opening) or privatizing industry simply increased the ranks of the "state bourgeoisie."[83] Thus, despite some increased investment, the private sector remained both firmly rooted in commerce and Palestinian in origin.

A second policy direction complemented the industrialization effort, albeit in different sectors. Beginning with the 1972 Encouragement of Investment Law, the Ministry of Commerce and Industry was given far greater discretion in awarding special tax breaks to new businesses. This had the effect of easing licensing requirements, since the ministry switched to using tax incentives rather than refusal of licenses as the principal means to dissuade start-ups in saturated sectors. Consequently, "around 1971–72 the government began to approve nearly all license applications without regard to the number of firms currently in existence."[84] Due to more license approvals together with the continuing influx in the 1970s of Palestinians – many of whom began small or medium-sized businesses – the size of the private sector as measured by the number of registered companies increased from 2,305 in 1970 to 12,439 in 1982.[85] In Amman, the number of registered ACC members increased from 2,100 to over 8,000 in the same period. As in Kuwait, the combination of industrial policies and a relaxed licensing regime helped lay the foundation for a new merchant elite. As the entrepreneurial ranks

---

[83] Alan Richards and John Waterbury, *A Political Economy of the Middle East: State, Class, and Economic Development* (Boulder: Westview Press, 1990), pp. 238–261.
[84] Manzur, *Economic Development*, p. 220.   [85] *Financial Times*, 13 August 1982.

expanded, so too did membership revenues, yet – recalling Samuel Huntington's institutional overload thesis – there would be an institutional cost. This change occurred precisely at the moment the state launched a third policy, one aimed directly against ACC interests.

Like many developing countries of the 1970s, Jordan experienced chronic high inflation. It was classic liquidity-induced inflation. Remittance increases, higher oil prices, and a greater volume of imports (so-called imported inflation) drove up prices, particularly in Amman. From 1973 to 1974 the consumer price index rose 17 percent in the capital. As housing shortages increased, land prices and rents went up correspondingly, nearly 200 percent in 1977.[86] Elite merchants who had built up (or been awarded) land tracts in the 1960s profited immensely. Given the political sensitivity of higher prices, the state stepped in forcefully to control them. In 1974, the state created the Ministry of Supply (MOS). Previously just a division within the Ministry of Commerce and Industry, the MOS was made a separate ministry with cabinet status. The MOS centralized government subsidization schemes and extended them to more classes of goods. It took over the importation and distribution of meat, rice, sugar, tea, flour, cooking fat, and some fuel products. Storage facilities were established for non-controlled goods to allow the state further leverage over distribution and prices. For other categories of goods, the MOS established set prices and published lists of the official prices in the local daily newspapers. These activities quickly made the MOS one of the most important economic ministries.

MOS officials regularly criticized merchants for "hoarding," "price gouging," and ignoring the needs of low-income citizens. Press and government rhetoric accused the minority of rich merchants of profiting at the country's expense.[87] In 1978, Prime Minister Mudar Badran in a major address issued not-so-veiled statements of the government's concern: "any government in power must aim at ensuring the prosperity and well-being of its citizens with an atmosphere of security and stability so they can produce and build." The next prime minster, 'Abdul Hamid Sharaf, continued the campaign by railing against "runaway consumption," emphasizing the need for "increased production and a cutback in luxuries," and suggesting that "free enterprise would be promoted as long as it is conducive to the welfare of society and lies within the constraints of social justice and balance."[88] Action followed words. The

---

[86] *Middle East and African Economist*, October 1974, p. 134; *Middle East*, March 1977, p. 73.
[87] *Al-Dustur*, 10–16 March 1980; *Al-Rai'* 7 September 1980.
[88] *EIU*, No. 1, 1980, p. 15.

cabinet approved a Citizens' Complaint Bureau to collect information about merchant price violations. Soon afterwards, a military-run, anti-corruption court was created to try price violators.[89] In 1980, the MOS expanded its reach by opening "parallel markets" designed to sell a wide range of commodities at below market prices. Minister of Supply Jawad Anani then announced the government would be creating a chicken supply company to slaughter, package, and market poultry at below market prices.[90] In addition to threatening ACC members' interests by competing through retailers, MOS policies reinforced the political aims of industrial and licensing strategies.

MOS import schemes relied on medium-sized merchants to import the subsidized commodities. These arrangements created instant monopolies and guaranteed profits for merchants close to the state bureaucracy. In the words of one former ACC official, "the MOS became a swamp."[91] Collusion, easy profits, and corruption helped create another niche for a class of merchants wedded to state distribution.

Institutional dynamics: strains on collective representation

Viewed at a distance, private-sector representation in Jordan appeared strong and durable in the 1970s. Business elites survived the civil war with no doubt about their loyalty to the monarchy. Elites profited from the boom in consumption and the rise in land prices. Elites invested some of their private savings in the West, and sent their sons and daughters to be educated or to live there. The widely respected Muhammed 'Ali Bdair remained president of the ACC, and the cream of the elite merchant families were represented on the board, including the 'Asfour, Touqan, Tabba, and Taher families. Despite these positive conditions, the ACC realized little lobbying success, particularly on the macro issues of economic policy. As witnessed in Kuwait, increased state autonomy translated into official disregard for business interests; however, in both cases there was much more to the boom period than simply this. In the Amman Chamber of Commerce, organizational and representation changes – the expansion of membership voting and obligatory membership – launched in 1961 coupled with the growing ranks of new merchants began to recast business's intra-associational politics. Let us first review the extent of these changes.

---

[89] *Jordan Times*, 11 January 1980; *Middle East Contemporary Survey*, vol. IV, *1979–1980* (New York: Holmes & Meier, 1981), p. 573 (subsequently referred to as *MECS*).
[90] *EIU*, No. 2, 1980, p. 14.   [91] Various interviews.

Under Bdair in the 1970s, the ACC instituted several changes. The chamber bought land and constructed a new headquarters in a developing upscale area of Amman, Shmeisani. Shmeisani was a booming business and residential area inhabited by Palestinian merchant elite. Many of the largest commercial and banking firms (including the largest, the Arab Bank) had moved their headquarters to the area. It was no coincidence that the ACC headquarters were built across the street from the Arab Bank building. Since office facilities were significantly expanded, the board approved an expansion of the permanent administrative staff. There was enough additional space to rent floors out to local businesses. The area quickly became the heart of the business sector of the city.[92] Along with the physical changes, Bdair created a Library and Documents Division to store and organize much of the economic statistical information that state agencies, such as the Central Bank and the Ministry of Planning, were producing annually. He also introduced one of the first computer systems in Amman. The rather unsophisticated (by today's standards) punch-card system was tasked with upgrading and handling the growing number of member registrations. No other private social institution operated such a system and only a handful of state agencies had followed suit.[93] In contrast with these organizational upgrades, more negative trends were taking root.

By 1973 the Palestinian character of the ACC was solidified. Not only were the vast majority of merchants in the Amman area Palestinian in origin, but also the significant Syrian board representation of the past had all but disappeared. Because municipal and state authorities only began consistent enforcement of the 1961 organizational regulations in the late 1960s, in the early 1970s one sees merely the onset of the effects that membership expansion and voting liberalization would have. There are few open records remaining on past chamber elections, so one must piece together the remnants with personal recollections to grasp how the election processes began to change in the 1970s and how elite cohesion subsequently weakened. What is documented is the membership breakdown. In 1975, of the total possible member voters (classes *mumtaz* through 4),[94] 9 percent fell into the category of old elite (those allowed to vote and nominate before 1961) and 91 percent fell into the newly enfranchised categories. By 1980, those figures were 13 percent and 87 percent, respectively (see table A.5 in appendix). Along with the obvious expansion of the overall electorate, the increased number of elites complicated the

---

[92] Interview, Tijani.
[93] Interview, Ma'atouq; ACC, *Al-Taqrir al-Sanawiyy, Ghurfat Tijarat 'Amman* [Annual report, Amman Chamber of Commerce], various years.
[94] The change in representation rules in 1961 extended voting to categories 3 and 4, but not category 5.

processes of elite compromise and cohesion. The elite increase included in part the new merchant rich and in part the sons of the traditional elite. The periodic clashes of perspective and bias alone would require constant attention to maintain elite cohesion. The leadership team of Bdair and 'Asfour in the 1970s was by all accounts respected, secure, and skilled enough to manage the larger elite grouping without any serious institutional or electoral repercussions. What eventually wrought changes was the addition of the mass of lower-category voters. The problems that arose were textbook examples from the literature on the difficulties of coalition-building and collective action. In line with Olson's early hypothesis, small groups have disproportionately strong powers for collective action and organization. Once they are no longer small, this power weakens, but what is the process involved?

Voting in elections for the twelve-member board in the 1970s began to show more evidence of being overtly influenced by origin and religious affiliation, signs that were first manifest early in the decade. For instance, running in alliance with Bdair, there might be among the Palestinians two Christian candidates, two with origins in Hebron, and two from Nablus; and besides the Palestinians, perhaps one Syrian, and so on. Surfacing possibly in the 1974 election but certainly in the 1978 election, formal lists of candidates appeared. These lists compressed eleven board candidates plus their leader (the presidential candidate) into a single vote list. A tool for coping with the larger and more diverse rank and file, lists allowed the presidential candidate to appeal to a broader range of potential voters by including elements representative of different sections of the larger voting membership. The electoral need to attract votes from category 3 and 4 members placed ascriptive concerns, such as garnering the Hebron vote, in front of more pragmatic ones, such as candidate profile or political skill. By the early 1980s, candidate lists reflected less sectoral balance and more narrow interests. Choices based on origin and religion meant that an entire ACC board might represent only one or two sectors of the economy. An unbalanced board could be expected to present proposals to the state that reflected particular rather than encompassing interests. This is a clear violation of Olson's thesis that encompassing associations, while impaired at policy advocacy, are better able to espouse more balanced economic policies. Evidence about the 1980s and 1990s and the role of voting rules, to be presented herein, will suggest amendments to Olson's thesis. Suffice it to say that, by the late 1970s, a trend was emerging that this Jordanian encompassing association was both impaired at policy advocacy and unable to free itself from particularist interests.

The effect on elites was clear. Not only winning elections, but also distilling diverse interests into policy initiatives were greatly complicated, because elites had to play a two-level game. At one level, elite compromise had to be made and cohesion ensured. At another, since some board members were chosen solely because of their ties to groups in the lower categories, rank-and-file concerns had to be met not only every election but during policy deliberations as well. This resulted in an overall weakening of elite cohesion, which now had to be based on something other than shared economic interests. The effects were not immediate, but hints of change during the 1970s were evident.

The first and most notable elite defection was one of Subri Tabba's sons, Tawfiq Tabba. Like many sons of prominent merchant families, Tawfiq sought to demonstrate his independence and success by serving on the board from 1966 to 1970. After 1970 he left the board, despite Bdair's attempts to bring him back.[95] His younger brother Hamdi would eventually take over Tawfiq's position, but the symbolism of the defection was clear. The ACC was not the association it had once been. One institution to benefit was the Chamber of Industry, which it will be remembered formed in 1961. Unburdened by the need to compromise with its rank and file – due to more restricted voting and a smaller ordinary membership – the ACI could attract leading merchants who chose to take on the "industrial hat." Even though membership in the ACC was obligatory, there was a consistent lack of industrial representation, for an industrial member running for the board could not necessarily attract category 3 and 4 votes.[96] The lack of this important sectoral representation was not lost on state officials. It should be remembered that the prime minister appointed Walid 'Asfour, the former ACI president, to the post of minister of commerce and industry in 1979. More evidence of the declining ACC position and its antagonistic relationship with the ACI was provided by Crown Prince Hassan's negotiation efforts in the 1970s.

Buoyed by the growing policy advocacy role of his Royal Scientific Society, Hassan took an interest in private-sector representation in the 1970s. He reasoned that the separation of the industrial and commercial sectors into two chambers injured private-sector representation and interest mediation by dividing their influence and encouraging them to compete to influence economic policy. In 1971, Hassan engaged the head of the Central Bank to mediate negotiations between the two associations with the aim of reuniting them. Occasional meetings took place until 1975. Bdair proposed that industrialists receive a one-third representation on the board – in other words a guarantee of four seats every election – and

---

[95] Interviews, Tijani and Tabba.
[96] The big vote-getters became textiles from Hebron, foodstuffs from Nablus, and retailers from Ramallah.

'Asfour responded with a demand for half the board. Neither side compromised and the issue receded after 1975. Though there are no open records on the deliberations, participants and observers suggest that a core issue for the ACC was the growing power of the lower categories.[97] Some of the executive board members who were most resistant (to ACI inclusion) were those whose base was composed of the newly assertive lower ranks. They stood to be sacrificed in any unification process, as industrial representation would be required on the board, and so raising the industrial percentage was not negotiable from their perspective.[98] This was possibly the last chance ACC elites had to alter the 1961 organizational changes.

Attempting policy coordination

The types of failed business–state coordination in Jordan closely resembled those in Kuwait. Business resistance to more aggressive economic intrusions by the state was generally ignored. Policies were adopted with little or no associational input. Some policies indirectly endangered elite interests, while others were a more direct challenge, with the aim of fostering rivals. One example of an indirectly threatening policy was the suspension of Jordan's parliament in 1976, leading to the creation of an interim appointed assembly which seemed to offer new access to state decisionmaking. This strategy of creating *ad hoc* policy venues through political appointment marked an increasingly frequent state alternative for more bureaucratized business–state interaction.

Access points for policy input underwent some change in the 1970s, but in the aggregate much was the same as it had been in the 1960s. Personal access to ministers (commerce/industry and finance) and to the prime minister remained the paramount points of influence. Permanent representation on the Investment Promotion Council (tasked with granting investor subsidies and tax exemptions) within the Ministry of Commerce and Industry remained in place. The high-profile policy role of Crown Prince Hassan, which had begun in the 1960s, added another point of access. However, in the 1970s Hassan was building his own advisory coterie within the RSS, and ACC elites had yet to make much headway there. Consequently, the details of Hassan's economic advocacy in the 1970s reflected little of the ACC's concerns. In the words of one ACC board member, "Hassan had his own ideas" in the 1970s.[99] Not until the

---

[97] Interviews, former chamber officials.

[98] To be sure, some observers suggest that neither Bdair nor 'Asfour was serious about reuniting. Negotiations occurred because the crown prince had requested them.

[99] Interview, Abu Hassan.

1980s, when the crown prince broached more consultation with the ACC, did merchant elites become more comfortable with Hassan. A noticeable addition to ACC access came with its permanent representation on the board of the Social Security Corporation (SSC) in 1980. Its primary task was to extend insurance coverage for Jordan's workforce; It – in addition to the Postal Fund and the JIC – acted as a principal funding arm for public investment in shareholding companies.[100] This public investment was an important function that clearly had an impact on ACC interests, but since patterns of public investment were already in place, representation within the SSC did not assume much lobbying importance until later in the 1980s. The more important change in policy access during the period was the suspension of parliament and its replacement with the National Consultative Council.

In 1974, Arab leaders at Rabat, Morocco, declared the Palestine Liberation Organization "the sole and legitimate" representative of the Palestinian people. King Hussein, ever vigilant over external politics and their potential domestic impact, returned from the meeting determined to change Jordan's electoral law to "reflect the new situation."[101] The previous separation of the Lower House into East and West Bank elections was to be limited to the East Bank only. However, in 1976 the king halted plans to elect an East Bank-only parliament and dismissed the sitting parliament. In its place, the king in 1978 proposed a temporary appointed body, the National Consultative Council (NCC). As its name suggested, the NCC was designed solely as a consultative body, with no legally binding powers. It was to deliberate on policy passed down from the prime minister and offer advice but, unlike parliament, it could not approve or reject policy. At first glance, the suspension of parliament appeared to be a gain for the ACC.

The sixty-member NCC had its own Finance Committee, and business representation was far greater than in past parliaments. Nine businessmen sat on the first council, including ACC board members Bdair and Abu Hassan. Other businessmen were either previous board members or were closely allied to ACC elites. Tribal representation (which traditionally was rarely in agreement with urban business interests) declined in contrast to that of urban-educated elites as a whole.[102] The creation of the NCC gave full control of the Finance Committee to business representatives, unlike

---

[100] *Official Gazette*, Social Security Law, No. 30, 1978.
[101] Nabeel Khoury, "The National Consultative Council of Jordan: A Study in Legislative Development," *International Journal of Middle East Studies*, 13, 4 (November 1981), p. 429.
[102] Khoury, "The National Consultative Council of Jordan"; and Bar, "The Jordanian Elite," p. 223.

in the elected parliaments of the 1960s. However, access proved easier than actual influence. Aside from the very limited power of the NCC, the royal invitation to participate was predicated on loyalty. Subri Tabba was appointed to sit on the first senates because of his loyalty and closeness to the king, and reciprocated with continuing dedication; similarly, the new generation was expected to show its gratitude for appointments through allegiance. Consequently, businessmen sat as individuals, rather than as representatives of their association. Mamdouh Abu Hassan describes the precarious position of business on the NCC:

> The NCC actually paralyzed business. We sat on the council without support from the business community or its associational representatives. We could do little. Because there was already an atmosphere of suspicion about business, our appointment was regarded with even greater caution by the other political elements on the NCC.[103]

The NCC represented what would become a common template to bypass weak business representation. As institutionalized engagement failed, more *ad hoc* informal arrangements, anchored outside associational channels, would replace them.

Two pieces of legislation and the 1976–1980 economic plan for Jordan best exemplified the ACC's lack of policy input. In 1972, the prime minister had pushed through parliament a key reform of the Labor Law. The purpose of the reform was to enact legal parameters for the establishment of professional associations.[104] ACC elites sought to have the reform stipulate that professional employer associations (covering subsectors such as foodstuffs, transportation, sweets, and so on) be legally obliged to fall either under the leadership of a local chamber or under the representation of the federation. In other words, they wanted encompassingness to extend not only to individual business licenses but to licensed economic associations as well. Since ACC elites feared that such institutions would compete for lobbying access or duplicate proposals, their appeal was based on the state's desire for one business voice on national policy. Officials at the Ministry of Commerce and Industry ignored the appeal and left the reform rather vague. Associations were given permission to form, and no legal guidelines on affiliation with the chamber were put in place.[105] The chamber had little control over associational formation since the minister granted permission for the founding of institutions. Seen in conjunction with other state policies to spur the growth of new merchants, decentralization of associations made sense.

---

[103] Interview, Abu Hassan.
[104] *Official Gazette*, Labor Law, 1972 (Article 69, section D).
[105] Interviews, Ma'atouq and Abu Hassan.

Another legal revision flowing from the 1976–1980 economic plan stirred significantly more ACC resistance. Following the exit of Western companies from war-torn Beirut in 1975, Jordan's state technocrats, led by Crown Prince Hassan, crafted a new vision of Jordan's economic role in the region.[106] The same group that had pushed the idea of Jordan's industrialization closed ranks with Hassan in declaring Jordan "the new Beirut." With much fanfare and international press coverage, in 1975 the crown prince unveiled plans to turn Amman into the new center of business in the Middle East.[107] President Robert McNamara of the World Bank reportedly agreed to back the plan with targeted loans.[108] The twin visions of an industrial Jordan and the new Beirut came together in the 1976–1980 economic plan for Jordan. The plan represented the low point for ACC involvement in planning for Jordan's economic future. Integral to the plan were calls for increasing investment in industry, mining, and tourism.[109] It projected a decrease in investment in commerce. To boost export-oriented industries, the plan called for a committee to reexamine Jordan's tariff structure. Though the theme of tariff reform was an annual concern of ACC policy papers and letters to the ministry, the committee had no ACC representation. In addition to ignoring any input role for the ACC, the plan called for expanding the capabilities of the ACI by funding the formation of subsections to cover specific industries.[110] In order to enhance Amman's regional role, the plan advocated modifying the 1972 Encouragement of Investment Law.

Hassan and his advisors argued that a first step in replacing Beirut would be to attract those firms which had left Lebanon. In November 1976, the Ministry of Commerce and Industry and the prime minister's office completed revisions to the law. No business representatives were consulted on the law or on the larger vision for remaking Amman into a Beirut for the 1970s. Foreign companies wishing to relocate to Amman were exempted from registration with the chamber, and from customs fees.[111] The committee (on which the ACC had representation) empowered in 1972 to rule on tax breaks for business was bypassed by this new legislation. Instead, the minister would henceforth directly adjudicate foreign business requests. Therefore, not only was the chamber deprived of fees and contacts from foreign business licensing, but leverage

---

[106] Even into the 1990s, this new economic vision of Jordan surfaces again and again. See Pete Moore, "The Newest Jordan: Free Trade, Peace, and an Ace in the Hole," *Middle East Report Online*, 26 June 2003.

[107] *New York Times*, 2 October 1975.   [108] *Journal of Commerce*, 8 December 1975.

[109] Jordan, Ministry of Planing, *Five-Year plan for Economic and Social Development, 1976–1980*, p. 39.

[110] *Ibid.*, pp. 173 and 176.

[111] *Official Gazette*, Law No. 46, 1975; *EIU*, No. 1, 1976, p. 14.

over granting breaks was lost. By spring 1977, businessmen in Amman were openly protesting the law. They argued that simply letting in foreign offices contributed little to the economy, and actually stretched already thin social services and increased competition for skilled workers.[112] In vain, ACC elites filed petitions with the ministry and the prime minister to repeal the law. The failure of these efforts solidified an already poor record of lobbying by the association up to that point, because the chamber was already losing a more important struggle over the Ministry of Supply.

The creation and operation of the MOS was the most injurious and difficult issue merchant elites faced in the 1970s. Jordan and its private sector had successfully weathered the waves of Nasser-inspired socialism of the 1950s. Imitation of Nasser's treatment of Egypt's once well-respected private sector was muted in Jordan.[113] However, the mood in the public sector in the 1970s, resounding with its injunctions against "runaway consumption" and demands that "free enterprise . . . lie within the constraints of social justice and balance," echoed – for Jordan's merchant elites – themes of the Nasserite era. Exaggeration was easy, but the MOS's activities and the Economic Security Committee's selective sequestrations departed from traditional state–business relations.

In the first place, state officials did not consult ACC representatives prior to the creation of the MOS. Bdair and 'Asfour reacted by petitioning the prime minster for ACC representation within the MOS to ease some of the import transitions and guard against unfair accusations against merchants, but to no avail.[114] The rapid expansion of the MOS's import lists and goods that fell under price control was not curbed by merchant complaints. The type of working relationship of the past in which ACC elites, such as Subri Tabba, worked with ministry officials to set up emergency storage facilities was gone. MOS officials made storage, distribution, import, and pricing decisions in the absence of any merchant or associational input. Mid-level merchants close to MOS officials were awarded monopoly import rights to bring in goods for the ministry.[115] ACC elites argued that merchants were simply setting prices in relation to demand and, to censure them for the rise in prices, ignored other more important external factors, notably oil prices. In the late 1970s, when the MOS began to establish retail outlets, "the private sector began to see the government as a competitor, since it owned so many businesses."[116] For instance, the MOS decided to spend JD 11 million to develop its

---

[112] *The Times* (London), 25 May 1976; *Middle East*, April 1977, p. 73.
[113] For an excellent history of that relationship, see Tignor, *Capitalism and Nationalism*, pp. 96–194.
[114] Interviews, Abu Hassan and Tabba.   [115] Interview, Jabber.   [116] Interview, Tijani.

own bakery capable of supplying Amman with 11,000 loaves of bread an hour.[117]

In 1979, the Citizens' Complaint Bureau came into effect and military-administered courts were empowered to try price violators. The new prime minister 'Abdul Hamid Sharaf gave special weight to the MOS and its policies.[118] Over the next year and a half, "hundreds of merchants" were tried before this court; additionally, retailers who violated price controls or "hoarded stocks" had their names published in local tabloids.[119] Amman merchants were exclusively targeted and, though none of the ACC elites were arrested, some were implicated in the tabloids. Despite protests that the MOS rein in such suspicion, the febrile climate continued. "MOS witch hunts" (as they had become known among merchants) proved impervious to ACC influence, even though Bdair and Abu Hassan led vocal criticisms of the government's pricing policies in the NCC.[120] Prime Minister Sharaf rejected the appeals, as well as proposals that the chamber's own Arbitration Department adjudicate some of the price violation cases. This marked a nadir of business–state relations in Jordan.

Conclusion

High inflows of capital to a country affect its politics. This much we know from structural/statist theorizing. Applied to the historical record, however, the revenue or sectoral emphasis misses a great deal of political importance carried by business–state relations during periods of high rent. External sources of revenue to Kuwait and Jordan clearly strengthened the fiscal autonomy of the state, increased patronage resources, and facilitated a reduction in the size of the private sector in relation to the public sector. However, the boom period did not break completely with the past. In both cases, previous patterns of public–private interaction and the earlier institutionalization of business representation conditioned state strategies toward economic policy and the private sector.

Though points of confrontation were evident, state strategies in each case did not entail replacing business. Instead, strategies in the 1970s involved expanding patronage through state-mediated intervention, while at the same time encouraging (actively and passively) the growth of rival business interests. In both countries, these efforts were only partially

---

[117] *Middle East*, February 1979.

[118] Umayya S. Tukan, "The Debate About Development," in Seale, *The Shaping of an Arab Statesman*, p. 109.

[119] *MECS*, vol. V, *1980–1981* (New York: Holmes & Meier, 1982), p. 639; Interview, Abu Hassan.

[120] *Al-Rai'*, 14 November 1979.

successful. The Kuwaiti effort to generate new private-sector growth through industrialization failed, but the overall effort to encourage groups not previously present in the private sector (Shi'a, Bedouins, and younger merchants) did succeed. The industrialization effort in Jordan also fell short, yet it too succeeded in expanding the ranks of the private sector and elites tied to state investment projects. Following these indirect challenges were state actions that tangibly reduced policy participation by organized business and in some cases took over private interests. In response, business representatives in both countries sought to revive public–private coordination through either resistance to specific proposals or advancement of new policy ideas. These reactions met with little success, in part because, in the words of John Waterbury, "Flogging the private sector is generally good politics."[121] Especially during boom times, flogging the private sector is attractive – even in the United States.[122]

A focus on business representation's adjustments to the boom period provides a window into how each business community came to accommodate its own changing ranks. By the 1970s, the structure of business representation and representational cohesion in Jordan began to mainfest the 1961 organizational changes (widening membership and voting). The use of candidate lists linked with presidential hopefuls in elections to the executive board of the ACC, for example, reflects these changes. Additionally, the task of balancing elite interests with coalition demands generated enduring leadership tensions. More and more, Jordanian elites were forced to construct compromise, taking into account rank-and-file concerns, ascriptive issues, and electoral needs. In contradiction to Mancur Olson's ideas on associative action, as the ACC became a more encompassing institution, its leadership and policy stances began reflecting less, not more, catholic views of the economy. Kuwaiti business representation, however, weathered the 1970s with little evidence of intra-associational tensions. Instead, KCCI leaders invested heavily in the institutional capabilities and public relations assets of the association. These were the seeds of the divergent patterns that manifested themselves in the 1980s and 1990s as the boom days faded.

[121] Waterbury, *Exposed to Innumerable Delusions*, p. 213.
[122] David Vogel, *Fluctuating Fortunes: The Political Power of Business in America* (New York: Basic Books, 1995).

4   Crises at century's end

Easy money and regrets in Kuwait

The economic historian David Landes best summed up the precariousness of the rentier state: "Easy money is bad for you. It represents short-run gain that will be repaid for in immediate distortions and later regrets."[1] In the case of Kuwait, what we see is a state beset by two fiscal crises: an externally imposed decline in oil rents and an internally generated fiscal collapse brought on by the crash of the Souq al-Manakh. Exacerbating the money problems were persistent regional security issues arising from the 1980–1988 Iran–Iraq war. These pressures culminated in the Iraqi invasion and coalition liberation of Kuwait in 1990–1991. If the fiscal crises of the 1980s had not already laid bare state vulnerability, then certainly Iraq's invasion did so. For Kuwaiti business, the decades of the 1980s and 1990s offered great economic peril but also significant opportunity to recast its relations with political authority. How it did so and the ensuing political ramifications challenge accounts of business–state relations based solely on structural incentives.

Turning to Olson's framework, we should expect Kuwait's non-encompassing business representation to respond to exogenous economic shocks by advancing particularist, protectionist policies. No doubt there is evidence of such rent protection during crisis, but this is a limited view. The wider political and economic consequences from Kuwait's crisis and the creation of what in many respects came to resemble a new business–state coalition follow in previous trajectories and flow from institutional features absent in the Olson schema. Most at variance with Olson's expectations is the fact that, in significant respects, the reengagement between organized business and the Kuwaiti state was a key factor in Kuwaiti reform and response to persistent economic shocks. The non-inclusive character of Kuwaiti representation did not present the obstacle to reform and implementation Olson theorized. If we step back from the Olsonian

---

[1] Landes, *The Wealth and Poverty of Nations*, p. 173.

120

frame to consider the expectations of the wider structural/statist perspective, we can see that the Kuwaiti experience stands the anticipated pattern on its head. Instead of business–state relations under crisis producing policy deadlock, it was renewed coordination between the two that surfaced and became a crucial ingredient in crisis management. The position and strength of Kuwait's Islamists as political and economic rivals to business and state proved to be an important factor as well. By the late 1990s and early 2000, institutionalized business–state coordination on economic reform began to encompass broader political collusion against the Islamist opposition.

The terrain of crisis politics: parliament and business as the opposition

The timing of Kuwait's crises coincided with the maturation of new social and oppositional forces. If in the 1950s and 1960s the merchants were dominant, and in the 1970s their position declined as the power of religious and tribal elements grew, then in the 1980s and 1990s we see the maturation of the new opposition. Therefore, on the one hand, once the fiscal crises took hold, the policymaking playing field was considerably more populated than in previous years. On the other hand, the presence of more organized groups pressing for policy access meant the state was significantly more vulnerable than previously. The political supporters that the state and the monarchy had helped create in order to counterbalance the elite merchants now needed counterbalancing themselves. In Crystal's words, "by developing new allies, he [the emir] had inadvertently politicized them."[2] Relying on its organizational capabilities and elite cohesion, the KCCI could trade support of governmental efforts in parliament for policy influence. The outlines of this arrangement were evident before the actual fiscal crises.

Iran's 1979 revolution had reverberated throughout the Middle East. For Kuwait and its substantial Shi'a minority, events in Iran could not be isolated from Kuwait's domestic politics. The larger Shi'a families (such as the al-Wazzans) had always been a bulwark of al-Sabah legitimacy, the monarchy looking to them to lead the larger community. Still, Iran's revolution and subsequent demonstrations by Kuwaiti Shi'as the same year cast doubt on the broader community's loyalty. To head off potential instability, one of the monarchy's responses was to call for the reinstitution of parliament.

---

[2] Crystal, *Oil and Politics*, p. 101.

In 1980, Crown Prince Sa'ad announced the creation of a Constitutional Review Committee to reform the electoral process and pave the way for new elections. Headed by KCCI board member Abdulrazzik Khaled al-Zaid, the committee included a number of KCCI loyalists. Some press reports directly criticized the chamber's presence, suggesting the government was reverting to the old power structure.[3] Interestingly, however, the committee approved a redistricting plan whereby the country was divided into twenty-five two-man constituencies instead of the previous ten (it should be remembered that the KCCI proposed reducing the number of districts to two in the 1960s). Lines were redrawn to favor Bedouin/tribal candidates and to divide the Islamist elements. The redistricting crippled the leftist/nationalists like Ahmed al-Khatib, who was not reelected. Tribal representatives increased their seats to twenty-three, and Sunni religious candidates, surprisingly, won five seats. This representation was split between the more traditional Muslim Brotherhood's Social Reform Society and the more conservative salafi Islamic Heritage Society, but an alliance between the two quickly developed.[4]

In supporting the electoral reforms, the KCCI was admitting to its loss of parliament as a lobbying venue. Its candidates were squeezed into fewer districts as tribal and religious districts grew. For example, the old Qibla district, a stronghold of KCCI asil merchants, was divided into three new districts.[5] This narrowed KCCI representation to one prominent candidate, Jassem al-Sagr, brother of 'Abdulaziz al-Sagr. Though Jassim al-Sagr's official role was to head the politically sensitive Foreign Affairs Committee, his voice in all matters was deemed to be official KCCI representation. To be sure, other asil merchants, affiliated with or related to board members, did win elections. Such merchants held about 10 to 20 percent of parliamentary seats in the 1980s and 1990s, but Jassim al-Sagr was the sole KCCI representative; hence, the contrast with the parliaments of the 1960s and early 1970s was stark. Regardless of the loss of representation, greater openings toward business representation were unmistakable. In addition to its presence on the Constitutional Review Committee, the post-election cabinet was noteworthy for the departure of two KCCI rivals, al-Atiqi from the Finance Ministry and al-Nafisi from the Ministry of Commerce and Industry.

---

[3] *MECS*, vol. IV, *1979–1980*, pp. 404–405.

[4] It was also in this period that Islamist control of the local cooperatives spread. In the same year as the parliamentary elections, salafi and Brotherhood candidates took over half of the local cooperatives: Crystal, *Oil and Politics*, p. 103.

[5] Ahmad Daher and Faisal Al-Salem, "Kuwait's Parliamentary Elections," *Journal of Arab Affairs*, 3, 1 (1984).

Government gerrymandering and plans for new elections did not quell radical elements. In 1983, six car bombings took place in Kuwait City. The attacks, tied to a Tehran-based Shi'a group, prompted the state to reverse course. In the 1985 elections, government support (overt and covert) turned toward the old leftist/nationalist elements. Their gifted leader, Ahmed al-Khatib, was profiled in a lengthy television interview. To discredit the Islamist opposition, an official at the office of the emir suggested that Islamist groups had violated Kuwaiti law by operating as political parties.[6] Election results marked a return of al-Khatib and his allies; tribal candidates repeated their previous victories, with twenty-two seats; and Islamist candidates fared badly by securing only six seats. In a surprise result, Jassim al-Sagr lost his seat. Though other prominent merchants (al-Mutawwa', al-Ghanim, and al-Qatami) won seats, the loss of al-Sagr marked the first time there was no "KCCI representative" in parliament.[7] As before, the government appeared to have an assembly of loyalists; and yet an anti-government alliance soon developed between the Islamists and nationalists.

By this point it was obvious that parliamentary elections did little to curb political instability. In May 1985 an unsuccessful assassination attempt on the emir, followed by several bombings, shook the country. Government preoccupation with internal security was aggravated by new crises within parliament. Opposition groups investigating accusations of fiscal impropriety by Minister of Oil Shaikh Ali Khalifia al-Sabah demanded his resignation. The combination of political instability with an unruly opposition convinced the emir to suspend parliament in July 1986.

It did not take long, however, for opposition groups to mount pressure for the recall of parliament. In late 1988 and early 1989, petitions surfaced demanding the restoration of parliament and a lifting of press restrictions, which had been put in place with the suspension of parliament.[8] Islamist and nationalist groups as well as business all participated in the petitions. 'Abdulaziz al-Sagr led the merchant community's demand for a return of parliament. *Diwaniyyas* held by al-Sagr and other KCCI elites provided important venues for the venting of opposition demands.[9] In a rerun of the events of 1921 and 1938, merchant elites were making a play for their "rightful place" in Kuwait's social and political life. By 1990, all strands of the opposition had come together in demanding a return of parliament. The emir responded by convening a 75-member

---

[6] *MECS*, vol. VIII, *1983–1984* (Israel [sic]: Holmes & Meier, 1986), p. 404.
[7] Candidate lists and vote totals can be found in *Al-Siyasa*, 22 February 1985.
[8] *MECS*, vol. XIII, *1989* (New York: Holmes & Meier, 1991), pp. 484–489.
[9] *Financial Times*, 13 March 1990.

National Council, similar to Jordan's National Consultative Council, to quell opposition demands and prepare for new elections. The process was barely underway when Iraq invaded on 2 August 1990.

Opposition groups in exile during the occupation acquired unparalleled leverage. With the global spotlight on Kuwait, the emir agreed to a national convention of opposition and government officials in Ta'if, Saudi Arabia. The meeting was, in many respects, business's show. They represented not only the traditional opposition but also a bedrock of al-Sabah loyalty in the face of Iraqi occupation. KCCI leaders Yousef al-Ghanim and al-Sagr remained in Kuwait during the invasion. Rumors at the time portrayed al-Ghanim as a key player in the resistance, supplying communications and support equipment for Kuwait's underground.[10] There was little doubt as to where the loyalty of KCCI elites resided. At the Ta'if meeting, a famous photo showed al-Sagr (who was smuggled out of Kuwait for the meeting) seated at the right hand of Crown Prince Sa'ad. The symbolism was not to be missed. Among the opposition demands at the conference was an assertion for the monarchy "to stop running Kuwait's finances as a family show."[11] The crown prince had no recourse but to commit to new elections after liberation.

Those elections, in 1992, witnessed the return of Jassem al-Sagr to parliament, this time under the banner of the KCCI's own political grouping, al-Tajammu'a al-Dustouri (the Constitutional Group). The group advanced a platform focusing on a greater role for the private sector in Kuwait's economic management and more decentralization of policymaking. Recapturing its role as loyal opposition and successfully pushing for the reintroduction of parliament did not mean the merchant victory was absolute. For instance, unsupported by the Islamist and tribal blocks, Jassem al-Sagr failed in his bid to become speaker of parliament in 1992.[12] The struggle for parliament in the 1980s and 1990s confirmed that the KCCI had returned as an important political player, but it did not dominate the scene as it once had. Well-organized tribal and Islamist groups occupied the public policy arena as well. Nevertheless, parliamentary politics reopened venues for business access to policymaking and amendment. Briefly reviewing the country's fiscal crises reveals other areas in which state vulnerability appeared and opportunities for business–state coordination increased.

---

[10] These stories are easily exaggerated. More legends than hard evidence concerning the extent of Kuwaiti resistance and its players survived the occupation. But, in this case, as in many others, perception was as important as fact.

[11] *New York Times*, 13 October 1990.

[12] *EIU*, No. 4, 1992, p. 9. It is worth recalling that the previous speaker of parliament from the KCCI was Jassem's brother, 'Abdulaziz al-Sagr.

The expansion of policy participation

Internal and external fiscal crises sparked in 1982 represented a reversal of the halcyon revenue days of the 1970s. The crash of the Souq al-Manakh (to be discussed in greater detail on pp. 128–134) crippled Kuwait's financial system. The 5,000 plus individual debts that came to light in the aftermath totaled $92 billion, more than seventeen times the foreign reserves of Kuwait and 4 times that of Saudi Arabia.[13] Most of these debts were backed by local banks, which could not meet the liability.[14] The political and economic fallout would dominate Kuwaiti politics for more than a decade. The blow could not have fallen at a worse time, as world oil prices declined by 15 percent from 1981 to 1983. Kuwait's own oil exports declined by 50 percent in the same period.[15] In aggregate terms, this meant the 2.5 million barrels a day that Kuwait exported in 1979 were down to 1.1 million by the mid-1980s. Oil revenue as a percentage of the state budget declined accordingly.[16]

To fund the shortfall, the state ran a deficit in 1981 for the first time in Kuwait's history. Chronic deficits would stretch into the 1990s. As GDP growth declined through the first half of the 1980s, the government drew down its own reserves ($3.35 billion by 1985) to inject liquidity into the banking system. In 1988, the Central Bank reached its lowest level of foreign reserves ($1.4 billion) since 1973. The Iraqi invasion, ostensibly sparked by fiscal disputes between Baghdad and Kuwait City, ended any hope for a short-term solution. Reports have suggested that the government, to fund costs of the war and postwar repairs, reduced its foreign investment portfolio, estimated at $100 billion, to the range of $15–35 billion.[17] Details on the exact amounts have never been released, but the haste of the liquidation was best exemplified by the government's sale of shares in Britain's Midland Bank at well below market prices.[18] The state's fiscal and political vulnerability opened the door for the reassertion of the political opposition and the reestablishment of parliament. Fiscal vulnerability also meant the state needed the private sector, if not to contribute economic solutions, then at least to share some of the political heat.

---

[13] Darwiche, *The Gulf Stock Exchange Crash*, p. 101.

[14] *Euromoney*, August 1985, p. 119.

[15] Mahmoud A. Kaboudan, "Oil Revenue and Kuwait's Economy: An Econometric Approach," *International Journal of Middle East Studies*, 20, 1 (February 1988), p. 46.

[16] Beginning in 1987, returns from Kuwait's overseas investments outstripped oil revenues every year.

[17] *MECS*, vol. XVII, *1993* (New York: Holmes & Meier, 1995), p. 496.

[18] *Middle East*, September 1992, p. 36.

Entering the 1980s, Kuwaiti business representation was in an excellent position. Despite the appearance of political rivals, the KCCI was one of the largest, best-organized, and best-funded independent institutions in the country. It was well situated to take advantage of the state's financial and political vulnerability. Three tasks defined the political return of organized business: (1) solving the interrelated problems of debtors and creditors from the Manakh crash and Iraqi invasion; (2) influencing the process of economic reform and privatization; and (3) curbing the growing power of the Islamist opposition. Besides these, KCCI elites still faced internal challenges arising from the evolution of new merchant elites beginning in the 1970s. Analyzing how Kuwaiti business forged a new relationship with political authority to address these issues requires looking beyond the decline in rents and abstract organizational logics. These variables tell us little of how business representation took advantage of the policy openings that resulted from crisis.

Whereas economic policy venues remained essentially stagnant during the 1970s, they multiplied during the 1980s and 1990s. The most obvious of these was parliament. Unlike its predecessors of the 1970s, assemblies of the 1980s focused far more on domestic political and economic issues. Ministerial corruption and financial impropriety were popular topics of debate. The powers of parliament remained as circumscribed as in the 1960s, but the better organization and aggressiveness of the opposition pushed the boundaries of that authority. Especially during the Souq al-Manakh debates, the Finance Committee in parliament quickly became a focal point for heated national debate. However, the reassertion of parliament also produced problems for organized business participation in policy. In one respect, Islamist and tribal elements proved more skilled than business representatives at parliamentary politics, complicating KCCI initiatives at key points. In another respect, despite its having only one representative through much of the period, respect for the KCCI's economic analysis and its leadership made the association a valuable ally for the government at key points in time. KCCI elites effectively exploited this position by playing off government and opposition to realize its own goals.

The return of political liberalization to Kuwait increased the profile and policy impact of the media. Already established in the 1970s, al-Sagr's annual economic report as president of the KCCI proved an authoritative and politically useful tool. In the mid-1980s, the association's Research Department was significantly upgraded with a computerized database and staff expansion. Just as the Kuwaiti government and financial institutions were known to recruit the Arab world's best and brightest,[19] the KCCI augmented its staff with well-educated Palestinian, Lebanese, and Syrian professionals. By the mid-1980s, the KCCI possessed a respected team of Gulf economic analysts.[20] In addition, given that board members owned some of Kuwait's largest companies and financial institutions, the chamber could count on the support of their research staff as well.[21] It should be remembered that the executive board members had controlled the *Al-Qabas* newspaper since 1970. Its editorial predilection was decidedly middle of the road. Unlike the more exciting and partisan Islamist *Al-Mujtama'* or the nationalist *Al-Anbaa*, *Al-Qabas* sought to antagonize few. It was a calculated strategy that gave *Al-Qabas* the profile of a sober, professional newspaper. In the early 1980s the Kuwait Centre of Gulf Studies found that *Al-Qabas* had achieved the country's largest circulation precisely because it offended few.[22] The paper figured as an important public relations tool for the KCCI throughout the decade. Every major government proposal or draft was printed along with the chamber's response or expert commentary. Chamber proposals were also given much coverage. To be sure, *Al-Qabas* was not the only media outlet comprising Kuwait's otherwise rancorous press of the 1980s and 1990s, but it was prominent and effective.

In contrast to the patterns of the 1970s, state officials turned to the private sector more often and more overtly. Throughout all phases of dealing with debts from the crash of the Manakh and efforts at economic reform, the prime minister's office created *ad hoc* committees either to generate policy options or to oversee their implementation. Without exception, the new committees included KCCI representatives. In 1985, the prime minister established the Supreme Planning Council (SPC). Its task was to submit policy recommendations to navigate problems arising from decreased state revenue. Of ten independent members, seven were appointed from the private sector by the KCCI.[23] Since the 1960s, KCCI elites had demanded less *ad hoc* state economic policy and more bureaucratized planning for the future. The SPC was a significant step toward that goal. In 1986, direct pleas by al-Sagr resulted in the creation of the Economic Reactivation Committee, a high-level advisory board of KCCI board members and state technocrats. Through these venues, business representatives could integrate proposals ranging from

---

[19] A good example of this is Ibrahim S. Dabdoub, Chief General Manager of the NBK (National Bank of Kuwait) since the 1980s, and a Jordanian of Palestinian origin. Many observers credit the success of the NBK over the years to Dabdoub's financial skills.

[20] Interview, Walid Khadurri, Executive Editor, *Middle East Economic Survey*, Nicosia, Cyprus, 10 July 1995.

[21] The research resources of the NBK alone surpassed those of most Kuwaiti ministries.

[22] *MECS*, vol. VI, *1981–1982* (New York: Holmes & Meier, 1984), p. 499.

[23] *EIU*, No. 1, 1986, p. 7.

debt relief to economic reactivation. However, it is clear these were not open government invitations for the private sector to take over economic policymaking. Similar to most developing countries, these state openings were fashioned with cooptation/survival strategies in mind to widen the blame should reform fail; consequently, consultation, not advocacy, was the intent. Since inclusion is but one ingredient in successful business advocacy and coordination with state authorities, the extent and success of policy engagement by organized business would hinge on other factors.

Aside from institutional openings, increased access occurred through personnel changes as well. One of the key headaches for KCCI elites in the 1970s was appointment of rivals at the top of important economic ministries. By 1982, however, al-'Atiqi and al-Nafisi were gone. A distinct turn toward traditional business elites took place as the monarchy granted key ministerial appointments to KCCI loyalists. The first of these was Jassim al-Khourafi's appointment to the Finance Ministry in 1985. One of the richest merchants, al-Khourafi was a persistent critic of government policies in the late 1970s and early 1980s. The al-Khourafi family was one of the founders of the chamber and Jassem's relative Muhammed al-Khourafi served on the board throughout the 1980s. In that same cabinet, KCCI board member Yousef al-Nisf was appointed minister of social affairs and labor.[24] The apex of chamber appointments came in the aftermath of the Iraqi invasion when 'Ali Hilal al-Mutairi, longtime director-general of the KCCI, was appointed minister of commerce and industry. Though he was not an elected deputy, and despite being a vocal critic of the government's economic management, al-Mutairi became the first head of this ministry to be appointed directly from the chamber.[25] Key personnel in these positions obviously increased KCCI access, but their presence also allowed business representatives extra leverage through threats to resign (as al-Nisf did in 1986) or timely leaking of reports.

The Manakh struggles

The crash of the Souq al-Manakh stock market in 1982 and its economic repercussions dominated Kuwaiti political life until well after the end of the Iraqi occupation. Aside from fiscal dislocations, the crash wounded Kuwaiti national pride, built in part on the country's past banking prowess. Consequently, much has been written dissecting the crash, and sharp debates among Kuwaitis have endured through the twenty years since. The crash and its effects were obviously complex. The task of this section, therefore, is to consider debates about the Manakh in

[24] *MEED*, 26 April 1985.   [25] *EIU*, No. 2, 1994.

light of changing business–state relations in Kuwait. Toward that end, it is useful to divide the fifteen-year task of addressing the debt problem into two phases: efforts to adjudicate debtors and support creditors before the Iraqi invasion, and the renewed efforts after liberation.

Opinions on how to achieve these aims stretched between two polar opposites. One group argued for a full government bailout of the debtors. Recalling government stock bailouts in the late 1970s, public, private, and royal family debtors assumed the state should again limit their liability to prevent deeper economic recession and capital flight. The second group favored bailing out only the small debtors and leaning on the larger ones for full repayment. Factions in the government and Islamist and tribal opposition groups supported this latter view. The KCCI's own proposals evolved toward a central position, essentially going easy on the small debtors but offering government assistance to help the larger debtors and support the creditors.

A few days after the crash, once the Byzantine network of debt became apparent, Crown Prince Sa'ad met with business leaders to discuss a way out of the crisis. On 17 August, the minister of commerce and industry held a press conference during which he stressed urgent measures, "in collaboration with the private sector," to address the situation.[26] On 21 August, resolution 21 from the Council of Ministers made official the government desire to work closely with the private sector. A door for the KCCI had been opened. An official KCCI position did not immediately crystallize. Instead, the first opinion to surface in public debate was the hard line. Finance Minister 'Abdullatif al-Hamad personified this position with his often-cited statement:

Those who have debts must repay them or they will be sent to prison. To honour one's obligation is the only way to restore confidence. Those who keep their word have nothing to fear. I have no regrets in adopting this harsh attitude because the reputation of Kuwait can only be restored if we are strong.[27]

Certainly, al-Hamad represented only a faction within the government and monarchy, but its voice was the loudest at the outset. Since some 5,000 large and small debtors were scattered among traders, government employees, and royal family members, rival views were slow to take shape. The KCCI itself waited until December 1982 before it issued its first official position.

The apparent indecision of the chamber was due in part to the fact that some large debtors held sway within the executive board. None of the sitting board members was seriously implicated, but observers agreed

[26] *Al-Anbaa*, 18 August 1982.   [27] *The Economist*, 4 December 1982, p. 86.

that family members and friends of some board members were among the debtors.[28] The core leadership (al-Sagr, al-Khourafi, al-Ghanim, al-Nisf) was not deeply involved in the Manakh, creating the generally correct perception that the debtors were composed mostly of *al-tabaqa al-jadida* (the new class of merchants) and the small dealers.[29] The lack of significant KCCI involvement is demonstrated by the fact that the National Bank of Kuwait, led by KCCI board members, came out of the crash carrying few debts. While Kuwait's other commercial banks had allowed postdated checks, the NBK had avoided involvement and had lived up to its well-earned reputation for financial probity. Despite not being deeply involved, the KCCI leadership was still greatly concerned about the debts and how they would be repaid. The crash depressed the official stock market and threatened to ensnare the wider financial system. It also provided an opportunity to curb the growing power of merchant rivals, many of whom were caught in the crash. Taken together, these were important internal and external reasons for action.[30] A balance had to be struck between the desire to go hard on the debtors and the need to protect against massive bankruptcies that could bring down the entire fiscal system. The chamber's first policy statement in December 1982 represented elite mediation of these interests.

Concluding that "all traders in this market should bear a large part of the responsibility," but admitting that "it is impossible to find a solution which satisfies all parties," the chamber proposed that premiums on the debts be reduced, on the order of 25 to 50 percent, to facilitate repayment. Though the KCCI cautioned against excessive reliance on the public treasury, it nevertheless called for the government "to provide funding . . . to facilitate the payment of dealers' liabilities."[31] It was a balanced proposal, avoiding the finance minister's *laissez-faire* attitude but still demanding a form of assisted repayment. Several three-hour meetings between KCCI representatives led by al-Sagr as well as a ministerial committee headed by the crown prince took place to discuss the proposal. There are no detailed records from those meetings, but al-Sagr's position won out over that of the finance minister and his faction. The crown prince agreed to go forward with the core KCCI proposal, premium reduction (known as premium stripping), and put the proposal before parliament.[32]

The chamber subsequently suggested that a clearing house be set up to register and sort out the outstanding checks. The prime minister

[28] Interview, al-Sadoun.
[29] The infamous "eight" were debtors who accounted for two-thirds of the total debt. Its leader was Jassem al-Mutawwa', previously a clerk in the government.
[30] *Middle East Economic Survey* (*MEES*), 28 March 1983, pp. B2–B3.
[31] *Al-Qabas*, 6, 15, and 16 December 1982.   [32] *Ibid.*, 22 and 28 December 1982.

appointed 'Ali Hilal al-Mutairi (KCCI director general and future minister of commerce and industry) to head the Kuwait Clearing and Financial Settlements Company (KUCLEAR). This body worked closely with the chamber's own Arbitration Department and experts at the National Bank of Kuwait to sort out, and where possible settle, the debts.[33] The chamber also sought to buttress its negotiating position by convincing debtors to sign power of attorney over to the association. In this way, any arrangements negotiated by the chamber would be binding for those who signed on. The collective-action move proved impressive, with over 85 percent of debtors signing on with the chamber.[34]

By February 1983 the parliamentary opposition responded. Government patience over the progress of KUCLEAR was wearing thin, and the al-Hamad faction appeared to regain the policy initiative, as the public tone shifted toward punishing "the manipulators" and dropping the premium-stripping proposal. The government placed some sixty investors under house arrest, seized assets, and confiscated luxury cars.[35] Chamber leaders felt "stabbed in the back."[36] They firmly believed that a deal had been struck with the government and that the process of arbitrating debts was still underway. KCCI leaders responded by arguing that, without the hope that some government backing to lower premiums would be forthcoming, investors would be less likely to agree to amicable settlements. Moreover, the threat of mass bankruptcies among the merchant and trading communities could cripple the financial sector. Islamist and tribal deputies responded that the previous KCCI plan would leave the smaller investors to bear the brunt of bankruptcy while the larger players would be bailed out.

In spring 1983, the emir called a special session of parliament to deal with the continuing crisis. Once more, KCCI elites took the lead, calling for meetings with cabinet ministers and the crown prince to discuss a new proposal. The KCCI's plan called for a halt to the government's actions (which they blamed for a rash of bankruptcies since January) and a return to KUCLEAR's power to reduce indebtedness and facilitate repayments. Several meetings resulted in an agreement on the basis for new government legislation.[37] To augment ministerial lobbying, the KCCI mounted

---

[33] Interview, Ibrahim Dabdoub, Chief General Manager, National Bank of Kuwait, Kuwait City, 25 April 1996. This was an interesting confirmation that rents weaken a state's extractive and information-gathering capabilities. No state ministries had the capability or expertise to deal with the debts, so the NBK and chamber officials were charged with collecting this vital data.

[34] Interview, Al-Din; *MEES*, 6 December 1982, p. B1.

[35] Crystal, *Oil and Politics*, p. 99.   [36] Interview, Al-Din.

[37] Darwiche, *The Gulf Stock Exchange Crash*, p. 120; *Al-Qabas*, 21 and 27 June 1983.

a fierce public relations campaign to support the premium-stripping formula within the context of voluntary multilateral settlements, which it would oversee. The battle lines were drawn.

On one side, Finance Minister al-Hamad, supported by the opposition in parliament, urged a hard line, while the KCCI, the Ministry of Commerce and Industry, and Minister of Oil Shaikh 'Ali countered with the premium-stripping formula. Media outlets were in full cry with the Islamist newspaper *Al-Mujtama'* publishing constant criticisms of business–state positions. *Al-Qabas* joined the fray by criticizing proposed amendments from the opposition.[38] In parliament, an *ad hoc* committee of deputies was convened to review the draft law and its various amendments. It met with government officials, KCCI representatives, and independent debtors and businessmen to canvass ideas. Headed by Islamist deputy 'Isa Majid al-Shahin, the committee proved a focal point for every lobby. According to al-Shahin, "We met with everyone. Some of the debtors had very good contacts and could offer huge bribes. Representatives from every district also made their presence felt." In describing the KCCI, al-Shahin acknowledged, "they came well prepared . . . usually the younger board members would make the presentations, and they were very professional and quite well informed about the details of the draft law."[39]

Eventually the committee approved only slight modifications to the original KCCI/government bill, and Law 100/1983 was passed by parliament on 11 August. Finance Minister al-Hamad promptly resigned. On the one hand, the premium-stripping formula was preserved, with some slight modifications in the levels of repayments. On the other hand, the law contained an element of compulsion, since the arbitration board would dictate the terms of settlement.[40] Opposition criticism did not relent. An editorial in *Al-Watan* on 1 September 1983 severely criticized the government for incorporating KCCI representatives into the Draft Law Committee.[41] Then in October, some parliamentarians proposed formation of a "jumbo bank" to replace the Arbitration Committee. KCCI loyalists within the Finance Committee effectively quashed the idea.[42]

With the immediate problem at least acted upon, the longer-term problem of Kuwait's financial markets and new guidelines for the stock market continued to plague policymakers. Early in the crisis, the government had expanded the powers of the Stock Exchange Committee to participate in

[38] 7 and 8 August 1982, respectively.   [39] Interview, al-Shahin.
[40] *MEES*, 15 August 1983, p. B1.
[41] Cited in Darwiche, *The Gulf Stock Exchange Crash*, p. 129.
[42] *Al-Qabas*, 13 October 1983.

the resolution. In 1984, the committee began moving on a series of KCCI proposals to strengthen the official market. Returning to chamber proposals from 1977, some closed-shareholding companies were allowed into a newly created parallel market and an entirely new circulation system was introduced. The committee also integrated some of the Manakh's more legitimate shares into the official market, so that by November 1984 the Souq al-Manakh could be closed.[43] The official stock market recorded some recovery and renewed trading, but overall Kuwait remained mired in a recession.

Stemming from meetings between KCCI leaders and the prime minister in April 1984, the government began considering macro policies to reactivate the economy and address creditors' problems. Using the KCCI's position on the Economic Reactivation Committee, al-Sagr sent select board members to make its case.[44] The committee allowed these KCCI representatives to work with state officials – in isolation from public or opposition pressure – to fashion a complete package of reforms. This (modified) example of Peter Evans's embedded autonomy[45] succeeded in crafting a number of measures which did not require approval by the Kuwaiti parliament: new protection for local industry; new priorities for awarding government contracts to local contractors; and a return to public purchasing of land. A key proposal that would have required parliamentary approval was for the state to take over non-performing bank debts by issuing bonds directly to the affected banks. This provision became the basis for future KCCI proposals to reform the financial sector. Politically astute enough not to underestimate the opposition, the chamber also publicly bowed to some of their ideas by espousing "draconian" measures for debtors who had concealed foreign assets from local creditors.[46] This approach served as much to quell opposition voices as to signal to recalcitrant debtors active in the KCCI to cooperate with KCCI proposals or else.

In May 1985, the prime minister presented the bank-bailout plan, but the opposition did not accede to it. In that same month, the unsuccessful assassination attempt on the emir aggravated government views of the opposition. The subsequent suspension of parliament in 1986 effectively cut short debate on the proposal, and paved the way for

---

[43] MEES, 5 November 1984; and Darwiche, The Gulf Stock Exchange Crash, pp. 130–139.

[44] Al-Qabas, 11 November 1985.

[45] Evans envisions embedded autonomy as involving state officials working first in isolation from business (and similar social groups), and later engaging business leaders. The Kuwaiti case, however, suggests a modified version, whereby business and state first engage in isolation from other social actors. This seems to be more often the case among the Arab countries.

[46] EIU, No. 5, 1985, p. 11.

extraparliamentary approval of the KCCI–government plan by the Council of Ministers in August.

Despite these policy initiatives, recovery lagged. Oil prices remained low and public debt increased. Despite all the debt legislation, significant amounts of unrecoverable debt remained on most banks' books. The government commissioned a long-term report by the Massachusetts Institute of Technology in 1988 to offer solutions. This report was followed by another extensive KCCI report in October 1989. In December 1989, KCCI and ministry officials once again met and drafted a joint plan, incorporating some of the MIT and KCCI recommendations, to establish new debt-alleviation measures and a national strategy for the 1990s.[47] A core element to resurface was the KCCI's idea of Central Bank support for domestic bank debts. Less than six months later, the Iraqi invasion ended any implementation plans. The economic and political repercussions of that event would hasten the need for deeper business–state coordination beyond merely debt resolution.

Expanding coordination: resolving the debts and pursuing economic reform

In economic terms, the price of Kuwait's liberation was quite high. Not only was the state forced to liquidate more of its assets, but many of the previous decade's legislative efforts were rendered null. Politically, many of the pre-war trends were strengthened. Despite the prominent role asil elites played in pushing for a return of parliament, KCCI representation there remained limited to Jassim al-Sagr. Islamist and tribal opposition to al-Sagr's bid for the post of speaker of the assembly promised little chance for rapprochement between business and the opposition. Still, the basic message from the KCCI remained consistent and convincing for many: Kuwait's economic troubles were the result of the monarchy's misguided policies formulated without the input of business. While once Kuwait and its fiscal system were the envy of the Gulf, the argument went, the UAE had now seized the mantle of the best place to do business in the Gulf.[48] Moreover, there was no recourse for the state. It had to rely on KCCI input to solve renewed debt problems and plan for economic privatization. Building on the lessons and successes of policy debates in the 1980s, business elites anchored in the KCCI broached more ambitious

---

[47] *MEED*, 15 and 28 December 1989, pp. 17–18.

[48] Part of the reason for Dubai's specific success was its free-trade zone, in place since the early 1980s. KCCI elites never tired of reminding state officials that they had pushed the same idea for Kuwait in the 1970s and had been ignored.

strategies. In the mid-1990s, the chamber attempted to undercut the power of its rivals by using its state access.

Kuwaiti banks emerged from the Iraqi occupation with KD 6,300 million in bad debt, some left over from the Manakh's collapse and the rest resulting from the invasion. Resolving chronic local bank debt was the first issue on the table. Returning to the chamber's original idea to exchange local bank debts for government bonds, the prime minister worked with KCCI representatives to fashion the legislation. Once the draft was passed to parliament, however, KCCI influence dropped precipitously. High-level business lobbying had proven easier since the 1980s, but opposition politics challenged the ability of organized business to limit amendments. An advisor to the executive board in the 1990s, Jamal Al-Din, expressed the perceived problems with parliament:

The majority in parliament do not understand economic issues. They are more interested in government employment and benefits. We have difficulty communicating with them to reach any compromise. We work closely with the government because they have people who understand the issues. The problem is with parliament since the government must turn around [after fashioning legislation] and deal and compromise with parliament.[49]

The first postwar step toward final debt resolution was Law 32 in 1992. KCCI elites and Central Bank officials devised a plan for local banks to exchange non-performing loans for government bonds. KCCI representatives and state officials worked closely to convince Finance Committee deputies of the necessity of the bailout. Opposition deputies were wary of a deal because they suspected it addressed the concerns only of the financial community. The Finance Committee proved less susceptible to KCCI facts and figures. Despite merchant beliefs to the contrary, opposition deputies had gained much experience in fiscal matters by serving on the committee throughout the 1980s. Although they caved in to the law, the opposition deputies still attempted to salvage some gain. In the same session, the committee also passed legislation requiring all companies with more than 25 percent public ownership to disclose their financial records regularly to parliament. It was a populist backlash against postwar revelations of public corruption and mismanagement. The strongest critic of the law was Jassim al-Sagr, who argued that the law would be a burden for those private companies with minority government shares.[50] This was one of the first overt instances of the presence of a *quid pro quo* between state officials and business leaders. Without the backing of

---

[49] Interview, Al-Din.   [50] *EIU*, No. 1, 1993.

the owners of the shareholding companies,[51] the law amounted to little more than a public relations victory. To follow up on the bank bailout, the KCCI waded into the debate over how those government debts should be repaid.

In addition to Central Bank proposals and Finance Committee suggestions, a small but influential group of debtors banded together to win more favorable repayment opinions. The group called itself the Economist Forum, and it targeted the KCCI leadership to push for near-absolution of the debts. The forum represented an organization of the internal debtors that had figured in the KCCI's delayed response in December 1982. Members of the Economist Forum claimed that the Iraqi invasion had impaired their ability to repay earlier debts.[52] Under the sponsorship of the KCCI and the Central Bank, a second piece of legislation was put forward. It outlined a final repayment scheme for all debtors, large and small, and proposed differential payment rates. Opposition deputies, still wary of a bailout only for the large debtors, resisted KCCI provisions and amended key parts of the draft to further reduce the burden of small debtors and raise that of the larger. The Central Bank was disappointed in the amendments to the KCCI's original proposal and the debtors' lobby was certainly not satisfied.[53] Therefore, even though the draft became Law 41 of 1993, repayment was slow and many debtors refused to provide financial data to the committee. The chamber feared that parliament's amendments had dissuaded the larger debtors from compromise, and that, even if payments went through, the economy would collapse under the weight of more liquidations. To some extent, the debtors' lobby had succeeded.

A final push to correct the problems of Law 41 took place throughout 1994 and 1995. The Finance Committee within the chamber drafted a lengthy report detailing Law 41's failings and its proposals for amendment.[54] In a speech before the chamber, the head of the Central Bank expressed support for the plan. Opposition deputies were infuriated that the government would attempt to subvert the law the parliament had previously approved. The fight was nasty and public. Opposition deputies had little support on their side. Debtors refused to go along with the previous scheme, and the state had not shown steady enforcement in the past. In the end, the KCCI proposal suffered the kind of amendment

---

[51] Many of the companies with small percentages of public ownership were controlled by KCCI elites; hence, they were tardy in reporting their data, or failed to report at all.

[52] Interview, 'Abdulaziz al-Sultan, President, Architects, Engineers, and Planners, Inc., Kuwait City, 5 March 1996.

[53] *EIU*, No. 2, 1993.

[54] KCCI, *Amendments to the Law Collecting Difficult Debts: Why and in Which Direction?*, notes submitted to the Finance Committee, 24 April 1995.

that had resulted in Law 41. Better repayment conditions were restored
for the large debtors. They were allowed five annual payments instead
of the previous September 1995 deadline for full repayment. Additionally, there would be no interest added for the period since 1990. The
sole opposition victory was the refusal to extend Law 41's ten-year repayment schedule to twenty years, as in the KCCI proposal. On the key
aspects, premium stripping and government support, the amendments
amounted to a KCCI victory.[55] The Economist Forum, however, continued to press for more lenient terms, but for the KCCI leadership the
end to the Manakh saga had been reached. In early 1996, 150 members of the debtors' lobby filed a suit challenging the legality of the bad
debts law. Their challenge went unsupported by the chamber.[56] Of more
importance to organized business representatives was reform of the wider
economy.

As a result of business elites' work in resolving the Manakh debt
situation, they gained leverage elsewhere. After liberation, the KCCI's
influence on the reform of Kuwait's economic policies was dominant. A
visit by an IMF team to assess the economy and provide recommendations echoed the chamber's own guidance. In 1994 and 1995, the KCCI
presented several documents to parliament and the government, outlin-
ing cuts in government spending, civil service reform, and privatization.
Some were enacted with little resistance, such as the KCCI's long-desired
free-trade zone. The chamber's hopes for privatization, on the other
hand, ran counter to opposition interests. Eventually, a government plan
responded to KCCI suggestions, calling for selling government-owned
enterprises such as the telecommunications ministry, the national airlines, and the tanker company. Opposition deputies complained about
the potential loss of jobs once such big entities became private. One of
the first to speak out against privatization was Islamic deputy Nasir al-
Sane, who attacked plans to sell off public utilities. Eventually parliament
demanded that no state-owned firm be privatized without its approval.[57]

State officials avoided the issue entirely by forging ahead with the
liquidation of public assets in the shareholding companies. The result
was a rather decentralized process whereby merchant elites moved in
to buy government shares in a variety of sectors. Curiously, the KCCI
appeared institutionally severed from the process. The Kuwait Investment
Authority (KIA), a state agency, entered negotiations with prospective buyers, haggled about price and share numbers, and then sold the
government shares. Profitable ventures such as the National Industries
Corporation, the United Real Estate Company, and the Holiday Inn were

[55] Ibid., pp. 9–12.   [56] EIU, No. 4, 1996.
[57] MECS, vol. XVIII, 1994 (New York: Holmes & Meier, 1996), p. 455.

purged of public interest in this collaborative way. In most cases, the state was liquidating shares purchased as a result of the stock market crashes. By 1996 all shares in companies with less than 10 percent public ownership were liquidated. By 2000, these sales had netted nearly $3 billion.

Bureaucratically excluded from the process, the KCCI appeared to resist the decentralized approach. Jassem al-Sagr, for example, attacked the government's privatization programs in parliament. He argued that the *ad hoc* nature of sales was creating monopolies that would damage the economy.[58] Behind the scenes, however, many of those buying government shares were tied to the KCCI leadership. Moreover, the KCCI's own policy statements on privatization did not differ significantly from the state's actions. Both sides agreed that first public shareholding funds should be sold. Selling public utilities or even privatizing ministries, while advocated by the chamber, was not a priority for either side.[59] Consequently, there was the strong impression that KCCI complaints were not serious and that the decentralized process fit their interests well.[60] In return, state officials could extract promises of limited job layoffs or even political support elsewhere. The appearance of a collusive tradeoff was strong.

Two specific examples of this were the sale of the National Industries Company and the United Real Estate Company. In each case, KIA authorities participated in closed-door meetings with prominent KCCI elites (al-Khourafi and al-Sultan, respectively). The state agreed to sell its majority share to each group, and in turn both new owners released minority shares on the stock market for public sale. It was probable that the negotiations involved commitments for continued employment.[61] Consequently, opposition fears notwithstanding, there was no real threat of unemployment from Kuwait's first phase of privatization. This process provided compelling evidence that successful policy advocacy and participation could overflow into collusion.

Consolidating business's position: external and internal challenges in the 1990s and 2000

The late 1990s and 2000 witnessed the full fruition of a business class to rival the KCCI; at the same time, new, well-organized opposition began

[58] *EIU*, No. 3, 1995.
[59] Kuwait, National Assembly, *Ijabat al-Ghurfa ila al-Lajna al-Maaliyya hawl al-Khaskhasa* [Responses of the chamber to the Finance Committee (of parliament) concerning privatization], 1995.
[60] Interview, Sadoun.
[61] Interviews, Sadoun and Khaled al-Sanna, President, Industrial Union, Kuwait City, 3 March 1995.

to challenge the KCCI in the political arena as well. Thus, challenges to the political position KCCI elites had achieved came in two forms: intra-business rivalries and Islamist opposition challenges. A notable difference between the Kuwaiti and Jordanian cases was the early founding of an industrial chamber in Jordan. No such rival appeared in Kuwait until the 1990s. When private business did invest in industry, it was usually KCCI elites who "chose to put on the industrial hat." So, the al-Sagrs managed the Pepsi agency and bottling company as well as operating the Gulf Cable Company, a manufacturer of underground cables. The small segment of industrialists not tied to the KCCI elite went unrepresented, but in 1989 that changed. A small group of these industrialists first approached the Ministry of Commerce and Industry to create a Chamber of Industry. This was blocked by the KCCI. The group then turned to the Ministry of Social Affairs, which granted them the status of an industrial union. Like other subsectoral and professional associations, a union (of employers or employees) has no legal relationship to the chamber, but neither does it have the latter's institutional advantages and capabilities.[62] With about 180 members in 1995, the Industrial Union struggled with the chamber for representation. KCCI leaders gave Khaled al-Sanna, president of the union, a seat on the chamber's Industrial Committee. In addition, the KCCI nominated him to sit as a private-sector representative on the Industrial Committee within the Ministry of Commerce and Industry.[63] Despite al-Sanna's attempts to secure the union its own seat at the ministry, the union continued to be dependent on grants of access from the chamber. Marginalization of the Industrial Union was a fair depiction of the relationship between the KCCI and most subsectoral employer associations.

Cooptation instead of competition has been the norm. Presidents of the unions frequently ran for the KCCI board because it promised better access for their union. 'Abdullah Beaijan, president of the foodstuffs union, ran for the board in 1992 because "we were having problems with the government, so taking a position on the KCCI [board] afforded us better lobbying leverage with the municipality and ministries."[64] Perhaps most symbolic of the KCCI's dominant position was its new headquarters, completed in 1997. The building contained more space not only for the KCCI's expanded staff but a "businessmen's club" and extra office space for unions wishing to relocate. Competition for that space was reported to be keen.[65]

By far the most significant threat to KCCI elites, however, has come from within its own ranks. In 1992, elections were held for all twenty-four

[62] There were some twenty approved unions in 1995.   [63] Interview, al-Sanna.
[64] Interview, 'Abdullah M. S. Beaijan, Kuwait City, 26 March 1996.
[65] Various interviews.

seats of the executive board.[66] This was to be the most important and most publicized election in its history. Lead-up to the election was highly politically charged. Al-Sagr emerged from the Iraqi invasion with even more stature than he had had previously. Having remained in Kuwait during occupation and adopted a high-profile role within the pro-democracy movement, al-Sagr commanded a great deal of respect from all Kuwaitis. He was also an elderly man and this election would be his last. The executive board set elections right before the first post-invasion parliamentary elections, and hence the chamber elections became an important precursor to the latter. Given that the business community would obviously play a crucial role in the rebuilding of Kuwait, whoever controlled it would be in a powerful position. The challenger was Khaled al-Marzouq.

Al-Marzouq hailed from an asil family of colorful origins. His ancestor, Yousef al-Marzouq, had been active in the Majlis movement, had been jailed in India for smuggling, and according to legend had won a bride courted by an al-Sabah "by preparing her tea over a fire of 10-rupee notes."[67] Khaled al-Marzouq had inherited his ancestor's flair. Al-Marzouq headed an impressive array of trading and construction companies, including the extremely profitable Kuwait Real Estate Company. His family owned a leading daily newspaper, *Al-Anbaa*, and was considered to be politically close to the ruling family. A charismatic and gifted speaker, al-Marzouq portrayed himself as a maverick, and he had the resources and stature to seriously challenge al-Sagr. Organizing a list of twenty-four candidates to face al-Sagr had never been done, and it was a serious challenge. Al-Marzouq called his list *Ahl al-Dera*, which is a Kuwaiti dialect term meaning "our home" or "the family home." It was meant to convey a more inclusive leadership role, one not limited to the asil. Of al-Marzouq's twenty-four candidates, eight were Shia and five were bedouin. No Shia or bedouin had ever sat on the executive board.

Al-Anbaa and *Al-Qabas* each gave a great amount of partisan coverage to the election campaign. In speeches and debates, al-Marzouq sought to make the race symbolically one of all merchants versus the politically obsessed few. He argued that his list "provide[d] opportunities to all qualified Kuwaitis and support[ed] them with no favoritism." He promised to "correct the path of the chamber" and steer it away from "political involvement" toward the service of all its members.[68] A stinging editorial in *Al-Anbaa* hammered at the theme of a politicized, elite chamber:

---

[66] Since there were no elections during occupation, all twenty-four seats were up for election instead of the usual twelve every two years.

[67] Recounted by Crystal, *Oil and Politics*, p. 208.   [68] *Al-Qabas*, 15 May 1992.

Politics entered the chamber and overshadowed the general interest of the members. It kept those who would work for the benefit of all members from reaching any post . . . we wonder if the current chairman ever put the members' interests before his own.

The *Ahl al-Dera* platform made explicit the call to inclusiveness. Among a list of its policies were:

maintaining equality in rights between small and large members by adopting their problems and protecting the interests of all members . . . [and] returning and backing the manufacturers, handicraftsmen, and farmers to their rightful position in the chamber.[69]

The general theme was to blame the politicization of the KCCI for the decline of Kuwait's economy. Khaled al-Marzouq contrasted this with the rise of the merchant community in the UAE and that country's status as the new business center in the Gulf. Despite Marzouq's *asil* status, this was a contest pitting the various new sectors of merchants against the traditional elites. Al-Sagr's own list was uninspiringly called "the economic family." The cream of Kuwait's merchant community, including the head of the NBK, Muhammed 'Abdulmohsen al-Khourafi, rallied to al-Sagr's side. This group cleverly pushed the idea that al-Marzouq was a government-supported candidate sent to rob Kuwait's opposition of one of its traditionally independent institutions.[70] More crudely, some accused al-Marzouq of being the ruling family's revenge for al-Sagr's pro-democracy role over the last decade. The message appeared to work. A heavy voter response returned twenty-three of al-Sagr's candidates to the board.[71] The win was so large and sensitive for the government that a Reuters correspondent who reported that al-Marzouq was the state's candidate was expelled. However, reasons for the failed challenge went deeper than the pro-government charge.

In one respect, al-Marzouq clearly hoped the inclusion of Shia and bedouin candidates and an appeal to the more numerous small merchant members would give him the edge. It was long suspected that before an election, board members would simply pay up dues for smaller merchants (usually those retailers that sold their goods) to increase the votes of their subsidiaries and establishment memberships (see table A.3 in

---

[69] Advertisement in *Al-Qabas*, 17 May 1992.

[70] For the Muslim Brotherhood, this was a convincing argument. According to their spokesman, 'Isa al-Shahin (interview), they encouraged their merchant members to vote for al-Sagr.

[71] Marzouq won his seat, but then in a long-drawn-out series of published letters tendered his resignation.

appendix).[72] Al-Marzouq and his *asil* supporters could certainly do the same, but the addition of the smaller non-affiliated vote could make the difference. Al-Marzouq failed to win this group because they were not in a position to vote. Many smaller merchants were those civil employees illegally operating private businesses. They cared little about KCCI politics since there was no threat to their livelihood. Moreover, registering and voting in such a high-profile election invited unwanted publicity. Intra-merchant ties limited the appeal al-Marzouq's candidacy could generate. In a second respect, al-Marzouq lost because al-Sagr appeared to beat him at his own game.

Al-Sagr responded to the diversity of the al-Marzouq list by breaking KCCI tradition. Of his twenty-four, al-Sagr recruited seven new, mostly young candidates, including three Shi'a, one Bedouin former parliamentarian, two with strong Brotherhood sympathies, and one young, successful entrepreneur (see table A.1, appendix). It was a far smarter list, since private business in Kuwait was no longer the sole domain of the traditional merchant elite. He selectively incorporated only the cream of the new class. Take two examples. The young 'Abdulwahab al-Wazzan headed the largest Shia family business and was close to the royal family. Even though the election supposedly pitted a pro-government candidate against the opposition, KCCI elites felt secure enough to allow a candidate with business ties to the ruling family on their own list. A second new candidate was Jamil al-Essa, who headed a string of private grocery stores. He was one of the more dynamic and younger entrepreneurs in Kuwait without any strong ascriptive or *asil* ties. Al-Sagr had not so much diluted *asil* dominance as expanded *asil* ranks. In this way, the election of 1992 confirmed the institutional strength of Kuwait's business representation and the continued autonomy and cohesion of its leadership.

Leadership cohesion at the KCCI and its varied institutional capabilities also had an impact on business's broader political struggles with Kuwait's Islamists and the position of the Kuwaiti state. By the 1980s, the Islamists had taken over the elite merchants' mantle as "the opposition." Even regionally, Kuwait's Islamists had taken over a role that was once the domain of the merchants. Whereas al-Sagr and other *asil* merchants were among the first Arabs to organize relief supplies for Palestinians in the 1930s, Kuwait's Brotherhood and *salafi* associations were the new players

---

[72] It will be remembered that each company registered, branch and subsidiary, receives a vote. Hence, large merchants with several registered companies and licenses enjoyed multiple votes.

in regional Arab politics in the 1990s.[73] Moreover, the Islamist leadership was professional and well received in *asil* society; they were not outsiders. Consequently, the relationship between business and political Islam is hardly black and white. One can find evidence of some KCCI board members sympathetic to the Islamist movement, while some Islamist businessmen supported privatization. Neither desired open conflict with the other; KCCI leaders did not wish to be viewed as anti-Islamic; and Islamist leaders did not want to alienate the private sector.[74] Still, clashes between the two camps have been persistent and multifaceted aspects of Kuwait's politics in the new century.

In the 1990s, an integrated political and economic network of Islamist organizations had taken shape. In addition to non-profit social institutions (e.g., the Sanabil Project), the Kuwait Finance House (KFH) had come to occupy a position of fiscal prominence.[75] Like the merchant-controlled NBK, the KFH weathered the debt problems of the 1980s with few liabilities. Unlike the NBK, however, the Islamic bank remained exempt from most Central Bank regulations. Its unique mandate allowed it to offer everything from consumer loans to investment banking. The fiscal resources of the KFH combined with the growing market importance of the cooperatives worried KCCI leaders.

Politically, the cooperatives had become extremely important in postwar Kuwait. Cooperative elections were excellent bellwethers for the way a district would vote in parliamentary elections. People who won a cooperative seat could then redirect an estimated 20 percent[76] of their local cooperative's profits back into the district in ways that would strengthen the leadership's political support. *Salafi* and Muslim Brotherhood candidates controlled the majority of these cooperatives and built secure, independent electoral and funding bases. Economically, the cooperatives held sway over a significant slice of Kuwait's consumer market. Operating with virtually no overhead, cooperatives accounted for roughly 80 percent of foodstuff sales, representing a KD 300 million market annually.[77] Angered by this market control and purchasing power, merchants complained of corruption. There were claims that cooperatives paid for goods with postdated checks and demanded kickbacks to

---

[73] Kuwaiti Islamist groups were reported to be some of the main benefactors of Hamas. Arafat's occasional complaints of foreign meddling in Palestinian affairs were aimed as much at these Kuwaiti groups as at Iran.

[74] This is also a reason why representatives from each side were reluctant to discuss the issue.

[75] See Kristin Smith, "Culture and Capital."   [76] Interview, Beaijan.

[77] Interview, 'Abdulwahab al-Wazzan, board member, KCCI, Kuwait City, 20 December 1995.

showcase commodities in certain areas of their stores.[78] In 1994, state and select private citizens quietly came together to discuss their respective concerns.

A special committee was formed with the Ministry of Social Affairs to review possible reforms to the Cooperatives Law.[79] The state naturally wished to weaken the cooperatives as a basis for Islamist electoral strength. Merchants wished to break their market control. The ministry assigned new KCCI board member 'Abdulwahab al-Wazzan to the committee. Though this ruse was quite transparent, al-Wazzan sat as a "private individual," not as a KCCI representative. His presence guaranteed KCCI support. The eventual report was confidential, but observers confirmed that the suggested reforms increased state control of the cooperative boards and established more fiscal oversight of cooperative activities.[80] The issue awaited future parliamentary debate. However, it was clear that a new direction in business–state relations had been launched beyond policy coordination and advocacy, and toward the type of political and economic collusion which Olson hypothesized should materialize initially.

In the mid-1990s, KCCI representatives and state officials coordinated strategies to limit the financial and political power of the Islamist opposition. First, reports surfaced suggesting that reform of the cooperatives would entail increased state control of the cooperative boards and more fiscal oversight. Then, in 1998 the government presented legislation to parliament designed to bring the Kuwaiti Finance House under the control of the Central Bank. That legislation would have restricted the KFH from involvement in trading, contracting, manufacturing, and retail sales,[81] all sectors in which the business community had long complained about unfair Islamist advantages. These efforts addressed longstanding private-sector concerns about the "unfettered" practices of Islamic banking. These coordinated policies were followed by the appointment of KCCI board member al-Wazzan to head the Ministry of Commerce and Industry. This was the second direct appointment of a KCCI official to head the ministry in the 1990s. Despite the fact that al-Wazzan had been a vocal critic of government economic policies, his appointment confirmed the continuation of business–state coordination that had been forged in the 1980s. Throughout the spring of 1999, the emir released a string of decrees, requiring future parliamentary approval, among them the

---

[78] Merchants noted that cooperatives – resembling strip malls – sat on public land and operated with healthy state subsidies. The cooperative board then rented out extra space at premium prices.

[79] Law No. 24, 1979, Ministry of Social Affairs and Labor.

[80] Interviews, al-Wazzan and al-Shahin.   [81] *MEED*, 9 October 1998.

now-famous extension of suffrage to women (scheduled to take effect in 2003 but since abandoned). Collectively, these decrees advanced issues that the liberal business elite was expected to exploit in the upcoming elections.[82] Those elections in July 1999 marked a reversal of two decades of Islamist political advancement. A new group combining business and nationalist interests, the National Democratic Grouping (NDG), won sixteen of fifty seats, while the Islamist groups accounted for roughly fifteen seats. In debates over the next speaker of the parliament, Islamist deputies were again defeated, as government and NDG deputies combined to elect Kuwait's richest businessman, Jassem al-Khourafi.[83] Not since 1961, when KCCI president 'Abdulaziz al-Sagr was the first elected speaker, had an *asil* businessman held the post. This was the fruition of a new coalition: a parliament comprising a government/business majority and built upon a foundation of intense institutional coordination across a spectrum of policy areas. Organized business used the state to contain an economic rival, and the state used business to limit political opposition.

Adjustment in Jordan

The intertwined nature of Kuwait's and Jordan's political-economic histories could not have been demonstrated more clearly than in the 1980s and 1990s. Just as Kuwait's economy was beset with external and internal difficulties, so was Jordan's. Amman's immediate fiscal problems stemmed foremost from a decline in foreign aid and remittances. Reduced economic growth and increased public debt followed. These trends fed on one another, making reform attempts as unworkable as they were in Kuwait. Politically, the monarchy responded by reconvening parliament and legalizing political parties. In the mid-1980s, economic measures were taken to encourage more private-sector investment. Business participation in these first steps was superficial. Renewed attempts at economic and political reform in the 1990s offered opportunities to recast business–state relations. By this time, however, elite exodus from the Amman Chamber of Commerce, the degradation of institutional capabilities, and the presence of strong rivals had limited business's engagement with political authority to making particularist demands. This inability to fashion institutionalized coordination adversely affected Jordan's economic reform efforts in the 1990s and 2000. Moreover, in place of institutionalized coordination, an informal *ad hoc* network of business elites

---

[82] The conventional wisdom is that allowing women to vote would increase votes for liberal and merchant candidates at the expense of Islamist and Bedouin candidates.

[83] *Middle East International*, 20 August 1999; and *EIU*, No. 3, 1999.

and state officials came to define business–state relations under King Hussein's successor, King 'Abdullah.

In contrast to the Kuwaiti case, these outcomes at first glance seem to support structural accounts of crisis in a highly dependent country. However, evidence from business–state relations in this period backs up a different assessment. First, the absence of effective policy responses to Jordan's economic crises did not result from policy deadlock or coordinated private-sector resistance, as the Karl/Shafer arguments would suggest. Instead, the institutional weakness of organized business impaired effective policy coordination. Peter Evans's ideal version of embedded autonomy is turned on its head as state actors found no administratively capable organization representing business with which to engage. Second, the encompassing ACC did fulfill at least some of Olson's expectations insofar as this large and unwieldy association proved inept at policy advocacy. Paradoxically, despite its broad base, ACC policy positions on major economic issues in the 1990s reflected not the wider interests of its rank and file, but the particular interests of its more narrow leadership.

Fiscal crises and state vulnerability in the 1980s

The year 1982 was bad for all Arab countries. The sudden drop in oil prices meant Gulf states that gave money were squeezed, and those such as Jordan that received money felt the pain. Of the seven Arab states that had promised annual subsidies to Jordan at the 1978 Baghdad Summit, only Saudi Arabia was able to sustain its level of aid. In 1980, aid comprised 40 percent of Jordan's state revenue; by 1984 it had declined to 16 percent (see table 1.2, p. 16). The stupendous annual 10 percent GDP growth of the 1970s had been cut in half by 1982. By the late 1980s, per capita GDP actually declined. Jordan responded, as did Kuwait, by deficit borrowing. The Central Bank drew on its foreign currency reserves to finance the loans, and by February 1985 reserves had dipped to their lowest level since 1973. World Bank figures revealed that Jordan's debt-service ratio had gone from 9.9 percent in 1985 to nearly 15 percent in 1987.[84] There was little exaggeration when the head of the Central Bank, Mohammed al-Said Nabulsi, described Jordan's economic situation "as the worse [sic] since the years immediately after the 1973 war."[85]

Under such fiscal strain, Jordan's currency, the dinar, did not escape harm. The spark was Jordan's disengagement from the West Bank. Intended as a political act, the disengagement carried severe economic

---

[84] *Financial Times*, 27 August 1987.   [85] *Jordan Times*, 19 January 1985.

repercussions.[86] Palestinians in the West Bank, worried about their future relations with the Hashemite state, reacted to the disengagement announcement by withdrawing an estimated $200 to $300 million from Jordanian banks.[87] Cashing in dinars for dollars combined with already low foreign currency reserves meant the Central Bank could do little to stop a run on the dinar. By November 1988 the dinar had lost two-thirds of its value against the dollar in only a few months.[88] By 1989 it was painfully clear to state elites that no quick solution to Jordan's debt problems was on the horizon. Unable to meet its mounting debt payments, Jordan concluded its first adjustment loan with the IMF. This first agreement, running from 1989 to 1993, contained many of the aspects common to IMF-sponsored adjustment programs: reduction in budget deficits, reform of the tax system, and pursuit of a tight credit system.[89] By the late 1980s, it appeared that the Jordanian state had taken decisive steps to address the economic situation. The problem was that much of this was done without private-sector participation.

"A head without a body": business representation in Jordan

Jordan's turn for the worse economically created new openings for the private sector, led by the Amman Chamber of Commerce. To understand what became of these opportunities and why, one must first review the situation of organized business itself.

While the 1970s were disastrous politically for the ACC, the association began the 1980s still a significant institution. Its membership in Amman alone topped 10,000. Its control of the Federation of Jordanian Chambers, comprising twelve local chambers, meant that it effectively represented about 70,000 members nationwide. This made it by far the largest independent institution in Jordan.[90] In 1982, the elderly and respected Muhammed 'Ali Bdair retired. Because he had led the chamber for twenty years, Bdair's retirement represented a generational changing of the guard. Distortions from the 1961 organizational changes and the maturation of new business groupings could be seen in subsequent electoral politics and elite cohesion.

---

[86] The disengagement and its aftermath provide a good example of how little interest King Hussein had in economic issues.

[87] *MECS*, vol. XII, *1988* (New York: Holmes & Meier, 1990), p. 604.

[88] *New York Times*, 7 November 1988.   [89] *EIU*, No. 3, 1989, p. 11.

[90] Compare this to the eleven professional associations in Jordan (speaking for lawyers, engineers, and so on), which, taken together, by the 1990s represented only about 50,000 members: Schirin H. Fathi, *Jordan: An Invented Nation?* (Hamburg: Deutsches Orient-Institut, 1994), p. 191.

The list headed by Hamdi Tabba, son of Subri Tabba, ACC president in the 1950s, won eleven of twelve seats in the 1982 elections. This new board consisted of six new members, one of whom was the first category 3 member to sit on the executive board. Tabba admitted that his selection of running mates depended foremost on "origin and religion to achieve a balance," at the expense of lobbying skill, business acumen, or sectoral representation. The tradeoff for gaining the voting power of the lower categories was that the new board lacked representation from the industrial, transport, or financial sectors. Three dynamics became evident.

First, observers noted that the board members Tabba brought with him were not representative of the business elite in Jordan. Aside from a few notables (Touqan and Qawar), the candidates were chosen to attract the lower-category votes.[91] The leadership transition from Bdair was more a break than a cohesive transfer. Many of the lower-category voters identified with faces and names they knew, and often these were businessmen (no doubt successful) who had only recently relocated from Hebron or Nablus. These were not individuals with close ties to the monarchy or state officials. On a board with twenty-four members, as in Kuwait, a handful with low profiles could be compensated for elsewhere, but on a board of twelve there was less room to accommodate this. Second, the unevenness of the board's talents meant that engagement with political authority was almost exclusively carried out by the president and the vice-president. Contrast this with the Kuwaiti debt debates, when al-Sagr was able to ask younger, more energetic board members to lobby on behalf of the association. Third, as elite cohesion decayed, other board members began to approach government ministries for their own (or a friend's) particularist interests. Tendencies toward individual lobbying had always been present but were generally kept in check when there were clashes with wider chamber interests. In the 1980s and 1990s, such particularist lobbying became routine. Still, Tabba himself was one of the country's leading businessmen and was able to undertake positive, albeit short-lived, reforms of the association.

A close friend of the monarchy, Tabba was the first ACC president to accompany King Hussein (who died in early 1999) on a foreign visit. Tabba also launched an important structural change, the formation of the ACC's Research and Studies Department in 1985. He initiated discussions among board members to change associational by-laws either to eliminate fourth category nomination/voting or to designate board seats by sector, measures designed to bring back greater elite control and representation. Despite Tabba's belief that the change would have government support, the idea failed to gain a consensus among board members. On

[91] Various interviews.

the one hand, the newer, low-profile board members stood to lose their associational access for personal lobbying under such a system. On the other, board members feared that, if the attempt to change the by-law failed, lower-category members would exact electoral revenge.[92] Tabba did not return for a second term, so these reforms were short-lived.

In 1986, Muhammed 'Asfour (grandson of the first ACC president) was elected to the ACC presidency. As in the 1982 race, the elections returned less than half of the sitting board members who ran, meaning there was little continuity from the previous board. Of the new members, two came from the third category. Like Tabba, 'Asfour admitted that, in choosing his candidates, "I selected individuals with business experience and community popularity, not education or lobbying skills." While some leading elites ran with 'Asfour (see table A.4 in appendix), others that had run with Tabba (Touqan and Qawar) simply chose not to return. In their place, new faces appeared, including a successful outsider, Haider Murad. With this new board, top positions within the chamber (vice-president, heads of internal committees, and so on) were completely replaced. The permanent staff had to adjust to new personalities, new techniques, and new expectations. By 'Asfour's second run for the presidency in 1992, it was clear there was an imbalance between the status and prestige of the president and the rest of the board.

Half of the previous board returned, with Haider Murad moving into the vice-presidency, by virtue of having won the second-highest number of votes. This board clearly expressed the weight of the lower categories and the reliance on candidates who could deliver that vote. The difficulty of managing the two-level game, balancing attraction of voters with the maintenance of elite cohesion, meant that the elections were yielding an executive board with no returning members after every election, even under the same presidency. A byproduct of this change was the hampering of institutional development. Not until 1990 was 'Asfour able to augment the vital Research and Studies Department. Until that point, it was staffed by only three permanent professionals and lacked basic resources, such as a computerized database. The monthly chamber magazine, *Al-Iqtisad al-Urdani*, rarely came out every month and by the late 1980s had become basically a bi-annual magazine with little content. What exact function the department served was unclear, since the chamber often hired outside consultants to aid its preparation of policy documents. Asfour sought to change this by bringing in Ministry of Finance employees to head the department and upgrade it. As was the case with Hamdi Tabba, 'Asfour would not remain in office long enough to follow through on the changes. In 1994, the ACC saw its most important and most heated election.

[92] Interviews, Tabba and 'Asfour.

Quite similar to the 1992 KCCI elections, the 1994 contest in Amman pitted a traditional merchant elite, 'Asfour, against a new presidential challenger, Haider Murad. The chamber elections came shortly before parliamentary elections, generating the type of publicity that had occurred in Kuwait. Also as in Kuwait, the election was less about contrasting economic visions and more about the character, leadership, and control of the chamber. Murad was the first presidential candidate not to hail from a pre-1948 Palestinian or Syrian merchant family. He was in every way a man of the small and middle merchants. According to one former ACC official:

While he served under 'Asfour, Murad spent more time in the chamber with the members. He had a good touch with small merchants; he identified with them, spoke their language, and appeared more humble in their eyes. As for 'Asfour, the small merchants did not respond to his personality or his stature [as an elite merchant] and this limited his support base.[93]

A successful businessman, Murad was nevertheless viewed by the merchant elite as an outsider. Indeed, one supporter admitted "because Murad was the first of the newer Palestinians, he made a bad impression on some by going overboard to portray himself as representing all merchants."[94] As in Kuwait, one theme emphasized a candidate for all versus a candidate for the elite few. Consequently, the election was heated, with a great deal of press coverage and accusations of voter fraud.[95] In a contest between elite merchants and the middle rung, the results were predictable. The top three member categories comprised only 8.9 percent of the electorate, whereas the fourth category alone accounted for over 50 percent (see table A.5 in appendix). Murad won by a large margin, securing ten seats. It was a watershed event for the business community and a historical change for Jordan's oldest social institution.[96] 'Asfour's loss was clearly an embarrassment. More importantly, it was a warning to other elites that challenging for a seat on the chamber's board risked public humiliation. With the new board, Murad replaced staff allied with 'Asfour. Any promise of structural reform or increased institutional capabilities would have to await the new administration.

As will become evident in the next section, a lack of leadership continuity shaped the (in)ability of business and state to coordinate during economic crisis. For instance, government ministers often complained of

---

[93] Interview, Muhammed Muhtasib, ACC board member, Amman, 6 December 1996.
[94] Interview, Muhtasib.   [95] *Al-Rai'*, 26 November 1994.
[96] More broadly, this victory was symbolic of the social maturation of the great numbers of Palestinians who came to Jordan as refugees after 1948. The Shi'a, the Bedouin, and the younger merchants in Kuwait came into their own by the 1990s as well. The difference was that incorporation of the new merchants in Kuwait took place smoothly, with the traditional elites sharing control.

changes in ACC proposals and style with each new leadership. Lessons learned or compromises reached with one board might be abandoned by the next. Competing in chamber elections became a winner-take-all affair with the winning list completely replacing staff management positions with their allies. The lack of an entrenched leadership encouraged some board members to lobby independently for their own interests. Since these members were on the board because of the number of votes they could garner, disciplining them carried high costs at election time. Businessmen outside the chamber commonly referred to ACC personnel as "bureaucrats" (the pejorative term *mas'oul* was used). Going to the chamber was likened to visiting a government ministry. Institutional representation was sacrificed, damaging state views of the ACC as a representative of the private sector, especially during periods of acute economic crisis.[97] A leading industrialist, Bassem Saket, aptly summed up what the chamber of the 1990s had become: "a head with no body."

The weakening in the 1980s and 1990s of elite cohesion in the ACC and its declining political and social status created opportunities for associative rivals. Defecting elites gravitated to the Chamber of Industry for intra-associational characteristics that were precisely the opposite of the ACC's – a restricted membership scope (7,000 in 1994) and exclusionary voting rules. Structurally, the ACI was more developed. It moved far more quickly and effectively in forming subcommittees to cover diverse sectoral interests and provide policy input. Its Research and Studies Division had more resources and staff than the ACC's department.[98] Consequently, though the ACI represented far fewer members of the business community in Jordan, it received far more press coverage. Its influential president of the 1990s, Khaldoun Abu Hassan,[99] outpaced ACC presidents in press conferences, press releases, and policy statements in the early 1990s. The ACI was viewed as more professional, less particularist, and more authoritative than the ACC, and the attitude of state officials reflected this.[100] In addition to the ACI with its gains, another rival to the ACC appeared.

---

[97] There was near-universal agreement on these views of the chamber from heads of various ministries under different prime ministers throughout the 1980s and 1990s. In interviews conducted for this study, such views were stated most clearly by: Dr. H. Khatib, former minister of energy and planning; Zaid Fariz, former minister of planning and industry; and Sami Ghammo, former minister of finance.

[98] Interview, Ahmed M. al-Sa'adi, Director, Research and Studies Division, ACI, Amman, 27 July 1995. A simple review of the ACI's publications tells the story. They produce far more useful documents of economic data, reprints and translations of economic laws, and member surveys.

[99] The Abu Hassans are an East Bank merchant family with a long history. They were one of the principal beneficiaries of Jordan's industrial policies in the 1960s and 1970s. Khaldoun's older brother and father served on the ACC's board in the 1960s and 1970s.

[100] Since unsuccessfully trying to bring the ACI and ACC together in the 1970s, the crown prince came to favor the ACI over the ACC.

In 1985, a group of prominent businessmen formed the Jordan Businessmen's Association (JBA). The initial purpose of the JBA was to coordinate with a similar association in Egypt as part of Jordan's rapprochement with Cairo. Quickly, however, elites realized the domestic usefulness of the new organization. The JBA's stated mandate was almost identical to that of the ACC's but the JBA stood apart as a non-profit, private association. Membership stipulations were highly select: capital requirements, a seat on the board of a shareholding company, and nomination by two members.[101] Drawing members and large investors from most major economic sectors, the JBA could portray itself as a private club for the business elite.[102] Moreover, many businessmen who served in the government came to join the JBA rather than the ACC after public service. With its superior flexibility and profile, the JBA has come to dominate representation of the private sector in the eyes of the government.[103]

The first reform opportunities in the 1980s

The Jordanian governments of the early 1980s under Ahmed 'Obeidat and Mudar Badran responded to the decline in state revenue by maintaining the level of government spending while escalating external borrowing. From 1982 to 1984, government spending increased by nearly 4 percent while foreign aid declined by 47 percent.[104] Obeidat enacted several conflicting policies meant to curb consumption but still boost business confidence, including stricter licensing requirements for private companies; increased subsidies for mixed companies; greater limitations on imports through an expansion of the Ministry of Supply's purview; and a new decree requiring all foreign banks to become at least 51 percent Jordanian-owned.[105] Virtually none of these measures involved prior business or ACC consultation. Consequently, business protests followed. The country's largest bank, the Arab Bank, in its 1984 annual report called the law on foreign bank ownership "inopportune" and "not consistent with the interests of a country such as Jordan which has chosen to be open to the outside world."[106] In the few meetings that did result, ACC representatives complained to the prime minister that continued

---

[101] Jordanian Businessmen's Association, *By-Laws*, 1985.
[102] In 1993, for instance, Hamdi Tabba was elected president of the JBA. Other defectors from the ACC included elite business names such as 'Asfour, Taher, Bdair, Bilbeis, Saket, al-'Azzeh, al-Salfiti, and Abu Hassan.
[103] Equally important, foreign businessmen wishing to invest in Jordan are more apt to contact the JBA before either the ACC or the ACI.
[104] Central Bank of Jordan, *Yearly Statistical Series*.
[105] *EIU*, No. 2, 1985, p. 17.   [106] *Ibid*.

government expansion in a time of declining rents was counterproductive. In a response to business representatives that would become quite common, Prime Minister 'Obeidat was unmoved by the protests:

> To be honest, in spite of their presence we did not feel they carried out their role; they acted as individuals rather than as representatives of the business community . . . Therefore I personally did not respect their interests; there was [on their part] no devotion to public interests.[107]

In April 1985, after just over a year in office, the government of Prime Minister Ahmed 'Obeidat resigned, ostensibly due to continued poor economic performance. A growing government concern was unemployment, which was estimated at between 10 and 20 percent depending on the source.[108] To set a new pace with a new prime minister, King Hussein appointed a close friend, Zaid al-Rifa'i, generally viewed to be supportive of private business and of the need for economic liberalization. The change was accompanied by official pronouncements that the new al-Rifa'i government was to chart a pro-business course. In his instruction speech to the new government, King Hussein – not known for an interest in economic affairs – asked for "steps toward reviving and reinvigorating the economic process in Jordan" and called for "programs geared towards stimulating the private sector."[109] Once in office, al-Rifa'i moved forward on a series of institutional and policy reforms.

The banking law was repealed, restrictions on private business hours were lifted, and new tax exemptions for export industries were enacted. Al-Rifa'i also introduced Jordan's first plan for economic privatization.[110] It was scarcely an outline, but the idea was to enhance the private-sector role by transforming public shareholding companies and some state-owned enterprises to full private ownership. Most importantly for the ACC, the power of the Ministry of Supply was sharply curtailed. For the first time since the MOS had been established, the incoming head of the ministry did not receive a separate cabinet portfolio. Instead, it was subsumed into the Ministry of Commerce and Industry. MOS import controls were also narrowed to cover only flour, sugar, rice, and meat.[111]

The al-Rifa'i cabinet decreed two further institutional changes. Within the MOS, a "higher supply council" was set up that allowed for chamber representation on decisions of hoarding and price gouging. Officials created a new civilian supply court where supply disputes could be

---

[107] Interview with Ahmed 'Obeidat, former prime minister, Amman, 5 June 1995.
[108] In 1984 a World Bank report, which was later amended after Jordanian protests, forecast a 30 percent unemployment rate by the 1990s: *Al-Dustur*, 24–25 March 1986.
[109] *EIU*, No. 2, 1985, p. 17.   [110] *Jordan Times*, 27 August 1986.
[111] *MEED*, 19 April 1985, p. 14.

adjudicated instead of in the military courts.[112] A direct plea from ACC president Tabba to the prime minister resulted in a key reform to the Economic Security Committee. It was renamed the Economic Consultative Council, and ACC representatives were given permanent seats in addition to the ministers of supply, commerce and industry, finance, and planning, and the head of Central Bank.[113] It was the highest policy body on which ACC representation had been allowed. New ground was also broken in choosing ministers: the first al-Rifa'i cabinet had the highest percentage of Palestinians since 1974. The prime minister reached out to business leaders by appointing Rajai al-Mu'ashshir as his first minister of commerce and industry. The al-Mu'ashshirs were a prominent Palestinian business family with historically close ties to the ACC.[114] In 1986, Hamdi Tabba replaced Mu'ashshir. The move directly from the presidency of the ACC to the Ministry of Commerce and Industry was a first. In sum, the change from 'Obeidat's tenure to Rifa'i's was stark. The end of the Rifa'i administration, however, was equally abrupt.

With little economic recovery registered by the late 1980s, the monarchy was nervous. In a series of interviews, King Hussein admitted Jordan was in a "stage of economic adaptation," and sacrifices would have to be made.[115] Alarmed by the drop in the dinar, stagnation in wages, and increases in debt, state and monarchy soured on the private sector and the ACC in particular. In 1989, the MOS went back into action, detaining and fining scores of merchants for price violations. New sources of supply were made available from the military and subsidies were boosted.[116] Four days of violent protest – due ostensibly to price rises – in the cities of Ma'an, Tafila, and Kerak were the last straw. King Hussein appointed a new government led by Prime Minister Zaid Ibn Shaker, a close contemporary of the king and former commander of the armed forces. The tilt of the new cabinet reversed the previous openness to business, particularly with the appointment of Zaid al-Fariz, a well-known critic of the ACC, to head the Ministry of Commerce and Industry. How did all of this come about? Many of the same trends in Kuwait in the 1980s (creation of new policy participation boards, business leaders as ministers, and more openness to policy debate) instead heralded business–state policy coordination leading to policy implementation in the 1990s.

Despite institutional openings, what appeared to be absent was genuine involvement by organized business in policy negotiation aimed at

---

[112] *EIU*, No. 4, 1985, p. 11.   [113] Interview, Tabba; *Jordan Times*, 14 September 1986.
[114] Samir al-Mu'ashshir sat on M. 'Asfour's ACC board.
[115] *MECS*, vol. XIII, *1989*, p. 456.
[116] *Al-Dustur*, 6 August 1989; and *Jordan Times*, 31 July 1989.

economic reform. First is the issue of policies. It is not uncommon for
state technocrats to develop ostensibly pro-business policies without the
active lobbying or participation of business representatives. The situation
under the al-Rifa'i administration resembled Eduardo Silva's description
of Chile's failed liberalization between 1975 and 1982: "Policymakers
with close links to specific conglomerates churned out liberalizing decrees
without significant participation from other business interests."[117] Plans
for Jordan's privatization, for instance, generated neither coherent
responses nor counterplans from business representatives. Consequently,
there was virtually no private-sector participation in state declarations to
sell off Royal Jordanian Airlines or the Aqaba Port Authority, for example.
There was simply little investor interest in these enterprises, and state
officials received little feedback. Reforms of the MOS were certainly welcomed, but observers suggested there was equal private-sector interest
in reforming customs guidelines and creating more transparency in economic legislation. The lack of any significant decrease in government
spending levels kept business acceptance of the new al-Rifa'i economic
program to the level of a "cautious welcome."[118] At best, Tabba admitted,
under al-Rifa'i the government "recognized the importance of the private sector,"[119] but, with virtually no organized business response, the
reforms were destined to languish. Overall, the institutional openings to
ACC representation were not exploited. Take, for example, the experience of the highest-level economic policy venue created during the 1980s,
the Economic Consultative Council (ECC).

While a far cry from the infrastructure of full-blown state corporatism,
the ECC and higher supply council marked a definite shift in state strategy, since no comparable public–private arrangement had ever been instituted in Jordan. It was an attempt to draw organized business into a
limited and managed quasi-corporatist arrangement. The ECC operated to facilitate consultation, not lobbying. The prime minister controlled the agenda and the schedule of ECC meetings. Not surprisingly,
successive prime ministers have differed in their use of this committee, with some holding monthly meetings and some calling very few.[120]
Consequently, some of the blame for weak private sector–state cooperation can be attributed to varying commitment on the part of state
authorities. However, it would be incorrect to conclude that business–
state coordination through bodies such as the ECC was doomed solely
because of state action. The KCCI used such openings, designed with no

---

[117] Eduardo Silva, "Business Elites, the State, and Economic Change in Chile," in Maxfield
and Schneider, *Business and the State in Developing Countries,* p. 179.
[118] *MEED*, 4 January 1985, p. 12.   [119] Interview, Tabba.   [120] Interview, 'Obeidat.

more state sincerity, to bolster comprehensive policy initiatives or provide specific evidence to counter government claims. Even Tabba admitted that at ECC meetings "we come and listen to forty different speeches and then leave." The ACC involvement that did occur was deemed by most participants to be "lacking in preparation," "narrowly crafted," or "unconvincing."[121] Thus, even though Tabba's influence resulted in the inclusion of the ACC at the highest level, the lack of institutional capabilities meant little could be made of the opening.

Personnel changes fared no better. The Tabba and al-Mu'ashshir appointments were deemed "an experimental failure" by the government.[122] Instead of providing the private sector's voice, the ministries were run as if nothing had changed. Some observers suggested this was due to fear, on the part of the new ministers, of being perceived as pursuing personal business interests.[123] With no active support of organized business, the pro-business ministers were left out in the cold. Any radical departure from set policy, without an engaged business base, would certainly appear as a personal crusade. The fact that every chamber leadership change meant complete institutional transformation also implied that former leaders or allies would be distanced from the chamber once they left. When KCCI allies headed ministries in the 1980s and 1990s, they could count on the support of their association. When the Kuwaiti business representatives put forward recommendations, this gave the minister enough bureaucratic maneuver to support or reject parts of it without appearing to serve personal interests. In the absence of a connected, proactive association, the pro-business minister was left with the prospect of personally advancing ideas that could be seen as self-serving.

The al-Rifa'i reforms and Jordan's first opening to business were a failure. The economy still languished, and subsequent IMF recommendations meant the private sector could not remain on the sidelines. A return of parliamentary elections in 1989 and the eventual dislocations following the Iraqi invasion of Kuwait imparted added pressures for reform.

Business, state, and limited political liberalization in the 1990s

Jordan's standby agreement with the IMF committed the government to economic policy changes (including budgetary restraint, privatization, and tax reform) in exchange for immediate budgetary assistance; however, the country's economic woes were far from resolved. The invasion

---

[121] Various interviews with former ministers.   [122] Interview, 'Obeidat.
[123] Interview, Bassem Saket, President, Jordan Cement Company, Amman, 5 December 1996.

of Kuwait, the expulsion of Palestinians working in the Gulf states, and an end to Gulf aid reinforced that fact. In part to cope with these pressures, King Hussein delivered on promises made earlier in the 1980s to restore parliament. In April 1989, riots broke out in several southern Jordanian cities in protest over government austerity measures. The riots sharpened two imperatives for the Jordanian state: the need to improve economic performance as well as that to deliver tangible political liberalization. The Amman Chamber of Commerce specifically and the private sector in general viewed each imperative as leverage to broker greater policy influence. By all accounts, the scene was set for a new pact to be established between merchants and rulers in Jordan, a pact that could economically support the political hopes of liberalization and return policy clout to organized business.

Similar to Kuwait's experience, two aspects of Jordan's liberalization were key to business–state relations: greater press freedom and the rein-stitution of parliament. Increased press freedom was the most visible and exciting aspect of Jordan's liberalization. Jordan joined Yemen and Kuwait as countries where a relatively free press injected itself into domes-tic policy debates. All private-sector representatives utilized the media to present their ideas on current policy debates. Though none of the major daily newspapers in Amman were controlled by pro-business interests (in contrast to Kuwait), there were columnists who frequently presented private-sector interests in these debates. Interviews with ACC officials, coverage of major banks' year-end reports, and opinion pieces by leading merchants were examples of uses of the new press freedom.[124] However, as was the case in Kuwait, the media playing field was densely popu-lated. Opposition groups – particularly the Islamists – quickly and more effectively pursued press exposure. The Muslim Brotherhood in Jordan proved itself a formidable counterweight to business interests through its own media and tabloids, *Al-Sabil* and *Shihan*.[125] These papers, along with the nationalist and leftist press, frequently made the claim that the business community was out to rob the state or impoverish working Jor-danians. Their defense of public employment and attacks on privatization paralleled those of their counterparts in Kuwait. The lesson from both cases is that, while press freedoms have certainly imparted new oppor-tunities, the larger impact has been an increased competition to express

---

[124] Fhadi al-Fanek and Mohammed 'Asfour represent this type of pro-business voice. Also, the daily newspaper *Al-Aswaq* came to be a forum for pro-business ideas in the 1990s.

[125] Jillian Schwedler, "Democratic Institutions and the Practice of Power in Jordan: The Changing Role of the Islamic Action Front," paper presented to the conference Social History of Jordan, Amman, March 1998, p. 9.

one's position amid many loud opinions. Reconvening parliament went some way toward institutionalizing this competition.

Elections for Jordan's first parliament in twenty-three years marked the beginning of wider policy participation. In 1984, King Hussein recalled parliamentary deputies from the disbanded 1976 assembly. Gradually, the government crafted a new electoral law to carry out elections only on the East Bank. The resulting electorate was similar to that achieved by Kuwait's gerrymandering, in that a clear rural and tribal bias was evident. Amman, with 41 percent of the population, for instance, commanded only 25 percent of the seats. The new parliament of November 1989 and the ones to follow did not differ in their power or purview from the parliaments of the 1960s. Consultation and approval were its primary functions. Still, the presence of parliament subjected economic policy-making more and more to Jordan's form of quasi-party politics. The 1992 Political Parties Law allowed political parties to be legally registered. By 1994, over twenty had been formed, and this definitively changed the lobbying methods of organized business. During the existence of the NCC and previously, the ACC had relied on personal government contacts, on meetings with ministers, or as a last resort on the crown prince to influence policy. Parliament added a new and complicated venue of policy participation. Structurally, the Finance Committee was the primary body before which business representatives went to plead their case. This mirrored the process in Kuwait; even after interaction at the level of the prime minister to influence draft legislation, business leaders could go before parliament to press for last-minute amendments not accepted in previous lobbying. To be a player in this process, however, business needed effective representation.

As we know from much comparative work on democratization, parliaments empower different groups differently. In Jordan, as in most Arab states, Islamist and tribal groups have benefited. In the 1989 elections, for instance, twelve of Amman's seventeen seats went to Islamist candidates. The opposition that evolved after these elections comprised a loose alliance between the Muslim Brotherhood-controlled Islamic Action Front (IAF) and ten small leftist parties. While some businessmen were elected (Qawar and Nabulsi in Amman), efforts to organize that representation generally failed. In 1989, ACC president 'Asfour attempted to create a pro-business, centrist party to give the private sector a voice. Executive board members were unable to agree on the basics of a strategy, either allying with a currently established party or establishing a completely new party. The initiative foundered. In the mid-1990s, JBA elites gravitated toward the small, centrist Al-'Ahd Party making this, more or less, the "business party."[126] Given that both Jordan's and Kuwait's elected parliaments presented similar opportunities for and constraints on policy participation, how can one account for the ability of organized business in Kuwait to make better use of the venue than was the case in Jordan?

One glaring difference is the historical role merchants have had in Kuwait's elected parliaments. As discussed in chapter 2, Kuwait's merchant elites were the parliamentary opposition until the 1980s. Jordanian elites enjoyed no such position in the parliament of the 1950s. Experience of campaigning, coordinating with allied candidates, and balancing campaign platforms was scant among Jordan's business elites. Oddly, the fact that parties in Kuwait were illegal while parties in Jordan were legalized actually benefited Kuwaiti elites. In the absence of a formal party structure, the KCCI, at times when parliament was active, served as the organizational focal point; at times when parliament was not active, the Kuwait chamber preserved the institutional memory of parliamentary politics. The Jordanian chamber was never forced into such a role. Moreover, as the ACC's elite cohesion began to weaken and institutional capacities atrophied, the knowledge and skills in parliamentary politics that had been gained disappeared with the outgoing leadership.

A second factor related to differences in institutional representation was the weakness of Jordanian organized business to provide input on policy prior to parliamentary debate. As will be discussed below, business representation weakened at precisely the time the Jordanian state began overhauling a number of economic laws to advance reform. The inability of business to provide comprehensive input, feedback, or rank-and-file reaction to proposed legislation meant that state officials all too often submitted draft laws to parliament with little business input. This placed even greater stress on the amendment process in parliament. Kuwaiti elites, on the other hand, could count on leverage and tradeoffs at both stages of the policy process. This capability allowed them to exchange policy input for assistance in helping government ministers pushing legislation through the Finance Committee. These points of access existed in Jordan as well, but organized business proved unable to take advantage of them in the 1980s and 1990s. In sum, political liberalization in Jordan complicated actual policy participation for business. In part, this was due to the limited nature of the process itself but, as we can see from the comparative treatment, it also hinged on the institutional weakness

---

[126] Interviews with 'Asfour, and Anis Mu'ashshir, General Secretary, Al-'Ahd Party, Amman, 3 December 1996.

and historical differences in the way business–state relations evolved in Kuwait and Jordan.

War and taxes

The invasion and liberation of Kuwait typified how Jordan and Kuwait were historically tied in economic development. Even before Iraq invaded Kuwait, remittances and state rents had already declined significantly. The political position King Hussein staked out at the onset of the crisis served to exacerbate this trend.[127] In 1986 the World Bank estimated annual remittance flows to Jordan at $1.1 billion; by 1991 that amount had dropped to $450 million.[128] In 1991, GDP growth almost came to a halt, increasing by only 1 percent. Nearly 300,000 workers, mostly of Palestinian origin, were forced to return to Jordan from Kuwait after liberation. The savings they brought fuelled a mini-boom in the early 1990s, principally in the construction sector.[129] Annual GDP growth increased to 6 percent in 1994 and 1995, inflation remained low, and exports increased modestly. Government statistics highlighted increased private-sector investment as measured by the capitalization of new companies in 1993 and 1994.[130] Short-term gains clouded deeper, long-term problems. The immediate benefits did little to increase overall investment, and business confidence remained low. While the boost in construction increased temporary employment, the addition of so many new workers from the Gulf increased unemployment since little of the new growth would generate medium- or long-term returns.

Aside from the economic fallout, the influx of Palestinians from the Gulf added a dimension to business–state relations that is hard to over-estimate. Similar to 1967, thousands of new entrepreneurs poured into Jordan, except many of the new entrepreneurs in this influx had extensive mid-level management experience with lifelong business experience

---

[127] King Hussein's position, like his disengagement decision in 1988, suggested that he had taken very little consideration of the economic implications. That, or the political necessity to back Iraq, was deemed to be more important than the economic dislocations.

[128] World Bank, *World Tables 1994* (Washington, DC: World Bank, 1995). Given the difficulty of tracking real amounts of remittances, the loss could easily be greater.

[129] From 1990 to 1991 the total area under construction in Jordan's major cities almost doubled (Central Bank of Jordan, *Yearly Statistical Series*). See also Nicholas Van Hear, "The Impact of the Involuntary Mass Return to Jordan in the Wake of the Gulf Crisis," *International Migration Review*, 29, 2 (1995), pp. 352–374.

[130] In 1994 the Ministry of Industry and Trade reported that 4,462 companies with JD 408.37 million in capital were registered, compared with 4,409 capitalized at only JD 242.99 million the previous year. Such statistics, however, fail to report how many companies went under in that same period (*Al-Aswaq*, 22 January 1995).

in the Gulf. Their entrance into the private sector placed greater pressure on the ACC to accommodate them. Inexperienced in the politics of business in Jordan and obligated to join the chamber, many new businessmen looked to it as a source of *wasta*, or influence, in their dealings with state and municipal authorities. These new members also complicated electoral and representation trends within the ACC, as few had previous ties to the established elite. These new businesses were (and continue to be) wild cards in the evolution of Jordan's economy and politics. Externally, pressure mounted on the chamber as well. Policy targets of the IMF structural adjustment agreement had achievement dates in the mid-1990s, and many in the private sector and the government expected a number of economic policy changes. This was a contradictory environment, offering growth and new entrepreneurial input into the economy, while at the same time laying bare the fact that few of Jordan's underlying economic problems had been addressed. Both state strategies and the private sector's outlook took account of these conditions.

From a government perspective, it became necessary to replace lost external revenue with taxation on the (anticipated) increasing private-sector activity. In 1994, Jordan's parliament prepared the final legislation for the country's first national sales tax. A sales tax, while not as direct as an income tax, nevertheless parallels quite strongly the type of state intervention that rentier theory envisions after rents decline. According to Luciani, "a sales tax, or VAT [value added tax], requires extensive administration and comes close to a direct income taxation on individuals in establishing a direct relationship between the tax-payer and the state."[131] Rentier state theory imbues this connection with great significance. External rent reductions force domestic taxation, to which, in exchange, are attached the strings of increased political liberalization and, potentially, democratization. The literature, however, is unclear as to whether this political–economic connection is to be seen as a linear relationship or as multi-dimensional. The case of tax reform in Jordan in the 1990s suggests the former. Evidence from the political sphere is less clear-cut, and how business reacted to and engaged the issue was contingent on more factors than the revenue imperative on its own. But it is the revenue issue around which interests expressed by organized business coalesced. Just as with the debt issue in Kuwait, a review of the various positions on the tax is first necessary in order to observe how Jordan's business representatives and state officials interacted on the issue.

[131] Giacomo Luciani, "The Oil Rent, the Fiscal Crisis of the State, and Democratization," in Salamé, *Democracy Without Democrats*, p. 133.

Any plan to boost domestic revenue required creating new laws, altering institutions to carry out previously neglected government tasks, and determining which activities to tax and at what level. This direction was balanced by another concern, specifically maintaining positive economic growth and creating jobs for the vastly expanded workforce. Economic policymakers were fully aware that IMF grants could neither deliver more employment nor ensure steady economic growth.[132] The failure of reforms under al-Rifa'i and the weak response by the private sector lowered government expectations for private-sector cooperation. Moreover, an entirely new ACC leadership was in place, which neither experienced nor learned from the past failures. Nevertheless, government officials expressed the need for private-sector involvement. This would include:

Reducing the government's role in direct production, enhancing the role of the private sector through improving incentives for domestic and foreign investment, and discouraging government competition with the private sector; and activating the role of the private sector in the areas of infrastructure and basic services and increasing private-sector participation in the management and ownership of public-sector institutions.[133]

The consensus was somehow to entice the private sector into a new pact to deliver greater domestic investment and spark new economic growth.

Among business representatives, there were competing concerns. On the revenue side, merchants and traders in the ACC opposed an increase in general tax revenue or in import/customs duties. Especially for traders, increases in the size and power of the Customs Department in the Ministry of Finance had become a key concern. Bureaucratic problems with this agency were legion, and a good number of contacts with the state were over customs disputes. If a tax was to be imposed, most wanted exemptions for their goods. The small and middling retailers in the ACC opposed *any* intrusive government tax scheme that would force record-keeping, or a national sales tax that would further depress consumption. On the expenditure side, industrialists led by the ACI opposed any reduction in subsides for their produced goods or taxes on imported raw materials. The largest elite merchant families, distributed between the JBA and the ACI, acknowledged and welcomed a state move toward greater domestic revenue extraction. Many operated multisectoral enterprises and were aware of the need for austerity and structural adjustment.[134]

[132] Interview, Sami Ghammo, former minister of finance, Amman, 3 July 1995.
[133] Jordan, Ministry of Planning, *Jordan: Economic and Social Development Plan, 1993–1997* (Amman: n.d.), pp. 103–104.
[134] One of the best examples of these multisectoral, dynamic entities was run by the al-Salfiti family. They headed the Union Group of Companies, a group of industrial, financial, and trading concerns.

What they wanted in return was a greater role in policymaking. In various guises, they considered the future of Jordan to be as a low-tax, regional service center, focusing on its areas of comparative advantage (tourism and pharmaceuticals, for instance). They advocated some government support, particularly in the tourism sector, but generally their desire echoed neoliberal mantras to reduce the presence of the government, both as regulator and supplier.

All groups, however, shared two goals. One was simply to lower the proposed rate of the tax (10 percent). On that everyone could demand compromise and claim victory. A second concern was over the authority of the later phases of the tax. The original government intent was that the next phases of the tax would be enacted through the authority of the prime minister; that is, parliamentary approval of the first sales tax would entail blanket permission for the state to enact further tax without consultation.[135] Business and opposition in parliament wanted further stages to be submitted to parliament for approval. Adjudicating conflicting viewpoints and presenting consistent, competent input on taxation policy is something one would expect from the encompassing ACC. By the 1990s, however, the association was hardly an institution that adjudicated different membership interests. Instead of mediating sectoral goals which at times conflicted, the executive board reflected them through increased particularist lobbying. Limits on managing policy advocacy and policy participation with government officials became painfully evident in the tax debates of the 1990s.

The idea of a national sales tax first emerged in 1989 as part of IMF recommendations to overhaul public revenue and replace an older consumption tax. The intent was to implement a comprehensive sales tax, which would eventually become a national value-added tax on all retailers and traders. Business lobbying came in two phases. The first phase came in 1992 after the government of Prime Minister Sharif Zaid bin Shaker announced that a draft sales tax law was near completion and would be enacted as a temporary law. Under the constitution, when parliament is not in session, the government can enact temporary laws, to be approved once parliament reconvenes. Bin Shaker sought to bypass opposition to the tax by using this loophole. Opposition in parliament vehemently protested this move. The leftists and Islamists saw the government as simply enacting a mandate from the IMF and the West.[136] The ACC and other business associations were angry over the lack of

---

[135] [About the draft sales tax law], Article 4, Item B, Finance Committee, Parliament, 1994.
[136] *Jordan Times*, 29–30 April 1993.

consultation. Though the idea for the tax dated back to 1989, business had not been included in the state's deliberations to create the draft law. Belatedly, the ECC and the Ministry of Finance began holding *ad hoc* meetings with ACC and ACI representatives. It was too little, too late.[137] With parliamentary elections scheduled for November 1993 (some government ministers were up for reelection) and Islamist/leftist opposition running strong, the government backed down in May 1993, agreeing to submit the law to parliament after elections.[138] The second phase of lobbying came once the formal submission process began at the end of 1993.

Though the government had completed the draft law, the previous retreat convinced state elites to be better prepared. Part of that preparation was to secure business support for the tax in order to undercut parliamentary opposition, something Kuwaiti state officials had achieved in their own struggles with parliament.[139] Thus, in December 1993, the prime minister created a special sixteen-person subcommittee under the ECC (with ACC representation) to study business concerns about the tax. The committee went through at least four drafts of the tax law before consultations ended.[140] ACC and ACI representatives used this opportunity to convince state officials of the need for exemptions for their members, lowering the basic rate from 10 percent to 5 percent, and changing the authority over future tax phases.[141] On the latter two points, ACC and ACI lobbying was complementary. They clashed over the imposition of the sales tax on imports and over ACC demands for exemptions on specific goods. According to state officials involved in the exchange, there was a marked difference between the two associations' lobbying.

Better organized, the ACI commissioned its own Research Department to poll its members on the issue. They inserted these concerns along with their proposals and comparisons with other countries' tax codes and estimates on the impact to industry. By contrast, the ACC appeared unable to mediate its own competing internal claims. Its own research staff being of little use, the chamber hired an outside consulting firm to assist its deliberations.[142] It did not canvass its members nor did it circulate elements of the draft tax to generate internal reaction. Instead, it was "hoped" individual board members would alert members in their sector and collect opinions.[143] Echoing Prime Minister 'Obeidat's

---

[137] *Ibid.*, 5 and 10 May 1993.   [138] *Ibid.*, 10 May 1993.
[139] Interviews with government officials suggested that they reasoned they could reach agreement with business on the tax, but that there was little they could offer the Islamist and leftist opposition groups to achieve compromise with them.
[140] Interview, Muhtasib.   [141] *Al-Rai'*, 28 December 1993.
[142] Interview, Ghammo.   [143] Interview, Muhtasib.

complaints in the previous decade, ministers were puzzled at the ACC's lobbying initiatives. One minister admitted that chamber representatives lacked "backup research and appeared ill-prepared." Another was more blunt: "I failed ever to hear a coherent argument from their representatives; there was never any new blood presenting their views."[144] Most damaging, however, were the particularist exemptions that were gradually achieved by ACC representatives. Outside associational channels, individual board members sent letters and pressed ministers attached to the consultations for specific exemptions for their businesses. Therefore, sectors in which ACC board members operated (such as textiles) comprised most of the exemption demands while unrepresented sectors (such as transportation) were not addressed. All of this damaged the image of the chamber in the eyes of decisionmakers. As a result, ministers tended to work more closely and share information more freely with the ACI and its president Abu Hassan.[145]

By January 1994, little compromise had been reached on the main issues. Impelled by the need to show some progress on IMF recommendations, the prime minister presented the draft law to parliament in February. The draft failed to lower the rate of the tax and did not include the necessity of submitting future taxes to parliament. Business representatives and opposition elements braced for a fight within the Finance Committee, where amendments and exemptions would be considered.[146] Unexpectedly, ACC president 'Asfour announced that the chamber would accept the draft law and end its resistance. This opened the floodgates for more particularist demands. The interchange was often three-sided. Government ministers attended to defend or clarify government positions; opposition MPs defended constituent concerns; and individual business representatives (many from the ACC) pressed their own claims. Unlike the Kuwaiti debt debates, business representatives and Islamists appeared to work together. Islamist deputies in particular railed against any idea of a tax since it came, partly, from IMF recommendations: "The draft law is a requirement of the new Middle East so that our economy will be marginal, to the benefit of the Israeli enemy and the capitalist economy."[147] Consequently, Finance Committee members sympathetically received ACC exemption petitions more to demonstrate

---

[144] Interviews.

[145] There are no open records of these meetings. Interviews with ACC and ACI officials were understandably one-sided. Hence, most of the information on these deliberations came from interviews with former ministry officials present and high-ranking civil servants.

[146] *Jordan Times*, 14 January 1994.

[147] IAF deputy Hammam Sa'id quoted *ibid.*, 21 April 1994.

their legislative power than in recognition of chamber arguments or skill. Outside parliament, opposition parties mounted an impressive public relations campaign against the tax. A number of associations banded together in opposition, including the largest: the Consumers' Protection Society, the Engineers' Association, and the Contractors' Association. Their primary claim was that the tax would injure the poor and increase the cost of living.[148] Here again the ACI took the lead, purchasing full-page advertisements in some of the daily newspapers to explain industry concerns.

Eventually, the government chose not to fight the Finance Committee's amendments. Finance Minister Ghammo admitted, "we have spent more than 30 months discussing and negotiating the draft and we are not going to waste any more time on this."[149] What parliament eventually passed and the government accepted was a tax law riddled with inconsistencies and loopholes. On the macro aspects, there was compromise. The agreed rate was 7 percent, a compromise between government's initial 10 percent and business's 5 percent. This victory proved temporary, however, when the government pushed through an increase to 10 percent in 1995.[150] The Chamber of Industry succeeded to some extent, since the tax was to be applied only to raw material imports and not to the finished good. What the ACC could point to as success was the myriad exemptions to the tax. Pages of addenda to the law specified what type, number, and style of goods and services would be exempted from the sales tax.[151]

The various loopholes in the sales tax were an inadequate first step toward the kind of tax overhaul business elites and government officials had in mind. Jordan's already complex import/export regime was given another layer of interpretation with the addition of the sales tax. Just to be an importer, in addition to annual registration with the ACC, an applicant had to obtain a clearance authorization at each import site, a license of operation from each locality, a license to import from the ministry, and an authorization for parcels. Completing a customs importation document required seventeen signatures.[152] Since over half of Jordan's imports enjoyed some form of duty-free status,[153] the addition of a sales tax with countless exemptions meant businesses then had to determine

---

[148] *Ibid.*, 5 March 1994; *Al-Dustur*, 17 February 1994.

[149] *Jordan Times*, 14 May 1994.

[150] *Middle East Executive Reports*, November 1995; *Jordan Times*, 6 June 1995.

[151] *Official Gazette*, No. 3970 [The sales tax law], No. 6 (1994); *MEED*, 30 September 1994; *Jordan Times*, 19 June 1995.

[152] World Bank, Private Sector Development and Infrastructure Division, Middle East Department, *Jordan: Private Sector Assessment* (Washington, DC: World Bank, 25 August 1995), p. x.

[153] World Bank, *Jordan: Consolidating Economic Adjustment*, p. 53.

if, and to what extent, each good was subject to the sales tax. The consistent chamber goal to reduce red tape and streamline customs regulations was actually thwarted by its own particularist lobbying. Government customs agents, who already exercised wide discretionary powers, were given greater leeway with the arrival of more complex levels of tax assessment. Instead of easing transaction costs, business engagement contributed to impediments to new entrants to the market. The results were delays in tax collection and extensive evasion.

Confusion over the tax, its details, and how the tax was to be levied endured well into 1995.[154] Many businessmen struggled with customs officials at Aqaba, petitioned the Ministry of Finance, and complained to the Finance Committee. More amendments were passed through parliament (including the increase to 10 percent) to clarify the earlier amendments. The number and complexity of exemptions encouraged a good degree of evasion by business.[155] In sum, Jordan's tax debate hardly presented a neat example of tying a revenue imperative to greater liberalization.

Working to attract foreign investment

Not all aspects of economic policy generate the divisiveness of the tax debate or Kuwait's debt struggles. Hosting foreign trade delegations and participating in overseas marketing initiatives are issues on which state and business usually share overlapping interests. Attracting foreign investment in a period of fiscal downturn would logically find common ground as well. The 1995 Amman Economic Summit provided such an opportunity and, at least publicly, was one of the most anticipated international events ever held in Jordan. The summit brought together countries of the Middle East (including Israel) to discuss economic issues focusing on cooperation and investment. It provided a stage upon which Jordan could sell itself to private foreign investors and international lending bodies. Both state elites and organized business desired such investment, and attempted to coordinate a unified approach.[156]

---

[154] Some parliamentary debate in 1995 and 1996 as well as public forums with government officials were held to address these problems.

[155] Interviews, Muhtasib and Ghammo.

[156] There is, however, a caveat. As the Amman Summit occurred directly after peace with Israel, the conference was tied to general government efforts to involve Jordanian groups (especially business) in exchanges and transactions with the Israelis. As a consequence, it would be an overstatement to suggest that the entire business community was thrilled with the Amman Summit, but certainly an overwhelming majority were interested and hopeful about its outcome.

A component of the larger regional peace effort, the Amman Summit was set to follow the 1994 Casablanca Conference. While the Casablanca Conference was a political gathering meant to lay the groundwork for Middle East economic cooperation, the Amman Summit was intended to provide the opportunity for actual deals to be made. In concrete terms, the summit would be a mad dash by some Arab states to secure foreign (principally Western) investment into their weakening economies. Peace with Israel, a well-publicized liberalization record, and its role as host of the conference placed Jordan in a very favorable position. Rhetoric ran quite high in Jordan that the summit would spark the awaited peace dividend. The story of that conference in terms of business–state relations demonstrates how economic issues that are apparently international are, in great measure, driven by domestic political stakes.

Shortly after the Casablanca Conference, the minister of planning approached the Canadian Embassy to solicit assistance on the preparation of Jordan's investment strategy for the forthcoming summit. The primary tool to lobby for foreign capital was a list of projects prepared by the government promoting joint-investment projects in Jordan. In a scheme financed by the Canadian Embassy, foreign consultants were hired in December 1994 to assess this list. Their conclusions stressed the need to involve Jordan's private sector in summit preparation.[157] A key element in any strategy to attract foreign investment is a stable investment climate. The most simple and direct means for the potential investor to assess this is to sample the local business community's opinions. One American participant in the summit put it this way: "If the private sector has all this cash, why doesn't anyone invest? If they think it's a risk, how can I get my company to take that risk?"[158] This predicament became a key concern for the Ministry of Commerce and Industry and prime ministerial officials as they worked toward the summit. To assist, the Canadians developed a list of private-sector representatives who would participate in meetings to prepare for the conference.

This was an excellent test of business–state relations, since an outside agency was given purview to examine Jordan's business community and attempt to select its elite members to work with the state. Their first task was to contact Jordan's leading business associations for lists of potential representatives. Instead of lists of "dynamic business leaders," the tardy response contained only "the names of family members of the organizations' leaders." Moreover, the Canadians concluded that these formal

---

[157] Interview with Daniel Joly, First Secretary, Embassy of Canada, Amman, 1 June 1995.
[158] *Middle East*, December 1995, p. 17.

representatives could not "deliver mobilization and that it would entangle the process in bureaucracy."[159] Consequently, of the sixty-one individuals invited to the first meeting in May 1995, only five were from the country's largest business representative, the ACC. The rest were businessmen (and one businesswoman) chosen through the Canadians' own research.[160]

The first meeting allowed the private sector to compile its own list of priorities for the summit. These called for projects at the summit to be "attainable and sustainable." Many of the projects the state had originally proposed were large-scale investments such as the Disi–Amman water pipeline and the Red–Dead Canal.[161] There was little private-sector interest in such endeavors. Suggestions from the private sector focused instead on well-known sentiments to reform customs regulations, re-educate civil servants, and involve the private sector to a greater degree in economic policymaking. The real problem remained: how should the private sector structure its involvement in the summit, aside from using it as a venue to exchange views?

Discouraged with the chamber's response to the first meeting, the Ministry of Commerce and Industry appointed a ten-member board of leading businessmen, the Private Sector Executive Committee (PSEC), to organize and supervise business involvement in the conference. The chairman of the PSEC was the vice-president of the JBA, Thabet al-Taher. The PSEC was cast as representing Jordan's business elite and it was telling that only one ACC board member was chosen to sit on the committee. Several officials involved in the summit confirmed that the chamber was not supportive of the PSEC because its leadership viewed the organization as a rival to its own authority. With fewer resources than the chamber, the committee organized eleven sectoral committees and appointed its members from among the leading businessmen in each sector. None of the chairmen of the committees came from the ACC. By all accounts, the PSEC was very effective. Raising its own funds, the PSEC produced several well-organized publications for the summit and, most importantly, interacted smoothly with state personnel organizing it. This interaction helped shape the final project list, which consisted of

---

[159] Interview, Joly.

[160] List of attendees provided by the Embassy of Canada, Amman.

[161] The Disi project was a multimillion dollar effort to build a water pipeline from the Disi aquifer in the south to Amman. The Red–Dead Canal aimed to build a joint Israeli–Jordanian canal from the Red Sea to the Dead Sea (*Investing in Jordan*, marketing documents for the Amman Economic Summit, prepared by the Ministry of Planning, Investment Promotion Department, Amman, 1995).

twenty-seven ventures totaling roughly $1.3 billion in private-sector projects and $3.5 billion in public-sector schemes.[162]

Though the Amman Summit proved an organizational success for Jordan's public sector, it demonstrated little in the way of an institutionalized pact between state and business or more coordinated relations. Instead, creation of the PSEC strengthened a trend – inaugurated with the National Consultative Council – whereby ineffective business representation was bypassed in favor of *ad hoc*, informal networks representing the rank and file. Beyond the institutional factors in this shift, a final factor to consider is the broader (and more historical) political constraints that shape business–state relations. Just as those factors in the Kuwaiti case were made clear in the evolving business–state alliance against the Islamist political opposition, similar trends became evident in Jordan.

A political economy of Jordan's peace with Israel

As in Kuwait, Islamist groups and their organizations have come to dominate the political opposition in Jordan. The economic and political strength of Kuwait's Islamists created openings in a number of policy areas for business and state to coordinate efforts at curbing those strengths. The Jordanian case presents a contrasting set of historical and institutional features that have hindered such a quasi-alliance. Instead, organized business in Jordan has proven a poor partner for state ends vis-à-vis political Islam. The issues of privatization and peace with Israel are prime examples.

Privatization in the sense of turning over significant portions of public-sector activities to the private sector has not been under consideration in Jordan.[163] Instead, as in Kuwait, state officials have contemplated the liquidation of an array of state investments in public shareholding companies. Such companies were substantial: the state held an average stake of 46 percent in 109 shareholding companies registered on the Amman Financial Market.[164] There was very little consideration of privatizing government-owned corporations (potash and phosphates, for instance) or ministries. Structurally, the process was as decentralized as in Kuwait. A technical committee for privatization, created to oversee the process, was

---

[162] Interview with P. V. Vivekanand, Editor, *Jordan Times*, Amman, 7 November 1996. None of the projects received start-up funding. In part this was due to the fact that the conference was overshadowed by the assassination of Israeli prime minister Yitzak Rabin.

[163] See Piro, *The Political Economy of Market Reform in Jordan*.

[164] World Bank, *Jordan: Consolidating Economic Adjustment*, p. 59.

located at the prime minister's office. However, since the Jordan Investment Corporation owned most of the state assets in public shareholding companies, it generated the decisions of what to sell and to whom.[165] Individual ministries held other shares, and hence each minister had input into sales decisions.

While individual outliers can be found, for the most part the resistance of Jordan's Islamic Action Front to privatization was as consistent as that of Islamist opposition in Kuwait. Parliamentary and press complaints about the ill-effects of privatization on lower income groups, public-sector employees, and rural elements typified the campaign. Since privatization was first broached during the al-Rifa'i administration of the mid-1980s, state officials launched a number of efforts and white papers to secure greater private-sector participation[166] to counter this criticism. There was very little, if any, discussion among Jordan's business representatives and state officials about the issue. The ACC's policy on the process was quite weak, with general agreement for the need to privatize, but little beyond that.[167] Business leaders commonly expressed ignorance over state intentions toward privatization, except those policies broadly recognized by the public at large. Like Kuwait's public divestments, the trend in Jordan privileged *ad hoc*, specific agreements among domestic investors and state officials. There are no open records of these privatization negotiations, but logically one can assume that Kuwait's previous patterns of institutionalized coordination and the cohesion of business representation actually facilitated and complemented the informal processes that defined the speed and efficiency of state divestments in the 1990s. With little such experience to learn from and help build investor confidence, Jordan's efforts at divestment have moved at a laborious pace. The task of building a network of potential investors while negotiating divestment details presents problems of coordination, collective action, and information that are not easily overcome, especially given the weakness of business organization. Moreover, as the foregoing analysis has shown, attempts at business–state coordination are embedded within larger historical and coalitional factors.

The East Bank/Palestinian division in Jordan is often overemphasized in discussions of the country's politics, but it should not be discounted.

---

[165] Interview, Saket.
[166] Laurie A. Brand, "Economic and Political Liberalization in a Rentier Economy: The Case of the Hashemite Kingdom of Jordan," in Iliya Harik and Denis J. Sullivan (eds.), *Privatization and Liberalization in the Middle East* (Bloomington: Indiana University Press, 1992), pp. 167–188.
[167] Various interviews with ACC officials. Also, research uncovered no privatization documents or policy statements by the chamber.

The building of a largely East Bank-staffed public sector and the evolution of a more or less Palestinian private sector still holds in twenty-first century Jordan. Consequently, privatization has presented state and business with rather delicate issues to adjudicate, in addition to how much and how many jobs. Selling large amounts of public shares to what are perceived as Palestinian capitalists threatened to alienate the state's and monarchy's support base among East Bank political elites. Add to this the fact that Jordan's largest private-sector representative, the ACC, has failed to produce an elite leadership that reflects all of the faces (Palestinian and East Bank) of Jordan's business community, and there has evolved little ground on which coordination was possible. One circuitous way around this impasse has been to arrange sales to investment groups headed by prominent East Bankers. The first major divestment was that of the Inter-Continental Hotel in 1996, which was sold to a consortium of sixteen investors (many of them of Palestinian origin) headed by a prominent East Bank notable.[168] This complication is one reason why Jordan's privatization program in the 1990s supplanted Egypt's as the region's most lethargic.

Finally, Jordan's role and position in the Middle East peace process provide stark evidence that business–state relations respond to more than simply economic stimuli. The economic benefits of peace with Israel have been an issue of significant concern in Jordan since the Oslo process began. Opinion, within as well as outside Jordan, viewed Oslo as a driver of regional peace and as a way (similar to the Amman Summit) of attracting direct foreign investment into Jordan.[169] Shortly after the signing of the Jordanian–Israeli peace treaty in September 1993, the prime minister's office began repeated efforts to engage the assistance and participation of the private sector in working with Israel's private sector, in order to – if not in actuality then at least rhetorically – demonstrate work toward realization of the peace dividend.[170] While there was some apprehension within the business community over dominance by Israel's larger economy,[171] at the elite levels there was less fear. It was no secret that

---

[168] *Jordan Times*, 3 September 1996.

[169] Shaul Mishal, Ranan Kuperman, and David Boas, *Investment in Peace: The Politics of Economic Cooperation Between Israel, Jordan, and the Palestinians* (Portland: Sussex Academic Press, 2001).

[170] However, some businessmen invited to participate in the Amman Summit preparation refused because of the involvement of Israel.

[171] For example, much of Jordanian industry (unlike Israel's) does not manufacture in accordance with European or American standards. Change is coming, however. One example is Hikma Pharmaceuticals, the first pharmaceutical factory in the Arab world to receive approval from the US Food and Drug Administration: *MEED*, 21 April 1995, p. 10.

segments of the private sector have long dealt with the Israelis through trade in the occupied territories. Moreover, some of the larger trading and industrial concerns with established international connections welcomed an opening to Israel, specifically in sectors like textiles. The dilemma, of course, was that, for Jordan's business representation, peace with Israel involved more than just economic factors.

Perhaps the only area of consistent business–state cooperation over the years has been in hosting foreign delegations to attract investment. Accordingly, in 1994 and 1995 the state quietly pursued the leading business organizations to participate in joint Palestinian–Israeli business meetings. One of these initiatives involved a three-day meeting in July 1995 with Israeli, Palestinian, and Jordanian businessmen at the Royal Court.[172] Among organized business, only the Jordanian Businessmen's Association flatly rejected any participation, albeit quietly. The Amman Chamber of Commerce and the Chamber of Industry did participate in some gatherings but kept a low profile, and their officials played down the significance of the meetings.[173] The Amman Summit marked the high point of state efforts to generate more interaction between the two private sectors. At the summit, Egyptian, Palestinian, Jordanian, and Israeli representatives committed to forming the Regional Business Center (RBC), a crossnational chamber of sorts, to promote private-sector involvement in securing the peace. Though a US-initiated idea, the RBC received strong support from King Hussein and Crown Prince Hassan.[174] Indeed, following the Rabin assassination in November 1995, the king took the leaders of Jordan's business associations with him to the state funeral.[175] None of these actions, however, generated serious coordination and, as opposition mounted among Islamists and the other professional associations, business representatives were being forced to reassess their low-profile position.

The opposition's first target was the RBC. Beginning in October 1996, articles began appearing in Amman's daily newspapers about the activities of the RBC. Leaders of all the business associations took the opportunity to come out strongly against any further dealings with the RBC because of Israeli actions in the occupied territories. Around the same time, leaders of all three business associations, along with opposition groups in parliament and professional associations, signed a declaration calling for an

---

[172] Interview, 'Asfour.

[173] Interview, Bill Fisher, American representative to the Regional Business Center, Amman, 4 October 1996.

[174] *Al-Dustur*, 2 October 1996; *Al-Rai'* 2 and 9 October 1996.

[175] This was a rare event. The author found that only once previously had the king taken a representative of Jordan's business community along on a state visit.

end to normalization and the withdrawal of Jordan's ambassador from Israel. This unprecedented political stance by Jordan's business associations was followed two months later by protests over an Israeli trade fair in Jordan. Former prime minister Ahmed 'Obeidat headed an organization of political opposition groups that, while unable to stop the trade fair, was able to stage protests outside the fair entrance. Though business associations did not officially join the opposition organization, the associations and many members did openly side with the aims of the opposition. Thus, comparason of the situations in Jordan and Kuwait, in terms of institutional capacity, historical trajectory, and political context, illuminates the complexities involved in crafting business–state coordination during economic crises, crises which are defined by more than their economic character.

Conclusion

By focusing on organized business representation in each case, this chapter highlighted obstacles to public–private coordination in responding to economic crisis. It also charted evolving divisions within each country's business communities and the political challenges elites faced. Divergent outcomes during almost two decades of fiscal crisis in Jordan and Kuwait pose challenges for theories of business–state relations that expect patterned responses to economic shifts. Kuwait's less inclusive business representation proved successful at crafting a new pact with state authorities, one which advanced and implemented reform, but which has also laid the groundwork for political collusion to limit parliamentary rivals. Paradoxically, the exclusive character of the KCCI contributed to the ability of Kuwait's business elite to incorporate new ranks of business and ease intra-merchant conflict during fiscal upheaval. The security of leadership and the ability to plan for the long term resulted in controlled inclusion. Jordan's more encompassing business representation, anchored at the Amman Chamber of Commerce, gradually lost policy and leadership cohesion as the crisis wore on. Waves of new merchants increased pressure on an already institutionally crippled association to accommodate them. Despite a number of policy openings, business and state failed to coordinate reform, particularist policy demands from the ACC dominated, and policy drift characterized Jordan's reform program at the close of the twentieth century.

Political differences in each crisis as well as previous political and institutional struggles shaped these outcomes. The 1960s expansion of membership in the Amman chamber and the extension of voting to lower categories of business set trends that would be fully expressed in the 1980s and 1990s. State strategies in the 1960s and 1970s to foster a more loyal business community would accentuate these pressures. Thus, once new ranks of business matured and came to the fore in these years, Jordan's leading business association was unprepared. Rival associations, though smaller, benefited from the ACC's inability to absorb and accommodate new business. Rentier and sectoral accounts are largely silent on such key institutional and political factors, which determine how interests are translated.[176] In the Jordanian case, these dynamics explain the general inability of business and state to coordinate during crisis.

Finally, the political context of each crisis was an important element in how business and state elites approached resolution. The abruptness and early timing of Kuwait's financial meltdown forged the conditions for early and intense business–state interaction. True, the KCCI responded effectively and consistently, but the suddenness of the Manakh crash and the administrative inability of state agencies to respond were fortuitous opportunities. Jordan's economic woes unfolded more gradually. State weakness was never laid bare all at once. Initial attempts at coordination in the mid-1980s failed and provided little in the way of a learning experience, even if the ACC had been equipped to adapt. The invasion of Kuwait and its liberation in 1990–1991 punctuated each country's ongoing economic problems. For Kuwait, the aftermath meant a return of an elected parliament, a more vehement Islamist opposition, and a greater reliance by the state on business. Jordan's external vulnerability not only resulted in thousands more joining an already fast evolving business community, but it also pushed state and society to the front of what would become a flawed and tenuous regional peace process.

---

[176] Haggard, Maxfield, and Schneider, "Theories of Business and Business–State Relations," p. 44.

5   Is business the solution?

> "An old merchant said to a person who wanted to find out the truth about commerce: 'I shall give it to you in two words [in short]: buy cheap and sell dear. There is commerce for you.'"[1]
>
> Ibn Khaldun, *The Muqaddimah*

After decades of economic dislocation and the added turbulence of the 11 September 2001 attacks, policymakers, scholars, and popular commentators have expounded endlessly on the problems of the Middle East and potential solutions. One does not have to look very far to find arguments that business is one solution. Thomas Friedman is one of the more prominent tellers of this story. In his popular book, *The Lexus and the Olive Tree*, Friedman repeatedly refers to what he terms "the silent invasion going on in the Middle East – the invasion of information and private capital through the new system of globalization." Friedman equates the olive tree with rootedness and tradition and the Lexus with the economic forces of globalization. In what Friedman cites as his favorite story of the Lexus trumping the olive tree, the author recounts a chance meeting with Jihad al-Wazir, son of Abu Jihad, Arafat's right-hand man, who was assassinated by the Israeli government in 1988. Friedman marvels to find that al-Wazir did not follow in his father's footsteps, but instead headed a trading firm in the Gaza Strip. "That's amazing [Friedman responds]. From Che Guevara to Dale Carnegie in one generation."[2] Such blanket assertions about the political role business will play have been echoed in recent US policy toward the Middle East. In his December 2002 speech launching the US–Middle East Partnership Initiative, Secretary of State Colin Powell set as the first of its three pillars: "We will engage with public- and private-sector groups to bridge the jobs gap with economic reform, business investment, and private-sector

---

[1] Ibn Khaldun, *The Muqaddimah*, vol. II, p. 337.
[2] Friedman, *The Lexus and the Olive Tree*, p. 209.

development."[3] Subsequent plans to create a US–Middle East free-trade zone and the sharpening focus of international lending agencies on correcting "behind the border" complications have put the Arab private sector front and center.[4] As both a liberal counterforce against radicalism and the linchpin of economic reform, Arab business seems to hold the solution.

Setting aside the irony of this new Western position,[5] these policies, much like the structural logics discussed in the first chapter, operate using a stylized portrait of business in the developing world. Business is, however, more than just buying and selling. Comparison of the Kuwaiti and Jordanian cases offers a more nuanced view of business. If how domestic business weathered previous political struggles (state creation of rivals and limits on participation) and the evolution of its institutional representation says something about its capacities for shaping political outcomes during crisis, then caution is warranted in assuming uniform political roles for business regardless of context. On the one hand, these findings confirm evidence from other parts of the world[6] that some level of business–state cooperation is necessary for successful reform and productive growth. Divergence between the Kuwaiti and Jordanian cases allows us to see that the institutional capacities of business representation and the context of coalition politics shape that cooperation. This means that, through greater institutional investment and political crafting, business–state coordination can be achieved in countries such as Jordan. This is no easy task, to be sure, especially given the prevalence of external pressures. On the other hand, these cases also reveal the disturbing disjuncture between economic and political liberalization in the region. In each case, moves to revitalize wider political participation occurred hand in hand with efforts to manage economic crisis. Some two decades later, the one-time regional leaders in political liberalization have halted deeper reform in this sphere and reversed earlier advances.

By way of conclusion, this chapter first discusses alternative arguments that can explain the observed outcomes. Second, I draw out the broader implications of current business–state relations in the Arab world with respect to the connections between economic crisis, economic reform, and deeper political liberalization.

[3] Speech, 12 December 2002, http://www.state.gov/secretary/rm/2002/15920.htm.
[4] Hoekman and Messerlin, *Harnessing Trade*.
[5] In the 1950s and early 1960s, American policymakers favored military strongmen like Gamal Abdel Nasser over what they considered weaker and untrustworthy private-sector elements. See Robert Springborg, "The Arab Bourgeoisie: A Revisionist Interpretation," *Arab Studies Quarterly*, 15, 1 (Winter 1993), pp. 13–40.
[6] Maxfield and Schneider, *Business and the State in Developing Countries*.

Addressing the alternatives

Response to fiscal crisis and implementation of economic reform by late-late developers require political skills, which are, in great part, shaped by the relations that prevail between organized business and the state. Generalizing from the cases of Jordan and Kuwait leads to the view that the organization of private-sector representation (structures of representation and membership), previous political struggles, and coalition politics during crisis account for the patterns of business–state cooperation. The impreciseness of broader structural explanations can be remedied with focused consideration of the political and institutional conditions of business–state relations. And, for any study that seeks to make particular as well as general claims, objections should be expected from both directions.[7]

One such objection involves a return to citing easily observable (and modeled) structural economic incentives as the ultimate source of divergence. Kuwait is one of the world's richest countries with proven oil reserves that guarantee significant levels of rent income well into this new century and possibly the next. By contrast, Jordan's sources of external rent (reported and unreported, such as aid, mineral exports, and "forgiveness" of international loans) have declined steadily since the 1980s. Few guarantees are attached to these sources. These different structural positions should translate into different incentives for state officials during economic crisis. The Kuwaiti state official may assume crisis is only short-term given large reserves of a finite resource. Consequently the state has the ability simply to "entertain" business demands (short of privatizing oil) and placate their desire for voice in the short term; institutional strength and previous political conflicts are secondary in explaining the emergence of policy coordination by business and state. This interpretation is faulty for two reasons. First, in a comparative context, the structural incentives for the Jordanian state official to work more closely with business would seem to be far greater than in Kuwait. Jordan cannot count on steady future aid or high phosphate prices as can Kuwait, with its significant oil assets. If anything, the structural "threat" in the Jordanian case should produce business–state coordination that is deeper than that

---

[7] Lisa Anderson, "Politics in the Middle East: Opportunities and Limits in the Quest for Theory," in Mark Tessler (ed.), *Area Studies and Social Science: Strategies for Understanding Middle East Politics* (Bloomington: Indiana University Press, 1999), pp. 1–10. Anderson states the dilemma this way: "The lesson that political institutions and mechanisms are abstracted from their economic and social context only at great peril is one I shall never forget. At the same time, however, the equal and opposite temptation – to elaborate that very context at the expense of identifying the universal or generic qualities of particular concepts or institutions – is no better a solution" (pp. 4–5).

which occurred in Kuwait. Second, any cursory review of Kuwait's fiscal problems in the 1980s would reveal genuine elements of crisis and fear on the part of public officials. Reverberations from the Iranian revolution and the ongoing Iran–Iraq war heightened the vulnerabilities created by massive public and private debt. The behavior of Kuwaiti public officials throughout this period demonstrated that immediate dislocations could not be endured in the long term.

A second, rival explanation targets more particular features, viewing broad sociocultural differences as the key. Some economists have argued that a society's cultural baggage (whether it is individually or collectively oriented) molds the business organizations that take shape and the way market problems are resolved.[8] Setting aside the fact that Kuwait and Jordan can be considered part of a common Arab-Muslim culture, differences between the two cannot be ignored. Kuwaiti business elites were cut from the same social fabric as the ruling al-Sabah family. A history of shared social origins and a founding story of consensual rule seems to make the case that cooperative relations between business and state are to be expected there. In contrast, Jordan's early business elite appear as strangers and have hardly enjoyed a tradition of equality with the Hashemites.[9] In the aftermath of the 1967 war and again after Kuwait's liberation in 1991, waves of new Palestinian merchants reinforced the distinction between a Palestinian business class and an East Banker state. In such a context, coordination and cooperation on economic reform, and especially on privatization, are fraught with political difficulties pitting the security and support base of state rule (East Bank elites) against the necessity of encouraging private-sector (Palestinian) investment. This position argues against generalizing from these cases, but it fails to provide a clearer picture of the cases themselves.

Sociocultural origins – because they do not change over time – fail to explain the shift in relations that occurred in Kuwait once massive oil revenues made their impact in the 1950s and again in the wake of the 1970s oil embargo. While Jordanian state actions against private capital during the same period demonstrate that "flogging the private sector is generally good politics,"[10] there is little evidence to show these policies are rooted in a distinction between East Bank and West Bank. In each case,

---

[8] Avner Greif, "Cultural Beliefs and the Organization of Society: A Historical and Theoretical Reflection on Collectivist and Individualist Societies," *Journal of Political Economy*, 102, 5 (1994), pp. 912–950.

[9] Even these characterizations gloss over contrary observations. For instance, despite similar origins, the elite merchant families of Kuwait have rarely married into the ruling family. By contrast, in Jordan there have been marriages between Hashemite family members and merchant family members.

[10] Waterbury, *Exposed to Innumerable Delusions*, p. 213.

sociocultural claims make sense only when placed within the institutional and political framework of economic crisis. They cannot account for the institutional and political factors that actually determine whether developmental and reform outcomes will take place. Formation of cohesive and capable business representation in Kuwait anchors and reproduces the story of equality and shared identity. In modified Olsonian terms, membership and investment in business representation pay a form of non-material selective benefit – group identity and expression – especially in times when other forms of political participation are reduced. During crisis, institutional capacities on the part of business representation, not shared sociocultural origins, provide the mechanism to craft business–state coordination. The threat of Islamist political opposition, from groups whose leaderships share similar elite social origins, contributes to the political rationale for a business–state alliance. In Jordan, the slow decay of elite cohesion and representation unhinge the control of traditional business elites and deprive business organization of the kind of institutional capacities necessary for sustained coordination. Likewise, a weaker political opposition in Jordan does not pose the kind of political challenge that encourages the state to ally with business.

Business, state, and economic liberalization in the Arab world

At stake in terms of theory are arguments privileging the revenue and sectoral logics of business–state relations in the developing world. For the cases at hand, business organizations' weak influence over policy and shifts in state strategies during the boom period confirm a link between a state's resource base, policy autonomy, and relations with the private sector.[11] Indeed, the early establishment of an industrial chamber in Jordan and the lack of one in Kuwait might lead one to conclude that greater sectoral differentiation in Jordan is what accounts for weak business–state coordination. Since the 1980s, Jordan's industrial sector has generated about 13 to 14 percent of GDP, while Kuwait's average was about 4 percent; these are small percentages, to be sure, but comparatively divergent. Upon closer examination, however, it becomes apparent that investment in industry is not exclusive. Jordan's large trading merchants are also the country's industrial investors. Thus, the sectoral focus takes us some way toward an explanation, but there is much more to the

---

[11] This literature, moreover, has broader – if often unrecognizable – significance for other developing areas. By 2005, it is expected that the former Soviet states of Kazakhstan, Azerbaijan, Uzbekistan, and Turkmenistan will begin receiving billions in windfalls from their oil exports (*New York Times*, 15 February 1998).

story. As Philippe Schmitter has argued, interest associations offer the advantage of "continuous representation." In times of crisis and instability, administratively weakened Arab states have turned to organized business, in part, for precisely this reason. Thus, one recommendation arising from this study is that business should be brought into the analysis,[12] not as a sole artifact of structural processes but as a social, political, and institutional actor with distinct strong and weak points. Moreover, the role of organized business representation and its historical relations with state authority in these cases support the conviction that economists' (particularly the new institutional economic accounts) treatments of institutions as simply aggregated rules responding to market problems unnecessarily and unhelpfully limits analysis.[13]

Some clarifications are necessary, however. The argument in this study is not that the associational aspects of business–state relations are the sole variable shaping economic policy outcomes during crisis, nor is it the idea that business–state coordination axiomatically translates into wider developmental goods. The literature on associational governance in Western societies makes the argument that associations may have dysfunctional consequences for other ordering principles (community, market, and state) or that the importance of associations may vary from country to country, but this does not obviate investigation into the associational aspects of political outcomes.[14] Furthermore, this study's investigation supports findings from other parts of the developing world that conclude intense institutional interaction between business and state is an increasingly important component of economic management and reform in a global economy. In the case of late-late developers in the Arab world, we need to unpack these trends with a more catholic perspective of what shapes business–state relations and what are the political and economic effects of this relationship.

Into the late 1990s, outcomes from Jordan's and Kuwait's efforts at economic reform confirm the consensus among social scientists that the interests and actions of the private sector are crucial issues of analysis

---

[12] This does not mean other social actors and professional associations should be left out. The growing use of and critique of the social movements literature among Middle East comparativists suggest other avenues of research.

[13] Roger J. Hollingsworth and Robert Boyer, *Contemporary Capitalism: The Embeddedness of Institutions* (Cambridge, UK: Cambridge University Press, 1997); Doner and Schneider, "The New Institutional Economics, Business Associations, and Development"; and Williamson, "The Institutions and Governance of Economic Development and Reform."

[14] Wolfgang Streeck and Philippe Schmitter, "Community, Market, State – and Associations? The Prospective Contribution of Interest Governance to Social Order," in Streeck and Schmitter (eds.), *Private Interest Government: Beyond Market and State* (London: Sage, 1985), pp. 2–6.

among developing world countries. Where weak administrative capabilities are the norm due to rent or sectoral reliance, the private–public nexus becomes even more important. To some extent, states can declare elements of structural adjustment, shift subsidies, create new oversight, and so on with little outside assistance. However, seeing reforms through, ascertaining employment effects, changing investment patterns, and planning for the future require more capacities than these states currently possess. Moreover, the next phase of reforms (so-called second-generation reforms), such as product standards, supply logistics, more flexible production, and greater regional cooperation, will require greater, not less, coordination with domestic business. Much of the Middle East, Jordan and Kuwait included, is still working through the first phases of reform and their effects, but one lesson is clear. While private-sector investment may be slow in emerging, business efforts at shaping policy, lobbying, and coordinating with state officials have not lagged. Therefore, the focus by international lending agencies on the important role domestic business plays should be fruitful. Though business and state officials search for reform, issues of common interest on which to coordinate, how business preferences are communicated, how they are shaped, and what explains different capacities for collective action among business groups[15] determine the effects of "unleashing" the private sector.

International lending agencies also base much of their analysis of the private sector on comparison with entrepreneurs and organized business in the capitalist democracies. Consequently, there is a great deal of literature drawn from North American and European cases as to what constitutes effective business representation; however, successful capacities are usually assumed and there is less attention to exactly why or how such institutions take form:

There are virtually no systematic empirical studies that investigate comparatively and over time success and failure of national business communities in formally integrating their collective action and representation . . . In particular, we know little about the causal connection between organizational cohesion and political access.[16]

The cases of Jordan and Kuwait demonstrate the complex, yet observable, links among elite cohesion, business representation, and coordination

---

[15] Michael Shafer, "The Political Economy of Sectors and Sectoral Change: Korea Then and Now," in Maxfield and Schneider, *Business and the State in Developing Countries*, pp. 90–91.

[16] William Coleman and Wyn Grant, "The Organizational Cohesion and Political Access of Business: A Study of Comprehensive Associations," *European Journal of Political Research*, 16 (1989), pp. 483–484. Though this article is fifteen years old, Coleman and Grant's point still holds true.

with the state on economic reform. The historical narrative shows that institutionalized business representation served to reinforce elite socialization and recruitment at times when structural and rentier arguments expect their defection. Somewhat paradoxically, the business association itself benefited, through the investment that flowed from sustained elite control. By the 1980s this circle was broken in Jordan. The earlier changes in the structure of representation gradually eroded elite cohesion during precisely the decades in which state officials turned to the private sector for crisis assistance. As the largest private-sector representatives weakened, external associational and internal rank-and-file rivalries consistently impeded effective engagement with state authorities. The prevalence of particularist demands by the Amman Chamber of Commerce and its near uselessness as a political ally and policy partner (in formulation and implementation) shaped state perceptions. The death of King Hussein and the accession of King 'Abdullah to the throne in Jordan marked a shift in state strategies that was foreshadowed in the creation of the National Consultative Council in the early 1980s and the Private Sector Executive Committee in the 1990s. One of King 'Abdullah's first acts was to convene his own, hand-picked, Economic Consultative Committee with little associational representation. Initiatives to attract information technology investment, take advantage of a free-trade agreement with the United States, and expand the kingdom's export-processing and free-trade zones embody what Steven Heydemann has termed "selective economic rationalization,"[17] all of which invite movement to more *ad hoc*, informal networks of business–state interaction. Still, many of the same coordination issues – which plagued the fitful reform efforts of the 1980s and 1990s – remain. Into the new century, rival business representatives remain incapable of adjudicating competing claims, and institutional capacities offer little beyond what a government ministry is capable of. Meanwhile, the prime minister's office has enacted[18] scores of pieces of economic legislation, which will likely see uneven – if any – implementation. Still, Jordan's role as the USA's ally in addressing regional tensions offers temporary solutions of external rent and support.

In contrast, the Kuwaiti experience demonstrates a positive link between organizational cohesion and political access. William Coleman and Philippe Schmitter have argued that, in much the same way as state autonomy is viewed as essential to increase state capabilities, similar

---

[17] Steven Heydemann, "The Political Logic of Economic Rationality: Selective Stabilization in Syria," in Henri J. Barkey (ed.), *The Politics of Economic Reform in the Middle East* (New York: St. Martin's Press, 1992), pp. 11–39.

[18] In Kuwait and Jordan, the prime minister can enact legislation when parliament is not in session, but each law must be approved once it reconvenes.

Table 5.1 *The structure of Kuwaiti and Jordanian business representation in the 1990s and 2000*

Kuwaiti attributes	Jordanian attributes
Horizontal differentiation	
Substructure differentiation by product and sector contributes to intra-associational interest mediation	*Little or uneven differentiation impedes intra-associational mediation*
Vertical integration	
Integration through interaction between committee and executive structures; executive board interacts and guides rank-and-file committees	*Flat structure and little interaction*
Horizontal links	
Good relations with other associations; other associations desire alliance; little competition for membership	*Competition with other business associations for individual members' exclusive loyalty*
Resources	
Diverse resource base and presence of professional staff; capable of ordering complex information and developing consistent policy and research skills	*Exclusively from member dues; dependence on executive board; weak research and information-gathering capacities*

Source: Adapted from William D. Coleman, *Business and Politics: A Study of Collective Action* (Montreal: McGill-Queens University Press, 1995), p. 55.

autonomy for a business association is key to enabling it to play its own policy role. Autonomous leadership can rise above the particulars of membership conflicts, seek out the longer-term advantage, and more easily mediate between members' and state interests.[19] This was clearly exemplified by the balanced debt proposals espoused by the KCCI leadership in the 1980s. The association effectively mediated conflicting internal interests to chart a clear, steady policy throughout the decade. Less encompassing and more restricted representation rules allowed Kuwaiti representation to avoid the spiraling circle of elite defections and institutional disarticulation experienced in Jordan. Institutional stability allows greater return on investments in the kind of capabilities that facilitate engagement with the state. Table 5.1 presents the divergent structural and administrative capacities that flowed from these larger dynamics.

The importance to economic reform and development of these extra-state institutional capacities highlights a final, general lesson. Though

[19] William D. Coleman, *Business and Politics: A Study of Collective Action* (Montreal: McGill-Queens University Press, 1995); and Streeck and Schmitter, "Community, Market, State – and Associations?"

similar external crises and price shifts have had an impact on the countries of the Middle East, the cases of Kuwait and Jordan are typical in displaying variations in their domestic responses and reforms. If one can therefore conclude that the line between domestic and international is at best blurred, then one must recognize that what may be considered as common obstacles to market reform in the developing world are better viewed as "local problems." Meaningful economic growth and effective reform in the face of external pressures are not achieved through boiler-plate solutions or pushing one-size-fits-all institutional arrangements through a consensus of international lenders. Solutions are achieved through an array of different institutional settings[20] and skill sets requiring attention to the origins and evolution of domestic institutions of economic governance.[21] These institutional arrangements and the factors that shape them "vary not only across countries but also within countries over time."[22] Consequently, the political environment in which business elites operate, changing coalition calculations, the expansion of policy participation, changes in the composition of the business community, and the institutional capacities to learn from the past all shape the character of developmental problems and their solutions. Little analytical purpose is served by resort to neat (often normative) distinctions between rent-seeking by organized business and its support of broader developmental policies. Evidence from these Middle Eastern cases echoes findings in other regions that it is the political context of rent-seeking that determines developmental and distributive impacts.[23]

Economic crisis, business representation, and the question of political reform

The fiscal crisis that gripped the entire Middle East in the early 1980s is broadly credited with sparking political reform, with Jordan and Kuwait demonstrating this most obviously. Confronted with increasing fiscal constraints, many Middle Eastern regimes faced the challenge of gradually

[20] Dani Rodrik, "Institutions for High-Quality Growth: What They Are and How to Acquire Them," *Studies in Comparative International Development*, 35, 3 (Fall 2000), pp. 3–32; and Rodrik, *The New Global Economy and Developing Countries: Making Openness Work* (Washington, DC: Overseas Development Council, 1999). One should note, however, that Rodrik's definition of an institution is restricted to the traditional conception of "behavioral rules" and not interests or associations.

[21] Kathleen Thelen, "Historical Institutionalism in Comparative Politics," *Annual Review of Political Science*, 2 (1999), pp. 369–404.

[22] Rodrik, "Institutions for High-Quality Growth," p. 7.

[23] See David Kang, *Crony Capitalism: Corruption and Development in South Korea and the Philippines* (Cambridge, UK: Cambridge University Press, 2002); and Khan and Jomo, *Rents, Rent-Seeking and Economic Development*.

replacing past social contracts with what John Waterbury labeled new "extraction contracts."[24] There were persistent hopes that deeper political liberalization and even democratization would take hold. What is now evident to all observers is the comparative insulation of Arab countries to the waves of democratization and political reform that swept many other regions in the late 1980s and 1990s. The hesitant steps toward liberalization that were taken in Kuwait, Jordan, Morocco, Yemen, Egypt, Tunisia, and Bahrain now appear to have stalled or to be in reverse. Elite splits within regimes (the soft-liner/hard-liner conflicts that Philippe Schmitter and Guillermo O'Donnell emphasized), which might advance liberalization, appear limited. The old leftist/nationalist elements in many Arab states are divided and ineffective. The powerful currents of political Islam, while not spent politically, appear unwilling or unable to challenge the status quo in ways that compare with the "resurgence of civil society" in Latin America and Eastern Europe.[25] Though this study's primary focus is not on the private-sector role in political liberalization, nevertheless, the fact that intensified business–state engagement in both cases occurred alongside elements of political liberalization requires discussion. Is Arab business the avatar of greater political liberalism and even democratization? Or perhaps a more useful inquiry follows Doner and Schneider, who argue that "the issue is not so much to determine whether capitalists exercise disproportionate influence and to seek ways to reduce it, but rather how to make the inevitable exercise of their power less dysfunctional for democracy."[26]

To begin in terms of theory, the role organized business representation plays in democratization is expected to be limited. The experience of Latin America and Eastern Europe suggests that associational interest representation is generally more important in determining what kind of democracy is consolidated than for the role it plays in the actual democratization itself.[27] Certainly in the Middle East, business and its representation can be expected to press for the rule of law where it affects issues such as investment, taxation, trade, and so on, and to be less eager to liberalize when it may have an impact on labor and human rights issues. The fate of deeper liberalization and democratization in the region certainly does

[24] John Waterbury, "From Social Contracts to Extraction Contracts: The Political Economy of Authoritarianism and Democracy," in John P. Entelis (ed.), *Islam, Democracy, and the State in North Africa* (Bloomington: Indiana University Press, 1997).

[25] Philippe Schmitter, "The Consolidation of Democracy and the Representation of Social Groups," *American Behavioral Scientist*, 35, 4/5 (March/June), p. 430.

[26] Richard Doner and Ben Ross Schneider, "Business Associations, Development, and Democracy," unpublished manuscript, Emory University, 1997, p. 23.

[27] Schmitter, "The Consolidation of Democracy and the Representation of Social Groups"; and Streeck and Schmitter, "Community, Market, State – and Associations?"

not, therefore, hang on the private sector alone. In the absence of strong political parties in the Middle East, interest associations, like business, can reasonably be expected to play a greater role in future transitions. With these caveats in mind, one can sketch both the positive and the negative ramifications of organized business's political reassertion.

In the parts of the Middle East where organized business was fully corporatized, the Jordanian and Kuwaiti models of business representation have provided a road map. For example, Egyptian, Syrian, and Qatari businessmen have succeeded in forming autonomous representative bodies or at least in achieving the right to elect their own leaders.[28] As large self-governing social institutions, business associations in Jordan and Kuwait have remained islands of participatory politics during periods of suspended parliaments. Internal struggles over representation and membership suffrage were key variables in the evolution of each institution. Though expansion of membership and voting in the Jordanian case and restriction of the same in the Kuwaiti case had divergent outcomes with respect to engaging the state, these elements of contestation and compromise are central to participatory politics. At the leadership level, Kuwait's more exclusive organizational characteristics actually facilitated greater inclusion of previously unrepresented elements of the private sector. Thus, can such associations operating within non-democratic contexts be thought of as types of Tocquevillean civilizing agents? The evidence suggests not. Cosmopolitan business elites hardly operate as prisoners of their own countries' political cultures. Extensive travel and dealings with businessmen from a variety of political contexts provide as much or more democratic socialization as associational service. From time to time during the 1980s and 1990s, when leaders of Kuwait's and Jordan's business associations were appointed to head government ministries, their behavior demonstrated little benefit from a background of associational participation. There was little that set them apart from other ministers from different backgrounds. What then of the external activities of organized business as direct or indirect factors in greater liberalization?

One of the lessons from the study of the transition to democracy in Latin America and Eastern Europe is that interest associations, like business, can play a role in "the resurgence of civil society" by withdrawing support for authoritarian rulers (among other ways). Generally, the role of associations in transitions may be great because, as Schmitter argues, "they [associations] will have been more tolerated by the ancien

---

[28] In the 1990s, the Damascus Chamber of Commerce elected a prominent critic of government economic policies to sit on its executive board. The Qatari government completely suspended government appointment of business organization leaders, and Egypt has allowed independent associations to form.

regimes than political parties." As noted above, this observation is particularly applicable to most Middle Eastern countries, where political parties are notoriously weak.[29] To date, however, decades of economic crisis have yet to yield circumstances in which organized business withdraws support from the state. Eva Bellin argues that Arab business is unlikely to play such a role, due to its dependence on the state and its fear of the possible results of the political opposition gaining power.[30] Dependence varies, especially as fiscal crises deepen, and political oppositions are not uniform in their capacities, as the Kuwaiti and Jordanian experiences reveal. While this evidence casts doubt on the expectation that Arab business will play a role in political liberalization through its withdrawal of support from the state, there remains important variation that is not captured through a binary distinction of pro- versus anti-democratic.

Though more exclusive in nature, Kuwait's business representation could claim the mantle of democratic actor, at least for a time. Heir to the 1938 Majlis movement, the KCCI served as a quasi-political party during periods when parliament was suspended. The KCCI and its leadership were a major force among the Kuwaiti opposition demanding a return of parliament after liberation from Iraq. Both Kuwaiti and Jordanian organizations used the increased freedom of the press that accompanied political liberalization to enter public policy debates and spur discussion of economic policies. In similar ways, though in a context of less political opening, Saudi, Egyptian, Qatari, Bahraini, Yemeni, and Syrian business elites have used their representative associations as venues to gain leverage in debates on public policy. The issue then becomes whether such associational adoption of quasi-state functions (setting product standards, adjudicating disputes, implementating policies) will enhance the prospects for greater political decentralization. Transparency and accountability won by an association might spill over into other areas.

No doubt from a pluralist perspective the participation of organized business in the public debates that defined Jordanian and Kuwaiti politics in the 1980s and 1990s is evidence of positive progression. In general, however, patterns of the reassertion of business throughout the region support the view that business will acquiesce to an authoritarian regime if it feels its interests are represented.[31] For instance, in Kuwait, once

---

[29] Schmitter, "The Consolidation of Democracy"; Lust-Okar, "The Decline of Jordanian Political Parties."

[30] Bellin, "Contingent Democrats."

[31] Ben Ross Schneider, "Business Politics in Latin America," unpublished draft manuscript, Northwestern University, 2002; and Dietrich Rueschemeyer, Evelyne Huber Stephens, and John Stephens, *Capitalist Development and Democracy* (Cambridge, UK: Cambridge University Press, 1992).

parliament was reinstated (along with greater economic policy consultation with the KCCI), organized Kuwaiti business pushed reform no further. The historical role of Kuwaiti merchants as the vanguard of participatory politics in the Gulf has been turned inside out. Evidence in the 1990s suggests that organized business representatives worked closely with state officials to increase, not decrease, central political control over elements of the opposition. The policy access created and exploited by KCCI elites has not widened to other social actors, and even efforts to create other associative interests have been resisted. Similar patterns appeared in Egypt and Syria, where government openings to business have excluded other actors.[32] Institutional weakness in the Jordanian case had similar results. At a crucial point during the sales tax debate, the ACC withdrew its support for parliamentary approval of future taxes, a potentially important lever in wider political decentralization. The ACC's weak participation in Jordan's broad opposition to normalization with Israel was emblematic of organized business's lack of support for opposition attempts to expand political participation in the 1980s and 1990s. Thus, in Kuwait it was a quasi-alliance between organized business and state that contributed to the stagnation of political liberalization, while in Jordan it was business's general aloofness from the political opposition.

Arab business associations are engaging state authority in a variety of new ways, yet their activities appear structurally isolated. In neither the Kuwaiti nor the Jordanian case did organized business craft backward linkages into a political party or movement. Kuwaiti business did participate in elections through the country's system of quasi-party politics, but its involvement was geared toward supporting a few strategic candidates. In parliament, business members often sided with state allies against Islamist and tribal deputies. Since the failed Majlis movement of 1938, Kuwaiti business elites have clearly opted for a strategy of internal solidarity and cohesion, instead of risking the compromise that comes with broader political appeal and mobilization. The same has been generally true in Egypt and Yemen, where businessmen have won election to parliament but often neither as members of a party nor with institutionalized private-sector support. Efforts to craft a "business party" in Jordan ran aground on the divisive politics that have plagued Jordan's business representatives. Those same representatives proved weak allies for the rest of Jordan's professional syndicates who banded together in the late 1990s to protest normalization with Israel. The institutional aloofness of

---

[32] See Volker Perthes, "The Private Sector, Economic Liberalization, and the Prospects of Democratization: The Case of Syria and Some Other Arab Countries," in Salamé, *Democracy Without Democrats?*, pp. 243–269; and Kienle, *A Grand Delusion*.

Appendix
Comparative associational data

Table A.1 *Membership of the executive board of the Kuwait Chamber of Commerce and Industry, 1965–1995*

1965

'Abdulaziz H. al-Sagr, President
Yousef Fulaij, 1st Vice President
'Abdullah Yousef Fahim, 2nd Vice President
'Abdulaziz al-Bahr
'Abdullah 'Aziz Ahmed al-Bahr
'Abdullah Yousef al-Ghanim
Yousef Ibrahim al-Ghanim
Yaqub al-Hamad

Hamoud al-Zaid al-Khaled
Muhammed al-Khourafi
Fahad al-Marzouq
'Abdullatif al-Nisf
Muhammed Yousef al-Nisf
Badr al-Saalam
'Abdulmohsen Faisal al-Thuwaini

1970

'Abdulaziz H. al-Sagr, President
Yousef Fulaij, 1st Vice President
Muhammed al-Khourafi, 2nd Vice President
Muhammed Yousef al-Nisf, Treasurer
'Abdullah 'Aziz Ahmed al-Bahr
Muhammed 'Abdurrahim al-Bahr
Sulaiman 'Abdullah al-Aiban
Yousef Ibrahim al-Ghanim
Yaqub al-Hamad
Yaqub Yousef al-Humaidi

Hussain Makki al-Juma'a
Hamoud al-Zaid al-Khaled
Nasser Abdulwahab al-Qatami
Ibrahim Abdullah al-Qatan
'Abdurrahman 'Abdullah Rowaih
Ahmed Salah al-Shayaa
Muhammed 'Abdulsalam Shu'aib
'Abdulmohsen Faisal al-Thuwaini
Badrassalem Abdullah al-Wahab
'Abdurrazzak Khalid al-Zaid

1975

'Abdulaziz H. al-Sagr, President
Yousef Fulaij, 1st Vice President
Muhammed al-Khourafi, 2nd Vice President
Muhammed Yousef al-Nisf, Treasurer
Muhammed Hamad al-'Aliqi
Muhammed 'Abdurrahim al-Bahr
Sulaiman 'Abdullah al-Aiban
Sa'ud 'Abdulaziz al-Fawzan
Yousef Ibrahim al-Ghanim
Yaqub al-Hamad
Yaqub Yousef al-Humaidi
Hamad Yousef al-'Issa

Hussain Makki al-Juma'a
Yousef 'Abdulaziz Mezaini
Barak 'Abdulmohsen al-Mtair
'Abdulbaqi 'Abdallah al-Nouri
Nasser 'Abdulwahab al-Qatami
Ibrahim Abdullah al-Qatan
Ahmed Salah al-Shayaa
'Abdulsalam Shu'aib
'Abdulmohsen Faisal al-Thuwaini
'Ali 'Abdurrahman al-'Umr
Badrassalem al-'Abdullah al-Wahab
'Abdurrazzak Khalid al-Zaid

1980

'Abdulaziz H. al-Sagr, President
Yousef Fulaij, 1st Vice President
Muhammed al-Khourafi, 2nd Vice President
Muhammed Yousef al-Nisf, Treasurer

Muhammed 'Abdurrahin al-Bahr
Sulaiman 'Abdullah al-Aiban
Sa'ud Abdulaziz al-Fawzan
Yousef Ibrahim al-Ghanim

(*cont.*)

Table A.1 (cont.)

Abdal-Majid al-Sayyed Ahmed al-Ghirballi
Yaqub al-Hamad
Yaqub Yousef al-Humaidi
Hamad Yousef al-'Issa
Hussain Makki al-Juma'a
Yousef 'Abdulaziz Mezeini
Barak 'Abdulmohsen al-Mtair
'Abdulbaqi 'Abdullah an-Nouri

Nasser 'Abdulwahab al-Qatami
Ibrahim 'Abdullah al-Qatan
Khaled 'Issa al-Saleh
Ahmed Salah al-Shayaa
Muhammed 'Abdulsalam Shu'aib
'Abdulmohsen Faisal al-Thuwaini
'Ali 'Abdurrahman al-Umr
'Abdurrazzak Khaled al-Zaid

1985

'Abdulaziz H. al-Sagr, President
Yousef Fulaij, 1st Vice President
Muhammed al-Khourafi, 2nd Vice President
'Abdurrazzak Khaled al-Zaid, Treasurer
Muhammed 'Abdurrahim al-Bahr
Ghanim Hamad Jasem al-Dabbous
Badr 'Ali al-Da'oud
Sulaiman 'Abdullah al-Aiban
'Ali Muhammed Thunayan al-Ghanim
Qays 'Abdullah Thunayan al-Ghanim
Yousef Ibrahim al-Ghanim
Yaqub al-Hamad

Ahmed Khalif al-Jasem
Salah Fahd al-Marzouq
Hilal Mushari Hilal al-Mteiri
Hamoud Yousef al-Nisf
'Abdulbaqi 'Abdullah an-Nouri
Nasser 'Abdulwahab al-Qatami
Ibrahim 'Abdullah al-Qatan
Khaled 'Issa al-Saleh
Ahmed Saleh al-Shayaa
Muhammed 'Abdulsalam Shu'aib
'Abdulmohsen Faisal al-Thuwaini

1990

'Abdulaziz H. al-Sagr, President
Yousef Fulaij, 1st Vice President
Muhammed al-Khourafi, 2nd Vice President
'Abdurrazzak Khaled al-Zaid, Treasurer
Muhammed 'Abdurrahim al-Bahr
Ghanim Hamad Jasem al-Dabbous
Sami 'Ali al-Ghanim al-Dabbous
Sulaiman 'Abdullah al-Aiban
'Ali Mohammed Thunayan al-Ghanim
Qays 'Abdullah Thunayan al-Ghanim
Yousef Ibrahim al-Ghanim
'Abdalmajid al-Sayyed Ahmed al-Ghirballi

Yaqub al-Hamad
Mubarak 'Abdulaziz al-Hasawi
Salah Fahd al-Marzouq
Hamoud Yousef al-Nisf
Nasser 'Abdulwahab al-Qatami
Khaled 'Issa al-Saleh
Jayer Badr Muhammed al-Sayer
Nasser Muhammed al-Sayer
Ahmed Saleh al-Shayaa
Muhammed 'Abdulsalam Shu'aib
'Abdulmohsen Faisal al-Thuwaini
Muhammed 'Abdullah Ahmed al-'Uraifan

1995

'Abdulaziz H. al-Sagr, President
'Abdurrazzak Khaled al-Zaid, 1st Vice President
Yousef Ibrahim al-Ghanim, 2nd Vice President
Yousef Fulaij, Treasurer
Muhammed 'Abdurrahim al-Bahr
'Abdullah Muhammed Sa'ud al-Baijan[a]
Sulaiman 'Abdullah al-Aiban
Jamil S. al-Essa[b]
Muhammed Hamoud Zamel al-Fajji[c]
'Ali Mohammed Thunayan al-Ghanim
Salah Khalifa Talal al-Jari[d]
Jawad Ahmed Bu-Khamseen[e]

'Abdurrazzik 'Abdullah Ma'arafi[f]
Salah Fahad al-Marzouq
Faisal 'Ali al-Mutawa'
Hamoud Yousef al-Nisf
'Abdulbaqi 'Abdullah an-Nouri
Muhammed 'Abdulmohsen al-Sayegh
Nasser Muhammed al-Sayer
Ahmed Saleh al-Shayaa
Muhammed 'Abdulsalam Shu'aib
'Abdulmohsen Faisal al-Thuwaini
Muhammed 'Abdullah Ahmed al-'Uraifan
'Abdulwahab al-Wazzan[g]

Notes: Various interviewees provided biographical details on selected board members new in 1995.
[a] Former Muslim Brotherhood.
[b] Young entrepreneur.
[c] Muslim Brotherhood sympathies.
[d] Bedouin; former parliamentarian, 1985.
[e] Shia; prominent in Manakh crash debts.
[f] Shia.
[g] Young, Shia.

Table A.2 *Kuwaiti Chamber of Commerce and Industry membership totals*

Year	Membership total
1960	1,579
1965	2,434
1970	2,994
1975	4,483
ANNUAL	
1976	4,890
1977	5,610
1978	6,341
1979	7,109
1980	8,616
1981	n.a.
1982	n.a.
1983	11,161
1984	12,483
1985	13,284
1986	12,114
1987	13,484
1988	13,040
1989	15,419
1990	21,952
1991	16,296
1992	22,905
1993	36,817
1994	n.a.
1995	47,014

Source: KCCI, *Al-Taqrir al-Sanawiyy, Ghurfat Tijarat wa Sana'at al-Kuwait* [Annual report, Kuwait Chamber of Commerce and Industry], various years.

Table A.3 *Kuwait Chamber of Commerce and Industry membership breakdown, 1990s*

Membership class	1990	1993	1995
Proprietor	661	661	535
Establishment	15,395	28,273	34,614
Partnership company	762	1,297	2,005
Joint liability company	959	1,381	1,874
With limited liability	3,855	4,857	5,502
Kuwait shareholding company	n.a.	n.a.	52
Kuwait shareholding company (closed)	236	259	289
Gulf shareholding companies	n.a.	6	6
Shareholding company (open)	49	49	1
Kuwait shareholding companies	n.a.	n.a.	4
Cooperative society	27	26	29
Craft	n.a.	n.a.	911
Branch (subsidiary)	n.a.	n.a.	81
Union	8	8	10
Branch with limited liability	n.a.	n.a.	220
Branch of partnership	n.a.	n.a.	59
Branch of joint liability	n.a.	n.a.	71
Branch of Kuwait shareholding	n.a.	n.a.	30
Commercial agency (trade)	n.a.	n.a.	576
Commercial agency (services)	n.a.	n.a.	53
Commercial agency (contracting)	n.a.	n.a.	92

Source: Figures provided by KCCI, Public Affairs Department.

Table A.4 *Membership of the executive board of the Amman Chamber of Commerce, 1923–1995*

1923

Yousef 'Asfour, President
Muhammed 'Othman al-Battikhi
'Ali al-Kurdi
Sa'id al-Kurdi
'Abdurrahman Madi
Ahmed Malhas

Amin Manku
Asad al-Saber
Khair al-Sa'udi
Hasan al-Shurbaji
Salim al-Wirr

1926

Muhammed Tahir al-Jaqqa, President
Muhammed Sharim, Vice President
Khair al-Diraniyya
Isma'il Haqqi
Ahmed Malhas

Hamdi Manku
'Awis al-Mosharbash
Asad al-Saber
Muhammed al-Sa'udi
Khalil al-Talhouni

Table A.4 (*cont.*)

1928	
Zaki al-Idlabi, President	Asad al-Saber
Muhammed Sharim, Vice President	Muhammed al-Sa'udi
Subhi al-Haj Hassan	Khalil Shuqair
Muhammed al-Kurdi	Hassan al-Shurbaji
'Abdurrahman Madi	Subri al-Tabba
Ahmed Malhas	Khalil al-Talhouni
'Awis al-Mosharbash	

1935	
'Abduldhiyyab, President	'Umar al-Mu'albaki
Muhammed Sharim, Vice President	Tawfiq Qattan
Shawkat 'Asfour	Jamil al-Safadi
Muhammed 'Ali Bdair	Khalil Shuqair
Ahmed Malhas	Hashim al-Tabba
Hamdi Manku	Subri al-Tabba

1941	
Subri al-Tabba, President	Rashid Darouza
Hamdi Manku, Vice President	Ramzi al-Haffar
'Umar al-Mu'albaki	Subhi al-Halabi
Shawkat 'Asfour	Hashim al-Tabba
Salem Bakhit	Yasin al-Talhouni
Isma'il al-Bilbaisi	

1943–1946
Records incomplete

1946	
Subri al-Tabba, President	Wajih al-Baghdadi
Hamdi Manku, Vice President	'Abdurrahim al-Nowari
'Adel al-Safadi	Faris al-Sa'udi
'Umar al-Mu'albaki	Hashim al-Tabba
Salem Bakhit	Yasin al-Talhouni
Khair al-Diraniyya	Subhi al-Halabi
Shafiq al-Hayek	'Abdurrahman Madi
Hashim Touqan	Ramzi al-Haffar

1948	
Muhammed 'Ali Bdair, President	Ilyas al-Mu'ashar
'Umar al-Mu'albaki, Vice President	Ibrahim Manku
Muhammed Khair Abu Arsheed	'Abdurrahim al-Nouri
Hassan Aziziyya	Tawfiq Qattan
Jawdat al-Bitar	Jawdat Sha'asha'a
Rashid Darouza	Mounir Shaqir
Khair al-Diraniyya	Hashim al-Tabba
Ramzi al-Haffar	Subri al-Tabba
'Abdurrahim Abu Hassan	Yasin al-Talhouni
Shafiq al-Hayek	Hashim Touqan
Husni Sidalkurdi	Subhi al-Usta

(*cont.*)

Table A.4 (*cont.*)

1949

Subri al-Tabba, President
Muhammed 'Ali Bdair, Vice President
'Abdurrahim Abu Hassan
Sami 'Asfour
Shafiq al-Hayek
Muhammed Madi

Sa'id Malhas
'Abdurrahim al-Nouri
Tawfiq Qattan
Hamdi al-Safadi
Jawdat Sha'asha'a
Yasin al-Talhouni

1954

Ibrahim Manku, President
Shafiq al-Hayek, Vice President
Da'oud Ahram
Salim Hassan Arafa
Munir al-Asmar
Arafat al-Bitar

George Dib
Shaher al-Hamli
Husni Sidalkurdi
Wajih Murad
Faisel al-Tabba
Hashim Touqan

1958

Ibrahim Manku
Muhammed 'Ali Bdair } President and Vice President[1]
Mustafa Abu Zaid
Salim Hassan Arafa
Zuhair 'Asfour

Jawdet al-Bitar
George Dib
Sa'id Malhas
Malik al-Masri
Hashim Touqan

1962

Ibrahim Manku, President
Tawfiq al-Tabba, Vice President
'Abdurrahim Abu Hassan
Hatim Alloush
Rashad Barakat
Farid Kassab

Malik al-Masri
'Adel al-Nouri
Musa Abu al-Raghib
Ahmed Yasin
Misbah al-Zamili
Ibrahim al-Zain

1966

Muhammed 'Ali Bdair, President
Zuhair 'Asfour, Vice President
'Abdurrahim Abu Hassan
Munir al-Asmar
Muhammed Tahir al-Haddad
George Khannuf

'Ali Manku
Malik al-Masri
'Adel al-Nouri
Sa'id Shaheen
Tawfiq al-Tabba
Hashim Touqan

1970

Muhammed 'Ali Bdair, President
Zuhair 'Asfour, Vice President
Ihsan Nimr Abu Dabbi
Mamdouh Abu Hassan
Muhammed Khalil 'Ashour
'Umar Muhammed al-Banna

Jamil 'Arif Barakat
Ahmed Ratib Ghanim
Muhammed Tahir al-Haddad
'Adel al-Nouri
Ibrahim 'Abdal Rajjal
Hashim Touqan

Table A.4 (*cont.*)

1974

Muhammed 'Ali Bdair, President	Muhammed Tahir al-Haddad
Zuhair 'Asfour, Vice President	Mamdouh Abu Hassan
'Umar Mustafa Abu Zaid	Muhammed Khair Bahjat al-Humsi
'Umar Muhammed al-Banna	Tawfiq Amin Qaawar
Jamil 'Arif Barakat	Khalil Yasin al-Talhouni
Ahmed Ratib Ghanim	Hashim Touqan

1978

Muhammed 'Ali Bdair, President	Ahmed Ratib Ghanim
Zuhair 'Asfour, Vice President	Sa'id 'Uthman Ma'atouq
Mamdouh Abu Hassan	Tawfiq Amin Qa'awar
'Umar Muhammed al-Banna	Hamdi al-Tabba
Jamil 'Arif Barakat	Hashim Touqan
Muhammed Khair Dib	Hassan Jamil Zakariya

1982

Hamdi Tabba, President	Muhammed Khair Bahjat al-Humsi
Muhammed al-Hajj Deeb, Vice President	Sa'id 'Uthman Ma'atouq
'Umar Mustafa Abu Zaid	Tawfiq Amin Qaawar
'Adnan 'Abdulkareem Darouza	'Abdulaziz Salhab
Ahmed Ratib Ghanim	Hashim Touqan
Hani al-Hajj Hassan	Muhammed Marwan Yousef Zubda

1986

Muhammed 'Asfour, President	Muhammed Khair Bahjat al-Humsi
'Adnan 'Abdulkarim Darouza, Vice President	Salim Mustafa Kharfan
'Umar Mustafa Abu Zaid	Samir Mansour al-Mu'ashshir
Muhammed al-Hajj Deeb	Haidar Murad
Ahmed Ratib Ghanim	Riyad al-Saifi
Hani al-Hajj Hassan	Yousef Ahmed al-Sardi

1990

Muhammed 'Asfour, President	Salim Mustafa Kharfan
Haidar Murad, Vice President	Walid Hashim al-Khatib
Muhammed al-Hajj Deeb	Muhammed al-Muhtasib
Hani al-Hajj Hassan	Riyad al-Saifi
Muhammed Khair Bahjat al-Humsi	Yousef Ahmed al-Sardi
Ghassan Shaqib Kharfan	Isma'il Marshad al-Taraira

Note: [1] This board alternated president and vice president each year.

Table A.5 *Amman Chamber of Commerce, membership by category*

Year	Mumtaz	1st	2nd	3rd	4th	5th	Total
		Membership category					
1923			23	34	34		91
1925			2	13	61		76
1930			11	14	58		83
1935		1	12	1	20		34
1937		1	6	10	17		34
1940							300
1950							500
1960							2,000
1970							2,100
1975	89	161	132	993	2,702	1,116	5,193
1980	323	223	253	2,652	2,887	1,249	7,587
1982							
1984							
1985	790	374	452	4,874	6,044	533	13,067
1986							
1987							
1988							
1989							
1990	663	371	416	5,589	10,726	1,636	19,401
1991	660	459	442	6,701	12,401	1,438	22,101
1992							
1993							
1994							
1995	1,044	869	569	9,413	16,008	1,007	28,910

Source: Amman Chamber of Commerce Data, Information and Research Department; ACC, *Al-Taqrir al-Sanawiyy, Ghurfat Tijarat 'Amman* [Annual report, Amman Chamber of Commerce] various years. Some data missing in original documents.

Note: Membership categories correspond to the member's stated capital. *Mumtaz* (excellent) is the highest category.

Select bibliography

Abidi, Aqil Hyder Hasan, *Jordan: A Political Study, 1948–1957* (London: Asia Publishing House, 1965).

Abu-Hakima, Ahmad Mustafa, *The Modern History of Kuwait* (London: Luzac, 1983).

Abu Nowar, Ma'an, *The History of the Hashemite Kingdom of Jordan*, vol. I, *The Creation and Development of Transjordan: 1920–1929* (Oxford, UK: Ithaca Press, 1989).

ACC (Amman Chamber of Commerce), *al-Kitab al-Dhahabi* [The golden book: 50th anniversary of the Amman Chamber of Commerce] (Amman: Amman Chamber of Commerce, 1973).

Al-Qanun wa al-Nizam, Ghurfat Tijarat 'Amman [By-laws and rules of the Amman Chamber of Commerce], 1995.

Al-Taqrir al-Sanawiyy, Ghurfat Tijarat 'Amman [Annual report, Amman Chamber of Commerce], various years.

Amawi, Abla, *State and Class in Transjordan: A Study of State Autonomy*, Ph.D. Dissertation: Georgetown University (1993).

Amman Chamber of Industry, *Nizam Ghurfat Sana'at 'Amman* [By-laws of the Amman Chamber of Industry], 1961.

Anderson, Lisa, "Politics in the Middle East: Opportunities and Limits in the Quest for Theory," in Mark Tessler (ed.), *Area Studies and Social Science: Strategies for Understanding Middle East Politics* (Bloomington: Indiana University Press, 1999), pp. 1–10.

"Remaking the Middle East: The Prospects for Democracy and Stability," *Ethics and International Affairs*, 6 (1992), pp. 163–171.

The State and Social Transformation in Tunisia and Libya, 1830–1980 (Princeton: Princeton University Press, 1986).

Anscombe, Frederick F., *The Ottoman Gulf: The Creation of Kuwait, Saudi Arabia, and Qatar* (New York: Columbia University Press, 1997).

Arab Bank (Amman, Jordan), *Annual Reports*, various years.

Assiri, Abdul-Reda and Kamal Al-Monoufi, "Kuwait's Political Elite: The Cabinet," *Middle East Journal*, 42 (Winter 1988), pp. 48–58.

Baer, Gabriel, "Land Tenure in the Hashemite Kingdom of Jordan," *Land Economics* (August 1957), pp. 187–197.

Barkey, J. Henri, *The State and Industrialization Crisis in Turkey* (Boulder: Westview Press, 1990).

Bates, Robert (ed.), *Toward a Political Economy of Development: A Rational Choice Perspective* (Berkeley: University of California Press, 1988).

Bates, Robert and Anne O. Krueger, *Political and Economic Interactions in Economic Policy Reform: Evidence from Eight Countries* (Cambridge, MA: Blackwell, 1993).

Bates, Robert and Da-Hsiang Donald Lien, "A Note on Taxation, Development and Representative Government," *Politics & Society*, 14, 1 (1985), pp. 53–70.

Beblawi, Hazem, *The Arab Gulf Economy in a Turbulent Age* (New York: St. Martin's Press, 1984).

"The Rentier State in the Arab World," in Luciani, *The Arab State*, pp. 85–98.

Beblawi, Hazem and Giacomo Luciani (eds.), *The Rentier State* (New York: Croom Helm, 1987).

Bellin, Eva, "Contingent Democrats, Industrialists, Labor, and Democratization in Late-Developing Countries," *World Politics*, 52, 2 (January 2000), pp. 175–205.

Bianchi, Robert, *Interest Groups and Political Development in Turkey* (Princeton: Princeton University Press, 1984).

Boone, Catherine, *Merchant Capital and the Roots of State Power in Senegal, 1930–1985* (Cambridge: Cambridge University Press, 1996).

Brand, Laurie A., "Economic and Political Liberalization in a Rentier Economy: The Case of the Hashemite Kingdom of Jordan," in Iliya Harik and Denis J. Sullivan (eds.), *Privatization and Liberalization in the Middle East* (Bloomington: Indiana University Press, 1992), pp. 167–188.

Jordan's Inter-Arab Relations: The Political Economy of Alliance Making (New York: Columbia University Press, 1994).

Brynen, Rex, "Economic Crisis and Post-Rentier Democratization in the Arab World: The Case of Jordan," *Canadian Journal of Political Science*, 25, 1 (March 1992).

Brynen, Rex, Baghat Korany, and Paul Noble (eds.), *Political Liberalization and Democratization in the Arab World*, vol. I, *Theoretical Perspectives* (Boulder: Lynne Rienner, 1995).

de Candole, E. A. V., "Kuwait Today," *Journal of the Royal Central Asian Society* (29 September 1964).

Central Bank of Jordan, *Yearly Statistical Series (1964–1993)* (Amman: Central Bank of Jordan, October 1994).

Chaudhry, Kiren Aziz, "The Myth of the Market and Late Developers," *Politics & Society*, 21 (September 1993), pp. 245–274.

The Price of Wealth: Economies and Institutions in the Middle East (Ithaca: Cornell University Press, 1997).

"Prices, Politics, Institutions: Oil Exporters in the International Economy," *Business and Politics*, 1, 3 (1999), pp. 317–342.

Clague, Christopher, "The Institutional Economics and Economic Development," in Clague (ed.), *Institutions and Economic Development: Growth and Governance in Less-Developed and Post-Socialist Countries* (Baltimore: Johns Hopkins University Press, 1997), pp. 13–36.

Coleman, W. D., *Business and Politics: A Study of Collective Action* (Montreal: McGill-Queens University Press, 1995).

Coleman, W. D. and Wyn Grant, "The Organizational Cohesion and Political Access of Business: A Study of Comprehensive Associations," *European Journal of Political Research*, 16 (1989), pp. 467–487.

Cook, M. A. (ed.), *Studies in Economic History of the Middle East* (London: Oxford University Press, 1970).

Corden, Max and J. Peter Neary, "Booming Sector and De-industrialisation in a Small Open Economy," *Economic Journal*, 92 (December 1982), pp. 825–848.

Cornett, Linda, "International and Domestic Causes of Economic Policy Reform," *Studies in Comparative International Development*, 32, 1 (Spring 1997), pp. 216–239.

Crystal, Jill, "Authoritarianism and Its Adversaries in the Arab World," *World Politics*, 46 (January 1994), pp. 262–289.

Kuwait: The Transformation of an Oil State (Boulder: Westview Press, 1992).

Oil and Politics in the Gulf: Rulers and Merchants in Kuwait and Qatar (Cambridge: Cambridge University Press, 1995).

Daher, Ahmad and Faisal Al-Salem, "Kuwait's Parliamentary Elections," *Journal of Arab Affairs*, 3, 1 (1984).

Darwiche, Fida, *The Gulf Stock Exchange Crash: The Rise and Fall of the Souq Al-Manakh* (London: Croom Helm, 1986).

Delacroix, Jacques, "The Distributive State in the World System," *Studies in Comparative International Development*, 15 (1980), pp. 3–22.

Deyo, Frederic (ed.), *The Political Economy of the New Asian Industrialism* (Ithaca: Cornell University Press, 1987).

Doner, Richard F. and Ben Ross Schneider, "Business Associations and Economic Development," *Business and Politics*, 2, 3 (December 2000), pp. 261–289.

"The New Institutional Economics, Business Associations, and Development," International Institute of Labor Studies, Discussion Paper Series N 110 (2000).

Doner, Richard F., Ben Ross Schneider, and Ernest J. Wilson, "Can Business Associations Contribute to Development and Democracy?," in Ann Bernstein and Peter L. Berger (eds.), *Business and Democracy: Cohabitation or Contradiction?* (Boulder: Westview Press, 1999), pp. 126–147.

Evans, Peter, *Embedded Autonomy: States and Industrial Transformation* (Princeton: Princeton University Press, 1995).

"The State as Problem and Solution: Predation, Embedded Autonomy, and Structural Change," in Stephan Haggard and Robert R. Kaufman (eds.), *The Politics of Economic Adjustment: International Constraints, Distributive Politics, and the State* (Princeton: Princeton University Press, 1992), pp. 63–87.

Evans, Peter, Dietrich Rueschemeyer, and Theda Skocpol (eds.), *Bringing the State Back In* (Cambridge: Cambridge University Press, 1985).

Fathi, Schirin H., *Jordan: An Invented Nation?* (Hamburg: Deutsches Orient-Institut, 1994).

Federation of Jordanian Chambers of Commerce, *Organizational Structure* (Amman: Federation of Jordanian Chambers of Commerce, 1989).

Frieden, Jeffry A., *Debt, Development, and Democracy: Modern Political Economy and Latin America, 1965–1985* (Princeton: Princeton University Press, 1991).

"A Pax on Both Their Houses: State, Society, and Social Science," *Contention*, 3, 3 (Spring 1994), pp. 171–182.

Frieden, Jeffry and Ronald Rogowski, "The Impact of the International Economy on National Policies: An Analytic Overview," in Robert Keohane and Helen Milner (eds.), *Internationalization and Domestic Politics* (Cambridge, UK: Cambridge University Press, 1996), pp. 25–47.

Friedman, Thomas, *The Lexus and the Olive Tree* (New York: Farrar, Straus, Giroux, 1999).

Gause, Gregory, *Oil Monarchies: Domestic and Security Challenges in the Arab Gulf States* (New York: Council on Foreign Relations, 1994).

Gourevitch, Peter, *Politics in Hard Times: Comparative Responses to International Economic Crises* (Ithaca: Cornell University Press, 1986).

Granovetter, Mark, "Economic Action and Social Structure: The Problem of Embeddedness," *American Journal of Sociology*, 91, 3 (November 1985), pp. 481–510.

Greif, Avner, "Cultural Beliefs and the Organization of Society: A Historical and Theoretical Reflection on Collectivist and Individualist Societies," *Journal of Political Economy*, 102, 5 (1994), pp. 912–950.

Haggard, Stephan, Sylvia Maxfield, and Ben Ross Schneider, "Theories of Business and Business–State Relations," in Maxfield and Schneider, *Business and the State in Developing Countries*, pp. 36–60.

Hamarneh, Mustafa B., *Social and Economic Transformation of Transjordan, 1921–1946*, Ph.D. Dissertation: Georgetown University (1985).

Hammad, Khalil, "The Role of Foreign Aid in the Jordanian Economy, 1959–1983," in Bichara Khader and Adnan Badran (eds.), *The Economic Development of Jordan* (London: Croom Helm, 1987).

Harrison, Paul, "Economic and Social Conditions in East Arabia," *Muslim World*, 14 (1924).

Herb, Michael, *All in the Family: Absolutism, Revolution, and Democracy in the Middle Eastern Monarchies* (Albany: SUNY Press, 1999).

Herbert, Simon A., "Organizations and Markets," *Journal of Economic Perspectives*, 5 (Spring 1991), pp. 25–44.

Heydemann, Steve, *Authoritarianism in Syria* (Ithaca: Cornell University Press, 1999).

"The Political Logic of Economic Rationality: Selective Stabilization in Syria," in Henri J. Barkey (ed.), *The Politics of Economic Reform in the Middle East* (New York: St. Martin's Press, 1992).

(ed.), *War, Institutions, and Social Change in the Middle East* (Berkeley: University of California Press, 2000).

Hirschman, Albert O., *Exit, Voice, and Loyalty: Responses to Decline in Firms, Organizations, and States* (Cambridge, MA: Harvard University Press, 1970).

The Strategy of Economic Development (New Haven: Yale University Press, 1958).

Hoekman, Bernard and Patrick Messerlin, *Harnessing Trade for Development and Growth in the Middle East* (New York: Council on Foreign Relations, 2002).

Hollingsworth, Roger J., "New Perspectives on the Spatial Dimensions of Economic Coordination: Tensions Between Globalization and Social Systems of Production," *Review of International Political Economy*, 5, 3 (September 1998), pp. 482–508.

Hollingsworth, Roger J. and Robert Boyer, *Contemporary Capitalism: The Embeddedness of Institutions* (Cambridge, UK: Cambridge University Press, 1997).

Hotelling, Harold, "The Economics of Exhaustible Resources," *Journal of Political Economy*, 39, 2 (April 1931), pp. 137–175.

Ibn Khaldun, *The Muqaddimah: An Introduction to History*, trans. by Franz Rosenthal, 2 vols. (New York: Pantheon Books, 1958).

Immergut, M. Ellen, "The Theoretical Core of the New Institutionalism," *Politics & Society*, 26, 1 (March 1998), pp. 5–35.

Inglehart, Ronald, *Culture Shift in Advanced Industrial Society* (Princeton: Princeton University Press, 1990).

International Bank for Reconstruction and Development, *The Economic Development of Kuwait: Mission Report* (Baltimore: Johns Hopkins University Press, 1965).

Ismael, Jacqueline S., *Kuwait: Social Change in Historical Perspective* (Syracuse: Syracuse University Press, 1982).

al-Jasim, Najat Abddalqadir, *Baladiyyat al-Kuwait fi Khamsin 'aman* [Fifty years of the Kuwait Municipality] (Kuwait City: Kuwait Municipality, 1980).

Jordan, National Planning Council (later Ministry of Planning), *Jordan's Social and Economic 5 Year Plans*, various years, Amman.

Jordan, Parliament, *Al-Qanun al-Dariba al-'Amma 'ala al-Mabi'at* [The Sales Tax Law], Number 6 (1994) The Official Gazette, Number 3970.

Jordan, Parliament, Finance Committee, *Hawl Mashru'a Qanun al-Dariba al-'Amma 'ala al-Mabi'at* [About the draft sales tax law], 1994.

Jordanian Businessmen's Association, *By-Laws*, 1985.

Kaboudan, Mahmoud A., "Oil Revenue and Kuwait's Economy: An Econometric Approach," *International Journal of Middle East Studies*, 20, 1 (February 1988), pp. 45–46.

Kang, David, *Crony Capitalism: Corruption and Development in South Korea and the Philippines* (Cambridge, UK: Cambridge University Press, 2002).

Karl, Terry Lynn, *The Paradox of Plenty: Oil Booms and Petro-States* (Berkeley: University of California Press, 1997).

KCCI (Kuwait Chamber of Commerce and Industry), *Amendments to the Law Collecting Difficult Debts: Why and in Which Direction?*, Notes Submitted to the Finance Committee by the KCCI, 24 April 1995.

Mudhakkara 'an Souq al-Ashum wa al-Nash'at al-'Iqariyy fi al-Kuwait [Memorandum on the stock market and real estate activity in Kuwait], 1977.

Al-Qanun wa al-Nizam, Ghurfat Tijarat wa Sana'at al-Kuwait [By-laws and rules of the Kuwait Chamber of Commerce and Industry], 1993.

Al-Taqrir al-Sanawiyy, Ghurfat Tijarat wa Sana'at al-Kuwait [Annual report, Kuwait Chamber of Commerce and Industry], various years.

Khader, Bichara and Adnan Badran (eds.), *The Economic Development of Jordan* (London: Croom Helm, 1987).

Khan, Mushtaq H. and K. S. Jomo (eds.), *Rents, Rent-Seeking and Economic Development: Theory and Evidence in Asia* (Cambridge, UK: Cambridge University Press, 2000).

Khazal, Husain Khalaf al-Shaikh, *Tarikh al-Kuwait al-Siyasi 1962–1970* [The political history of Kuwait, 1962–1970], vol. I (Beirut: Matabu Dar al-Kutub, n.d.).

Khouja, M. W. and P. G. Sadler, *The Economy of Kuwait: Development and Role in International Finance* (London: Macmillan Press, 1979).

Khoury, Nabeel, "The National Consultative Council of Jordan: A Study in Legislative Development," *International Journal of Middle East Studies*, 13, 4 (November 1981), pp. 427–439.

Kienle, Eberhard, *A Grand Delusion: Democracy and Economic Reform in Egypt* (London: I. B. Tauris, 2001).

Kochanek, A. Stanley, *Interest Groups and Development: Business and Politics in Pakistan* (Delhi: Oxford University Press, 1983).

Konikoff, A., *Transjordan: An Economic Survey* (Jerusalem: Economic Research Institute of the Jewish Agency for Palestine, 1946).

Krueger, Anne O., "The Political Economy of the Rent-Seeking Society," *American Economic Review*, 64, 3 (June 1974), pp. 291–303.

Kuwait, Ministry of Planning, *Statistical Abstract in 25 Years* (Kuwait City: Central Statistical Office, 1990).

Kuwait, National Assembly, *Ijabat al-Ghurfa ila al-Lajna al-Maaliyya hawl al-Khaskhasa* [Responses of the chamber to the Finance Committee (of parliament) concerning privatization], 1995.

Landes, David S., *The Wealth and Poverty of Nations: Why Some Are So Rich and Some So Poor* (New York: W. W. Norton, 1998).

Layne, Linda (ed.), *Elections in the Middle East: Implications of Recent Trends* (Boulder: Westview Press, 1987).

Levi, Margaret, *Of Revenue and Rule* (Berkeley: University of California Press, 1988).

Lin, Justin Yifu and Jeffrey B. Nugent, "Institutions and Economic Development," in J. Behrman and T. N. Srinivasan (eds.), *Handbook of Economic Development*, Volume IIIA (Amsterdam: North-Holland, 1995).

Lindblom, Charles E., *Politics and Markets: The World's Political-Economic Systems* (New York: Basic Books, 1977).

Lorimer, J. G., *Gazetteer of the Persian Gulf, Oman, and Central Arabia*, 2 vols. (Shannon: Irish University Press, 1970).

Luciani, Giacomo "Allocative vs. Production States: A Theoretical Framework," in Luciani, *The Arab State*, pp. 65–84.

(ed.), *The Arab State* (Berkeley: University of California Press, 1990).

Luke, Harry and Edward Kieth-Roach (eds.), *The Handbook of Palestine* (London: Macmillan and Co., 1934).

Lust-Okar, Ellen M., "The Decline of Jordanian Political Parties: Myth or Reality?," *International Journal of Middle East Studies*, 33, a (November 2001), pp. 545–569.

Mahdavy, Hussein, "The Patterns and Problems of Economic Development in Rentier States," in M. A. Cook (ed.), *Studies in Economic History of the Middle East* (London: Oxford University Press, 1970), pp. 428–467.

Mahoney, James, "Strategies of Causal Inference in Small-*N* Analysis," *Sociological Methods & Research*, 28, 4 (May 2000), pp. 387–424.

El Mallakh, Ragaei, *Economic Development and Regional Cooperation: Kuwait* (Chicago: University of Chicago Press, 1968).

  Kuwait: Trade and Investment (Boulder: Westview Press, 1979).

  "Planning in a Capital Surplus Economy," *Land Economics*, 42, 4 (November 1966), pp. 425–440.

El Mallakh, Ragaei and Jacob K. Atta, *The Absorptive Capacity of Kuwait* (Toronto: Lexington Books, 1981).

Mamdani, Mahmood, "Beyond Settler and Native as Political Identities: Overcoming the Political Legacy of Colonialism," *Comparative Studies in Society and History*, 43, 4 (October 2001), pp. 651–664.

Manzur, Michael P., *Economic Growth and Development in Jordan* (Boulder: Westview Press, 1979).

Martinez, Luiz, *The Algerian Civil War, 1990–1998* (New York: Columbia University Press, 2000).

Maxfield, Sylvia and Ben Ross Schneider (eds.), *Business and the State in Developing Countries* (Ithaca: Cornell University Press, 1997).

Mishal, Shaul, Ranan Kuperman, and David Boas, *Investment in Peace: The Politics of Economic Cooperation Between Israel, Jordan, and the Palestinians* (Portland: Sussex Academic Press, 2001).

Moore, Mick and Ladi Hamalai, "Economic Liberalization, Political Pluralism and Business Associations in Developing Countries," *World Development*, 21, 12 (1993), pp. 1895–1912.

Moore, Pete W., "Business–State Relations After Liberalization in Jordan," in Remonda Bensabat Kleinberg and Janine A. Clark (eds.), *Economic Liberalization, Democratization and Civil Society in the Developing World* (New York: St. Martin's Press, 2000), pp. 180–200.

  "The Newest Jordan: Free Trade, Peace, and an Ace in the Hole," *Middle East Report Online*, 26 June 2003.

  "Rentier Fiscal Crisis and Regime Stability in the Middle East: Business and State in the Gulf," *Studies in Comparative International Development*, 37, 1 (Spring 2002), pp. 34–56.

  "What Makes Successful Business Lobbies? Business Associations and the Rentier State in Jordan and Kuwait," *Comparative Politics*, 33, 2 (January 2001), pp. 127–147.

Moore, Pete W. and Andrew Shrank, "Commerce and Conflict: How the US Effort to Counter Terrorism with Trade May Backfire," *Middle East Policy*, 10, 3 (September 2003), pp. 112–120.

National Bank of Kuwait (Kuwait City), *Annual Reports*, various years.

North, Douglas C., *Structure and Change in Economic History* (New York: W. W. Norton, 1981).

Offe, Claus, *Disorganized Capitalism: Contemporary Transformations of Work and Politics* (Cambridge, UK: Polity Press, 1985).

"Political Authority and Class Structure: An Analysis of Late Capitalist Societies," *International Journal of Sociology*, 2 (1972).

Okruhlik, Gwenn, "Rentier Wealth, Unruly Law, and the Rise of the Opposition: The Political Economy of Oil States," *Comparative Politics*, 31, 3 (April 1999), pp. 295–315.

Olson, Mancur, *The Rise and Decline of Nations* (New Haven: Yale University Press, 1982).

Owen, Roger, "Government and Economy in Jordan: Progress, Problems and Prospects," in Patrick Seale (ed.), *The Shaping of an Arab Statesman: Sharif Abd al-Hamid Sharaf and the Modern Arab World* (New York: Quartet Books, 1983).

Patai, Raphael, *The Kingdom of Jordan* (Princeton: Princeton University Press, 1958).

Philby, J. B., "Trans-Jordan," *Journal of the Royal Central Asian Society*, 10, 11 (1923–24).

Piro, Timothy, *The Politics of Market Reform in Jordan* (Lanham, MD: Rowman & Littlefield, 1998).

Polanyi, Karl, *The Great Transformation* (New York: Reinhart & Co., 1944).

Popkin, Samuel L., "Public Choice and Peasant Organization," in Bates, *Toward a Political Economy of Development*, pp. 245–271.

Records of Jordan, Jane Priestland (ed.) (London: Archive Editions, 1996–).

Records of Kuwait, Alan deLancy Rush (ed.) (London: Archive International, 1989–).

Richards, Alan and John Waterbury, *A Political Economy of the Middle East: State, Class, and Economic Development* (Boulder: Westview Press, 1990).

Rodinson, Maxime, *Islam and Capitalism* (London: Penguin, 1974).

Rodrik, Dani, "Institutions for High-Quality Growth: What They Are and How to Acquire Them," *Studies in Comparative International Development*, 35, 3 (Fall 2000), pp. 3–32.

Rogowski, Ronald, *Commerce and Coalitions: How Trade Affects Domestic Political Alignments* (Princeton: Princeton University Press, 1989).

"Structure, Growth, and Power: Three Rationalist Accounts," in Bates, *Toward a Political Economy of Development*, pp. 300–330.

Ross, Michael L., "Does Resource Wealth Cause Authoritarian Rule?," *World Politics*, 53 (April 2001), pp. 325–361.

Rueschemeyer, Dietrich, Evelyne Huber Stephens, and John Stephens, *Capitalist Development and Democracy* (Cambridge UK: Cambridge University Press, 1992).

Ruggie, John, "International Regimes, Transactions, and Change: Embedded Liberalism in the Postwar Economic Order," *International Organization*, 36, 2 (Spring 1982), pp. 379–415.

Rush, Alan, *Al-Sabah: Genealogy and History of Kuwait's Ruling Family, 1752–1986* (London: Ithaca Press, 1987).

Al-Sabah, S. M., *Development Planning in an Oil Economy and the Role of the Woman: The Case of Kuwait* (London: Eastlords Publishing, 1983).

Al-Sabah, Y. S. F., *The Oil Economy of Kuwait* (London: Kegan Paul International, 1980).

Salamé, Ghassan (ed.), *Democracy Without Democrats? The Renewal of Politics in the Muslim World* (London: I. B. Tauris, 1994).

Satloff, Robert, *Troubles on the East Bank: Challenges to the Domestic Stability of Jordan* (New York: Praeger, 1986).

Schmitter, Philippe C., "The Consolidation of Democracy and the Representation of Social Groups," *American Behavioral Scientist*, 35, 4/5 (March/June), pp. 422–450.

"Transitology: The Science of the Art of Democratization?," in Joseph Tulchin (ed.), *The Consolidation of Democracy in Latin America* (Boulder: Lynne Rienner, 1995), pp. 11–41.

Schmitter, Philippe C. and Wolfgang Streeck, "The Organization of Business Interests: Studying the Associative Action of Business in Advanced Industrial Societies," Max-Planck-Institut für Gesellschaftsforschung, Discussion Paper 99/1 (March 1999).

(eds.), *Private Interest Governance* (London: Sage, 1985).

Schneider, Ben Ross, "Business Politics in Latin America," unpublished draft manuscript (2002).

Schumpeter, Joseph, "The Crisis of the Tax State," in Alan T. Peacock (ed.), *International Economic Papers*, No. 4 (London: Macmillan, 1954), pp. 5–38.

Schwedler, Jillian, "Democratic Institutions and the Practice of Power in Jordan: The Changing Role of the Islamic Action Front," paper presented to the conference, Social History of Jordan, Amman (March 1998).

Shadlen, Kenneth C., *Democratization Without Representation: The Politics of Small Industry in Mexico* (College Station, PA: Penn State University Press, 2004).

"Orphaned by Democracy: Small Business in Mexico," *Comparative Politics*, October 2002, pp. 43–62.

Shafer, D. Michael, *Winners and Losers: How Sectors Shape the Developmental Prospects of States* (Ithaca: Cornell University Press, 1994).

Shambayati, Hootan, "The Rentier State, Interest Groups, and the Paradox of Autonomy," *Comparative Politics*, 26, 3 (April 1994), pp. 307–331.

Siegel, Fred, *The Future Once Happened Here: New York, DC, LA, and the Fate of America's Big Cities* (New York: Free Press, 1997).

Smith, Adam, *An Inquiry into the Nature and Causes of the Wealth of Nations*, edited by Edwin Cannan (Methuen & Co., 1904; Library for Economics and Liberty, 1 March 2002, http://www.econlib.org/library/Smith/smWN5.html).

Smith, Kristin, "Culture and Capital: The Political Economy of Islamic Finance in Kuwait," paper presented to annual meeting of Middle East Studies Association (November 2001).

Springborg, Robert, "The Arab Bourgeoisie: A Revisionist Interpretation," *Arab Studies Quarterly*, 15, 1 (Winter 1993), pp. 13–40.

Stauffer, Thomas, "Accounting for 'Wasting Assets': Measurements of Income Dependency in Oil-Rentier States," *Journal of Energy and Development*, 11, 1 (1986).

"The Dynamics of Petroleum Dependency: Growth in an Oil Rentier State," *Finance and Industry*, 2 (1981), pp. 7–28.

Susser, Asher and Aryeh Shmuelevitz (eds.), *The Hashemites in the Modern Arab World* (London: Frank Cass, 1995).

Tatwir Souq al-Ashum fi al-Kuwait [Development of the stock market in Kuwait], papers from KCCI-sponsored conference, Kuwait City, November 1981 (supplied by KCCI Research and Studies Department).

Tétreault, Mary Ann, "Autonomy, Necessity, and the Small State: Ruling Kuwait in the Twentieth Century," *International Organization*, 45, 4 (Autumn 1991), pp. 565–591.

  Stories of Democracy: Politics and Society in Contemporary Kuwait (New York: Columbia University Press, 2000).

Thelen, Kathleen, "Historical Institutionalism in Comparative Politics," *Annual Review of Political Science*, 2 (1999), pp. 369–404.

Tignor, Robert L., *Capitalism and Nationalism at the End of Empire: State and Business in Decolonizing Egypt, Nigeria, and Kenya, 1945–1963* (Princeton: Princeton University Press, 1998).

Tilly, Charles, *Coercion, Capital and European States, AD 990–1990* (Oxford, UK: Blackwell, 1990).

Van Hear, Nicholas, "The Impact of the Involuntary Mass Return to Jordan in the Wake of the Gulf Crisis," *International Migration Review*, 29, 2 (1995), pp. 352–374.

Vandewalle, Dirk, *Libya Since Independence: Oil and State-Building* (Ithaca: Cornell University Press, 1998).

Vitalis, Robert, "Black Gold, White Crude: An Essay on American Exceptionalism, Hierarchy, and Hegemony in the Gulf," *Diplomatic History*, 26, 2 (Spring 2002), pp. 185–213.

  When Capitalists Collide: Business Conflict and the End of Empire in Egypt (Berkeley: University of California Press, 1995).

Vogel, David, *Fluctuating Fortunes: The Political Power of Business in America* (New York: Basic Books, 1995).

Waldner, David, *State Building and Late Development* (Ithaca: Cornell University Press, 1999).

Walpole, G. F., "Land Problems in Transjordan," *Journal of the Royal Central Asian Society*, July 1947.

Waterbury, John, "Democracy Without Democrats? The Potential for Political Liberalization in the Middle East," in Salamé, *Democracy Without Democrats?*, pp. 22–47.

  Exposed to Innumerable Delusions: Public Enterprise and State Power in Egypt, India, Mexico, and Turkey (Cambridge, UK: Cambridge University Press, 1993).

Williamson, Oliver, "The Institutions and Governance of Economic Development and Reform," in Williamson, *The Mechanisms of Governance* (New York: Oxford University Press, 1996), pp. 322–343.

Wilmington, Martin, *The Middle East Supply Center* (Albany: SUNY Press, 1971).

Wilson, Mary C., *King Abdullah, Britain and the Making of Jordan* (Cambridge, UK: Cambridge University Press, 1987).

Wilson, Rodney (ed.), *Politics and the Economy in Jordan* (London: Routledge, 1991).

World Bank, *Claiming the Future: Choosing Prosperity in the Middle East and North Africa* (Washington, DC: World Bank, 1995).

Jordan: Consolidating Economic Adjustment and Establishing the Base for Sustainable Growth, vol. I (Washington, DC: World Bank, 24 August 1994).

Jordan: Private Sector Assessment, Private Sector Development and Infrastructure Division, Middle East Department, (25 August 1995).

Yapp, M. E., *The Near East Since the First World War: A History to 1995* (London: Addison Wesley Longman, 1996).

Zu'bi, Ali Sharif and Sharif Ali Zu'bi (eds.), *Business Legislation and Incentives* (Amman: Allied Accounts, 1995).

Index

ACC, *see* Amman Chamber of Commerce
ACI, *see* Amman Chamber of Industry
Algeria 107
Amman Chamber of Commerce (ACC)
    by-laws 61–62, 148–149
    and civil war 101–102
    creation of 60–61
    and crown prince 112–114, 116
    decline of influence 115–118, 145–146
    effect of Palestine immigrants 68,
        110–111, 160–161
    elite cohesion 83, 110–112
    new elites 105–109
    defections 112
    weakness 119, 150, 151, 163
    executive board 194–198
    and Federation of Jordanian Chambers
        of Commerce 74, 147
    and foreign investment 167–170
    institutional capacities 184
    institutional change 72–77, 110, 119
        effects of 147–151, 184
    and intra-merchant relations 65, 148
    lobbying 105–109, 113–118
    membership 107, 110–111, 147, 198
        encompassingness 111, 119
    in parliament 70–71, 72, 158
    political liberalization 157–159
    positions on sales tax 162
    relations 65
    relations with ACI 112–113, 151
    relations with ministries 117–118
        (*see also* Jordan, Ministry of Supply)
    relations with other associations 115
    rivals 152
    representation in 61, 110–111
    elections 110–111, 148–150, 151
    structure of 61–62, 148–149, 184
Amman Chamber of Industry (ACI) 76,
    112–113, 151, 152, 162–163,
    164–166, 173
    relations with ACC 112–113

Anderson, Lisa 21, 178
Arab Bank 110, 152
ascriptive divisions 6
'Asfour, Muhammed 149, 150, 158,
    165
Asian tigers 2, 28
authoritarianism 29

Bahrain 6, 186
Bdair, Muhammed 'Ali 71, 73, 74, 76,
    102–103, 109, 110, 111, 112, 113,
    114, 117, 118, 147, 148
Beblawi, Hazem 19
business associations 3, 180, 181
    comparison of 6–8, 81–84
    and economic reform 181–182
    and elites 183, 184
    encompassing 25–26
    institutional evolution 12–13
    new institutional economics 24–27
    organization of 5
    and political liberalization 187–190
    and political parties 189
    predictions about 21–24
    and press 188
    rent-seeking 185
    sociocultural factors 179–180
business elites 8, 27, 182–183
    collective action 24–27, 180
    mobility of in Kuwait 30
business–state relations 2–3, 5, 181
    ascriptive factors 179–180
    association level 24–25, 181
    comparing Jordan and Kuwait 81–84
    coordination in 6, 7, 28–29, 177, 180,
        182–183, 184
    in crisis 21–24
    and economic growth 177, 181–182
    historical factors 11, 26, 159
    and Islamist groups 190
    and political liberalization 186–190
    and press 187, 188

rent-seeking 185
sociocultural factors 179–180

Chaudhry, Kiren 9, 15, 17, 20
clientelism 7
colonial rule 6
comparison
    bust period 9–10
    of business associations 6–8, 180
    of Jordan and Kuwait 4, 5–10, 16, 26,
        89, 101, 174–175, 177, 180
    time frame 9–10
corporatism 6, 75, 155–156
Crystal, Jill 30, 33, 35, 36, 45, 86, 100, 121

Delacroix, Jacques 19
democratization 6, 9, 22
    resulting from crisis 21–24
Dutch Disease 20

economic adjustment 2, 3, 177, 185
        (see also liberalization, economic)
    role of business associations 3, 177,
        181–182
    role of private sector 3, 177
economic crisis 12–13, 178, 179, 180
        (see also fiscal crisis)
Egypt 3, 6, 15, 17, 80, 82, 104, 107, 186,
        187, 188, 189
Egyptian Businessman's Association 7
Evans, Peter 28, 133, 190
embedded autonomy 28, 133, 146, 190
external resources 9, 12, 14–15, 178
        (see also oil)
    decline in 21–24
    effects of 118
    in relation to domestic economy 22
    measuring 13, 15, 16, 21–22, 62
    as patronage 118
    remittances 15

fiscal crisis 1–2, 21–24, 178, 185 (see also
        economic crisis)
    predictions about 24
foreign aid 1, 6
free trade 177, 183
Frieden, Jeffry 8
Friedman, Thomas 176

Gerschenkron, Alexander 106
globalization 2, 7
Gourevitch, Peter 4

Abu Hassan, Khaldoun 151, 165
al-Hamad, 'Abdullatif 129, 132

Hashemite monarchy 6, 102, 107, 179
    'Abdullah Ibn Hussein 57, 102, 183
    Hussein bin Talal 80, 148, 153, 154,
        157, 160, 173
    Al-Hassan Bin Talal 80, 112–114, 116,
        173
Hirschman, Albert 1, 21
Huntington, Samuel 108

Ibn Khaldun 11–12, 19, 72, 73, 176
Inglehart, Ronald 83
institutions (definition) 24–25, 181
Iraq 80, 107
Ismael, Jacqueline 31, 32, 33

Jordan
    1970 civil war 101
        effects of 102–103
    Amman Economic Summit 167–170,
        172
        Private Sector Executive Committee
            169–170, 183
    Amman Financial Market 106, 170
    British Mandate 57, 58–59, 62–66
    business–state relations 70
    Arab Common Market 79–80
    and civil war 101
    contested relations 105–109, 113–118
    cultural factors 89
    coordination 77–81; lack of 145–146,
        150, 154–156, 183
    economic laws 78–79
    economic planning 80–81, 116
    foreign investment 167–170
    and Islamists 170, 173–174
    and Israel 173–174
    land distribution 59–60, 70
    lobbying 77; failure 105–109,
        115–118; sales tax 163–167, 189
    peace process 172–174
    political liberalization 157–159
    Private Sector Executive Committee
        169–170
    Mandate's effect upon 62–63
    and Ministry of Supply 108–109,
        117–118
    new economic elites 105–109, 119
    Palestinian factor 68, 179–180
    private sector; expansion of 107–108
    role of crown prince 80, 112–113, 116
    role of parliament 70–72, 114, 158,
        159, 165–166
    and taxation 66, 161–163, 167, 189
        (see also lobbying, sales tax)
    during World War II 65

Jordan (*cont.*)
  Central Bank 77, 106, 110, 112
  debt 147, 152
  devaluation 146–147
  East Ghor canal project 70
  economic crisis 145, 146, 160
    responses to 145
  economic elites
    attitude toward Israel 172–173
    cohesion of 83
    creation of new 105–109
    in parliament 70–72
  Economic Consultative Council 154,
    155, 164, 183
  economic planning 80–81
  Economic Security Committee
    102–103, 154
  external revenue 67
    foreign aid 103, 104, 183
    mining 103
    remittance income 101
  foreign ownership 78
  gross domestic product 89
  import substitution industrialization 66,
    105–107
    failure of 107, 119, 180
  Industrial Development Bank 68, 69,
    106
  inflation 108
  International Monetary Fund 147, 156,
    161, 162, 165
  Islamists 123, 170 (*see also* Jordan,
    parliament, Islamic Action Front)
  relations with Israel 167, 168, 172–174
    opposition to 173–174
  Ministry of Supply 108–109, 117–118,
    152–153, 155
  Palestinians 67–68, 157, 171–172,
    179–180
  parliament 70–72, 158–159
    and business representation 159,
      165–166
    elections 156, 158
    contrast with Kuwait 71
    Islamic Action Front 158, 163,
      165–166, 171 (*see also* Jordan,
      Islamists)
    National Consultative Council
      114–115, 124, 158, 183
    powers of 158
    and sales tax debate 165–166
    suspension 114
  political liberalization 157–158
    stagnation of 177, 189
  political parties 71, 158, 159

  pre-colonial merchant community 58, 59
  press 103
    contrast with Kuwaiti 58
    institutions 59
  privatization 153, 155, 170–172
    Palestinian factor 171–172
  public-sector employment 104, 105
  as a rentier state 68–69
    creation of 62–63
  riots 157
  Royal Scientific Society 105, 112
  shareholding companies 104, 106
  state-owned enterprises 69, 105
  taxation 63–64, 79, 106, 116, 153,
    161–167
    pre-independence 66
  unemployment 153
  and US Free Trade Agreement 183
  workers, professionals 1
    in Kuwait 1, 98
Jordan Investment Corporation 104, 171
Jordanian Businessmen's Association 152,
  158, 162, 173

Karl, Terry Lynn 15, 17, 18, 20, 22–23,
  25, 146
Kuwait
  Bani Utub 30–32
  British protectorate 33–36
  business–state relations
    appointments to economic ministries,
      effect on 128
    cabinet crisis 49
    coordination 51–57, 134–138, 145;
      breakdown of 94–101
    collusion 121, 135, 137, 138, 144
    and debts 135–137
    decline of private-sector employment
      87
    early changes 34–36
    and economic ministries 96–97
    founding economic laws 53–55
    and industrialization 87–89
    inter-war period 37–38
    intra-elite competition 137, 138–145
    and Iraqi occupation 124
    lobbying venues 127–128
    oil's effect on 40, 42–43, 45–46
    and political liberalization 126–128
    press 98, 126–127
    privatization 137–138
    rent-seeking 53
    role of Islamist groups 90–91, 98,
      121, 142–145, 180
    role of ministries 96–97

role of National Assembly 49–51, 121, 122, 126, 135–137
and al-Sabahs 100–101
Souq al-Manakh 100
World War I period 36
cabinet 49, 94
Central Bank 134, 136, 144
Constitution 50
cooperatives 90–91, 122, 143–144
creation of rentier state 34
debts 125, 135
diwaniyya 50, 123
economic crisis 120, 121–124, 125
economic elites (asil) 30, 31, 32, 36, 40–41, 45–46
  cohesion 83
  intra-elite coordination 52–53
  Islamists 90–91
  new elites 86, 87–94, 137, 138–142, 145
Economic Reactivation Committee 127, 133
free-trade zone 96, 134
gross domestic product 89
industrial representation 139
industrialization 87–89
  weakness of 89, 119
inflation 95
Iranian Revolution 121
invasion by Iraq 1, 120, 124, 125, 128, 134, 156, 160, 187, 188
land purchases 86
loans to Iraq 1, 27
Majlis movement 37–38, 40, 123, 140
  failure of 40
  precursors 35, 36
  results of 39–40, 187, 188, 189
National Assembly (parliament) 121, 122, 126
  in 1960s 56
  and debts 135–137
  elections 49–51, 98, 145
  formation of 48–51
  and Iraqi occupation 124
  Islamist groups 98, 121, 122, 123, 124, 126, 129, 132, 135–137, 141, 142–145
  reinstitution of 122, 123
  and Souq al-Manakh debates 131–132
  suspension of 97, 123, 133–134
nationalism 38, 39
nationalization 86–87
oil
  discovery 34
  impact on business–state relations 40, 46, 179

impact on state 41–42
institutional effects 42–43
and National Assembly 98
revenues 39
and ruling family 41
Ottoman rule 33–34
patronage 32
  means of distribution 43–45, 86
pearl industry 31, 35
Planning Board 42, 55–56 (*see also* Supreme Planning Council)
political parties (groups) 50
political liberalization 126–128
  stagnation of 177
pre-colonial labor force 31
privatization 137–138
  political opposition 137, 138
public spending 86
ruler–merchants relations under Mubarak 33–36
shareholding companies 85, 133, 136
Shiites 32, 38, 39, 88, 93, 94, 121, 123, 142
Souq al-Manakh 1, 93, 100, 125, 126, 128–134, 175
  closing of 133
stock market 87, 91–93, 98–100, 132–133
structure of merchant community 31–32
Supreme Planning Council 127
taxation 34, 39, 97
Kuwait Chamber of Commerce and Industry (KCCI)
  arbitration role 53
  appointments to ministries 49, 128
  by-laws 47
  control of *Al-Qabas* 57, 95
  creation of 46–48
  creation of rivals 87–94
  and debts 135–137
  early organization 37–38
  economic planning 55–56
  economist forum 136, 137
  elections 139–142
    role of press 140–141
    finances of 47–48
  executive board 191–192
  financial reform 133–134
  free-trade zone 96
  institutional capacities 95, 127, 184
  and intra-merchant relations 52–53
  and Iraqi occupation 124

Kuwait Chamber of Commerce and
    Industry (*cont.*)
  leadership cohesion 36, 40–41, 48,
    52–53, 83
    contrast with Jordan 119
    new leaders 142
  lobbying
    failure 94–101
    goals 53–54
    venues 127–128
  members in government 49
  membership 93, 141–142, 193, 194
  ministerial relations 96–97
  and National Assembly 49–51, 56,
    122–123
    advantages in 50–51
    problems with 126, 135–137
  and political liberalization 126–128
  policy coordination with state 134–138,
    145
  precursor institutions 37–38
  privatization 137–138
  representation in 47, 141–142
  rivals in 1990s 137, 138–145
    associations 139
  Souq al-Manakh 100
    policies toward 129–132, 134
  stock market 98–100, 132–133
  use of media 127
Kuwait Clearing and Financial Settlements
    Company (KUCLEAR) 131
Kuwait Finance House 90, 143, 144
Kuwait Investment Authority 137,
    138–145
Kuwait Oil Company 41, 86

labor 7
late development 9, 11, 12
Latin America 8
liberalization, economic 180–185 (*see also*
    economic adjustment)
liberalization, political 2, 3, 10, 29,
    186–190
  resulting from crisis 21–24
  role of private sector 3–4
  US policy 4, 176
Lindblom, Charles 72
Luciani, Giacomo 15, 17–18, 21

al-Marzouq, Khaled 140–142
Middle East Partnership Initiative 176
Middle East Supply Company 64–66, 107
Migdal, Joel 97
Morocco 3, 6, 186
Murad, Haider 149, 150

National Bank of Kuwait 45, 57, 127, 141,
    143
  and Souq al-Manakh 130, 131
neoclassical economics 11, 13, 24
new institutional economics 11, 181
  approach to organized business 24–27
North, Douglass 1, 24, 27

'Obeidat, Ahmed 152–153, 164, 175
oil 2, 18–20, 23, 88, 101, 178, 179 (*see also*
    external resources)
  price decline 21–24, 146
Olson, Mancur 8, 20, 24, 25–27, 28, 29,
    48, 75, 111, 119, 120–121, 146,
    180
Oman 6

path-dependency 12
patronage 3, 118
Polanyi, Karl 11
political opposition 5
political parties 8
Popkin, Samuel 19
Powell, Colin 176
productive growth 2

Al-Qabas (newspaper) 57, 95, 99, 127,
    132, 140
Qatar 3, 31, 51, 187, 188

regional peace 4
rentier state thesis 5, 15, 44, 161, 175,
    180–181
  counterintuitive outcomes 21–22
  critiques of 81, 178, 180–181
  measuring rents 15 (*see also* external
    resources)
  rent decline expectations 21–24
  semi-rentier 15, 17
rent-seeking 7, 19–20, 52, 53, 83
al-Rifa'i, Zaid 103, 153–154, 155, 162,
    171
Rogowski, Ronald 26

al-Sabah ruling family 6, 30–32, 41, 107,
    179
  'Abdallah Salim al-Sabah 89
  Ahmad Jaber al-Sabah 89
  in business 100–101
  and National Assembly 49
  Sa'ad 'Abdallah al-Sabah 124, 129
al-Sagr, 'Abdulaziz 35, 46, 48–49, 51, 87,
    100, 123, 124, 127, 130, 140, 145
Saudi Arabia 3, 9, 20, 38, 82, 125, 146
Schumpeter, Joseph 14

sectors 17–18
Shafer, Michael 15, 17–18, 20, 22–23, 25,
    146
al-Shahin, 'Isa Majid 132
Smith, Adam 14, 19
smuggling 36
state formation 12
Stauffer, Thomas 21–22
structural/statist theories 4–5, 11, 26, 27,
    51, 72, 118, 146, 175, 177,
    178–179 (*see also* rentier state
    thesis)
  confirmation of 85, 101
  counterintuitive outcomes 21–22
  critiques of 81, 178, 180–181
  fiscal crisis 21–24
  patronage 118
  view of organized business 20–21

Syria 3, 15, 17, 80, 187, 188, 189
  business associations 7, 46, 187

Tabba, Hamdi 147–149, 150, 154, 155,
    156
Tabba, Subri 73, 115, 117, 148
taxation 18, 22
Tétrault, Mary Ann 34
Tunisia 3, 6

underdevelopment thesis 33, 83
United Arab Emirates 92, 134, 141

Waterbury, John 68, 69, 119, 186
al-Wazzan (family) 88, 93, 121, 142,
    144

Yemen 3, 6, 9, 15, 20, 186

1 Parvin Paidar, *Women and the Political Process in Twentieth-Century Iran*
  0 521 47340 3 hardback 0 521 59572 X paperback
2 Israel Gershoni and James Jankowski, *Redefining the Egyptian Nation,
  1930–1945*   0 521 47535 X hardback 0 521 52330 3 paperback
3 Annelies Moors, *Women, Property and Islam: Palestinian Experiences,
  1920–1990*   0 521 47497 3 hardback 0 521 48355 7 paperback
4 Paul Kingston, *Britain and the Politics of Modernization in the Middle East,
  1945–1958*   0 521 56346 1 hardback 0 521 89439 5 paperback
5 Daniel Brown, *Rethinking Tradition in Modern Islamic Thought*
  0 521 57077 8 hardback 0 521 65394 0 paperback
6 Nathan J. Brown, *The Rule of Law in the Arab World: Courts in Egypt and the
  Gulf*   0 521 59026 4
7 Richard Tapper, *Frontier Nomads of Iran: The Political and Social History of
  the Shahsevan*   0 521 58336 5
8 Khaled Fahmy, *All the Pasha's Men: Mehmed Ali, his Army and the Making of
  Modern Egypt*   0 521 56007 1
9 Sheila Carapico, *Civil Society in Yemen: The Political Economy of Activism in
  Arabia*   0 521 59098 1
10 Meir Litvak, *Shi'i Scholars in Nineteenth-Century Iraq: The* Ulama *of Najaf
  and Karbala*   0 521 62356 1 hardback 0 521 89296 1 paperback
11 Jacob Metzer, *The Divided Economy of Mandatory Palestine*   0 521 46550 8
12 Eugene L. Rogan, *Frontiers of the State in the Late Ottoman Empire:
  Transjordan, 1850–1921*   0 521 66312 1 hardback 0 521 89223 6 paperback
13 Eliz Sanasarin, *Religious Minorities in Iran*   0 521 77073 4
14 Nadje Al-Ali, *Secularism, Gender and the State in the Middle East: The
  Egyptian Women's Movement*   0 521 78022 5 hardback 0 521 78504 9
  paperback
15 Eugene L. Rogan and Avi Shlaim (eds.), *The War for Palestine: Rewriting the
  History of 1948*   0 521 79139 1 hardback 0 521 79476 5 paperback
16 Gershon Shafir and Yoav Peled, *Being Israeli: The Dynamics of Multiple
  Citizenship*   0 521 79224 X hardback 0 521 79672 5 paperback
17 A. J. Racy, *Making Music in the Arab World: The Culture and Artistry of* Tarab
  0 521 30414 8 hardback 0 521 31685 5 paperback
18 Benny Morris, *The Birth of the Palestinian Refugee Problem Revisited*
  0 521 81120 1 hardback 0 521 00967 7 paperback
19 Yasir Suleiman, *A War of Words: Language and Conflict in the Middle East*
  0 521 83743 X hardback 0 521 54656 7 paperback